Henry VI, Margaret of Anjou and the Wars of the Roses

A Source Book

Keith Dockray

SUTTON PUBLISHING

First published in the United Kingdom in 2000 by
Sutton Publishing Limited · Phoenix Mill
Thrupp · Stroud · Gloucestershire · GL5 2BU

British Library Cataloguing in Publication Data
A catalogue record for this book is available from the British Library

ISBN 0 7509 2163 3

Typeset in 10/15.5 pt New Baskerville.
Typesetting and origination by
Sutton Publishing Limited.
Printed in Great Britain by
Biddles, Guildford, Surrey.

Contents

Preface

This book, like its two predecessors *Edward IV: A Source Book* and *Richard III: A Source Book*, is very much aimed at sixth-formers, undergraduates and general readers interested not only in the political history of later fifteenth-century England but the primary sources on which historians depend.

Henry VI, Lancastrian politics *c.* 1450–61 and the Wars of the Roses formed a major part of my Special Subject teaching at Huddersfield Polytechnic (now University) in the later 1970s and 1980s; since moving to Bristol a few years ago, Peter Fleming and I have made the years *c.* 1450–71 central to our joint BA and MA teaching at the University of the West of England. Therefore I must express my gratitude to former students at both universities for many vigorous seminar discussions, as well as Peter Fleming himself and Peter Allender. Ralph Griffiths has been immensely encouraging and supportive, even though, as he put it in a characteristically helpful letter, 'we don't quite see eye to eye on poor Henry and his capacious shoulders bearing the weight of practically all undesirable things in the fifteenth century'. Michael Hicks and Tony Pollard, too, have helped spur me on.

Two BA (Hons) dissertations I supervised at the University of Huddersfield have proved helpful and informative: Stephen Garrett, 'Fifteenth Century Politics and Government: The Minority and Personal Rule of Henry VI *c.* 1422–1450' (1994), and Chris Marks, 'Henry VI, Margaret of Anjou and the House of Lancaster' (1995). Peter Fleming kindly let me have, in advance of publication, a copy of his most informative survey of 'Kent Political History 1400–1540', for *A History of Kent: The Later Middle Ages*, ed. Nigel Ramsey, Kent Archaeological Society/Kent County Council. Various anonymous and unpublished translations of Latin chronicles that circulate in fifteenth-century circles have proved invaluable. The discussion of primary sources for *c.* 1450–1471 derives in part from my earlier survey in *Edward IV: A Source Book* (1999) and I have also drawn considerably on three of my articles: 'The Origins of the Wars of the Roses', *The Wars of the Roses*, ed. A.J. Pollard (1995); 'The Battle of Wakefield and the Wars of the Roses', *The Battle of Wakefield* (Ricardian pamphlet, 1992); and 'William Shakespeare, the Wars of the Roses and Richard III', *History Teaching Review Year Book (Journal of the Scottish Association of Teachers of History)*, Vol. 11 (1997).

The documentary material in this source book is divided into sections focusing on particular aspects of the Wars of the Roses era *c.* 1450–1471. Each chapter is prefaced by a commentary providing a focus for the extracts, with numbers in round brackets referring to the documents which follow. Passages from Latin and French sources are given in translation. Vernacular sources I have rendered in modern English. Apologies are clearly in order for any inadvertent infringement of copyright.

Keith Dockray
Bristol,
September 1999

Abbreviations

Annales	'Annales Rerum Anglicarum' in *Letters and Papers Illustrative of the Wars of the English in France*, ed. J.S. Stevenson, Vol. 1 (1864)
Benet	'John Benet's Chronicle for the years 1400 to 1462', ed. G.L. and M.A. Harriss, *Camden Miscellany* (1972)
Blacman	*Henry the Sixth: A Reprint of John Blacman's Memoir*, transl. M.R. James (1919)
Brut	*Brut or Chronicles of England*, ed. F.W.D. Brie (1908)
Crowland	*Crowland Chronicle Continuations 1459–1486*, ed. N. Pronay and J. Cox (1986)
CSPM	*Calendar of State Papers and Manuscripts existing in the Archives and Collections of Milan*, Vol. 1, 1385–1618, ed. A.B. Hinds (1913)
Davies	*An English Chronicle of the Reigns of Richard II, Henry IV, Henry V and Henry VI*, ed. J.S. Davies (1856)
EHD	*English Historical Documents*, Vol. 4, 1327–1485, ed. A.R. Myers (1969)
Flemming	*England under the Lancastrians*, ed. J.H. Flemming (1921)
Flenley	*Six Town Chronicles of England*, ed. R. Flenley (1911)
Gairdner	*Three Fifteenth-Century Chronicles*, ed. J. Gairdner (1880)
Giles	*Incerti Scriptoris Chronicon Angliae de Regnis Henrici IV, Henrici V et Henrici VI*, ed. J.A. Giles (1848)
Great Chronicle	*Great Chronicle of London*, ed. A.H. Thomas and I.D. Thornley (1938)
Gregory	'Gregory's Chronicle' in *Historical Collections of a Citizen of London*, ed. J. Gairdner (1876)
Hallam	*Chronicles of the Wars of the Roses*, ed. E. Hallam (1988)
Ingulph	*Ingulph's Chronicle of the Abbey of Croyland*, ed. H.T. Riley (1854)
Lander	J.R. Lander, *The Wars of the Roses* (1965)
Paston Letters	*Paston Letters 1422–1509*, ed. J. Gairdner, 6 vols (1904)
Robbins	*Historical Poems of the 14th and 15th Centuries*, ed. R.H. Robbins (1959)
Rotuli Parliamentorum	*Rotuli Parliamentorum*, ed. J. Strachey and others, 6 vols (1767–1777)
Thornley	*England under the Yorkists 1460–1485*, ed. I.D. Thornley (1920)
Vergil	*Three Books of Polydore Vergil's English History*, ed. H. Ellis (1844)
Warkworth	John Warkworth, *A Chronicle of the First Thirteen Years of the Reign of King Edward the Fourth*, ed. J.O. Halliwell (1839)
Whethamsted	*Registrum Abbatiae Johannis Whethamstede*, Vol. 1, ed. H.T. Riley (1872)
Wilkinson	B. Wilkinson, *Constitutional History of England in the Fifteenth Century* (1964)

Edward III
(1327–1377)

Edward the
Black Prince

Richard II
(1377–1399)

Lionel Duke of
Clarence

Philippa = Edmund
Mortimer Earl of
March

Roger Mortimer
Earl of March

Anne Mortimer =
Richard Earl of
Cambridge

Richard Duke of
York

Edward IV
(1461–1483)

John of Gaunt
Duke of Lancaster

Henry IV
(1399–1413)

Henry V
(1413–1422)

Henry VI
(1422–1461)

Edward of
Lancaster

Edmund of Langley
Duke of York

Richard Earl
of Cambridge

Richard Duke of
York

Edward IV
(1461–1483)

Introduction:
Sources and Historiography

Jane Austen, a self-confessed 'partial, prejudiced and ignorant historian', declared, in her *History of England* (written in 1791) that:

> I cannot say much for [Henry VI's] sense. Nor would I if I could, for he was
> a Lancastrian . . .
> This king married Margaret of Anjou, a woman whose distresses and
> misfortunes were so great as almost to make me, who hate her, pity her . . .
> There were several battles between the Yorkists and Lancastrians, in which
> the former (as they ought) usually conquered.

The great novelist's youthful scribblings on Henry VI, Margaret of Anjou and the Wars of the Roses have long since been forgotten. By contrast, William Shakespeare's *Henry VI, Parts 1, 2* and *3*, a trilogy of plays written in the early 1590s, remain firmly embedded in English consciousness, most notably the dramatist's presentation of the fifteenth-century civil wars as a series of dynastic struggles, his emphasis on their bloody nature and the prevalence of blood feuds, and his compelling portraits of the leading participants in this traumatic tale of power politics, perfidy and paranoia. Yet, since Shakespeare so firmly reflected Tudor tradition on the struggles of Lancaster and York, he is, arguably, no more to be relied on than Jane Austen.

Contemporary and near-contemporary commentators certainly disagreed about both Henry VI and Margaret of Anjou; historians, too, have brought in contrasting verdicts. For John Blacman, a Carthusian monk who served as the king's chaplain for several years, the 'upright and just' Henry VI deserved admiration as a man 'more given to God and to devout prayer than to handling worldly and temporal things'; yet John Whethamsted, Abbot of St Albans, another well-informed contemporary, judged him 'a son greatly degenerated' from his father Henry V who proved 'half-witted in affairs of state'. Henry VI's modern biographer B.P. Wolffe argued that, at any rate until his mental breakdown in 1453, the king himself was 'the essential unique feature of the reign', actively presiding over the liquidation of the Lancastrian empire in France and responsible, too, for 'creeping paralysis in home affairs and a consequent collapse of respect for law and order by the great'; John Watts, by contrast, concluded (in his 1996 study of *Henry VI and the Politics of Kingship*) that, such was Henry's lack of independent will, he 'never came to perform the role expected of an adult king'. Much contemporary English comment on Margaret of Anjou was critical, not least a letter of February 1456 where she is described as 'a great and strong laboured woman' who 'spares no pains to pursue her objectives towards an end and conclusion favourable to her power'; yet one of her servants, in October 1458, remarked on his mistress's 'wise and charitable disposition', while the queen's own letters certainly supply evidence of her good ladyship and compassion for the poor and needy. Moreover, although Margaret's modern biographer J.J. Bagley particularly chose to highlight, in 1948, her 'intense bitter feeling' towards her opponents, her 'refusal to compromise' and her single-minded championing of Prince Edward of Lancaster's right to inherit his father's throne, Patricia-Ann Lee has recently questioned the reliability of hostile male judgements (both in her own time and since) on a woman who clearly failed to conform to their stereotype of apt queenly behaviour.

Virtually everything pertaining to the Wars of the Roses has provoked controversy, even the term itself. S.B. Chrimes, in his 1964 survey *Lancastrians, Yorkists and Henry VII*, saw no justification for the continued employment of so erroneous and misleading an expression: the white rose, he argued, was only one Yorkist symbol among many, while the red rose (a Tudor device) was never used by Henry VI. Charles Ross, by contrast, considered it 'surely pedantic' in 1976 to reject a phrase whose genesis at least was contemporary. The second continuator of the *Crowland Chronicle*, writing in 1486, remarked on the red rose avenging the white at Bosworth the previous year; Polydore Vergil, in the early sixteenth century, learned that 'the white rose was the emblem of one family and the red rose of the other'; Sir John Oglander referred to 'the quarrel of the warring roses' in 1646 and David Hume the 'wars of the two roses' in 1762: consequently, when Sir Walter Scott (in his 1829 novel *Anne of Geierstein*) highlighted 'the civil discords so dreadfully prosecuted in the wars of the White and Red Roses', he simply immortalized an already well-established usage of the term. Historians cannot agree either about when the wars commenced (1399, 1450, 1452, 1453, 1455 and 1459 have all been put forward at one time or another) or when they ended (1471, 1485 and 1487 have found favour here). As for the causes, nature and impact of the wars, historical debate remains as vigorous as ever.[1]

CONTEMPORARY AND NEAR-CONTEMPORARY SOURCES FOR 1450–1471

Traditionally, historians of Henry VI, Margaret of Anjou and the Wars of the Roses have relied heavily on contemporary and near-contemporary narratives but, as twentieth-century scholars have delved ever more thoroughly into the vast bulk of surviving records for 1450–71, their shortcomings have become ever more apparent. Many chronicle accounts are short, their authors often anonymous and their sources of information unclear or even unknown. Narratives were often written years after the events they describe, their chronology is sometimes faulty, and they contain factual inaccuracies and incorrect dates. Frequently, they not only reflect the political propaganda of the times but present clearly partisan explanations and interpretations of events: indeed, almost all the chronicles covering the period 1450–71 (many of them written after Henry VI's deposition in 1461) are pro-Yorkist, favouring Richard of York in the 1450s and Edward IV thereafter. True, the *Chronicon Angliae* (1450–55) and *Warkworth's Chronicle* (1461–71) do contain some critical comment on Richard of York's behaviour in the early 1450s and Edward IV's policies after 1461, but it was not until Polydore Vergil put pen to paper in the early sixteenth century that Lancastrian tradition on the Wars of the Roses found a narrative spokesman of distinction. Also, since most chroniclers reflect a southern, often London, bias, their accounts of events in the north tend to be thin at best and seriously confused at worst. Moreover, although chronicles occasionally provide meaty accounts of battles (for instance, *Gregory's Chronicle* on the second battle of St Albans in 1461 and the *Arrival of Edward IV* on Barnet and Tewkesbury in 1471), too often they are ignorant of topography, uncertain about the details of fighting and unreliable on the nature and size of armies: most notably, Wakefield in 1460, a northern battle and a Yorkist defeat, tends to be passed over rapidly, and chroniclers provide hardly any coverage at all of the Northumberland battle of Hexham in 1464. Nevertheless, for all their shortcomings, historians cannot dispense with narratives in favour of records. Much of our chronology of politics and war 1450–71 comes from them; they supply invaluable details of events not available elsewhere; and, if handled with care, they can provide real insight into men's motivations and behaviour. Records certainly supplement chronicles – plugging gaps in the storyline, correcting details and inaccuracies, and even on occasion offering alternative explanations of what was going on – but they can never replace them entirely.

Records, Letters and Papers

English governments since the later eleventh century had become ever more prone to accumulate records and, by the mid-fifteenth century, well-established departments of state such as Chancery and Exchequer were generating large quantities of documents: indeed, most new material on Henry VI, Margaret of Anjou and the Wars of the Roses that has come to light in recent times has been gleaned from central government (or public) records. *Chancery Patent Rolls* have proved a particularly rich quarry of information, providing insight into the exercise of government power in a whole range of respects and invaluable for evidence of who benefited from royal patronage, and who did not, during these turbulent years. There are also supplementary Chancery rolls recording pardons granted for offences, containing interesting indications of men's political affiliations and possible military involvement in the wars. The Exchequer archive throws much light on the dire state of late Lancastrian government finances, while the records of the central criminal court of King's Bench not only provide evidence of lawlessness, riot and even rebellion but also tantalizing glimpses of how Henry VI and his government may have been perceived by ordinary folk.[2]

Parliament almost invariably enjoyed a higher profile during periods of political turmoil and warfare in later medieval England than when peace and stability prevailed. This is certainly true of Henry VI's reign: in 1439, for instance, there were complaints in Parliament about royal extravagance; in 1445 Parliament attempted, albeit with little success, to limit the size of the king's household; and, in 1449/50, ferocious attacks on government waste and corruption led R.A. Griffiths to dub this Parliament 'the most difficult assembly with which an English king had to deal since 1399'. Unfortunately, the records of Parliament are by no means as substantial as we would like: there is a dearth of information about the day-to-day workings of Lords and Commons; not a great deal is known about parliamentary procedure; and virtually nothing survives of parliamentary debates or votes. Consequently, we are forced to rely on documents which, while telling us a fair amount about *what* was done in Parliament, say very little about *how*. The rolls of Parliament formally record parliamentary proceedings and legislation but clearly omit a great deal of material that might have proved invaluable to the political historian. Occasionally, they do come alive: for instance, there is interesting evidence of Henry VI's incapacity in March 1454 and on the Courtenay/Bonville feud in south-western England in November 1455. Commons' petitions – such as that of March 1453 calling for a responsible and wise council – certainly point to concern among MPs about the king's government. And even relatively formal parliamentary documents like the records of William de la Pole Duke of Suffolk's impeachment in 1450, Jack Cade's attainder in 1451 and the Coventry Parliament's comprehensive indictment of Yorkist leaders in the autumn of 1459 can prove very informative.[3]

Propagandist intentions clearly underpinned many of the proclamations, manifestos, broadsheets, newsletters, even political ballads and poems, promulgated and circulated during the period 1450–71, particularly at times of political crisis and military confrontation such as 1450, 1455, 1459–61 and 1469–71. Moreover, although the Lancastrian regime did increasingly recognize the need to defend its record and behaviour following the upheavals of 1450, it was the government's critics who most effectively exploited the potential of carefully slanted propaganda. Indeed, as Charles Ross emphasized in 1981, the Yorkist dynasty 'came to power in 1461 in the wake of a veritable flood of propaganda', when 'all the then known propaganda devices' had been employed.[4] As early as June 1450, a manifesto put out by the Cade rebels not only demanded the dismissal of 'the false progeny and affinity of the Duke of Suffolk' but also that Henry VI should 'take about his noble person men of his true blood', particularly 'the high and mighty prince the Duke of York'. Later in the year Richard of York himself, in a public bill directed to the king, remarked on 'the great complaining and rumour' universal throughout the realm that 'justice is not duly administered' against men indicted of treason; in February 1452, in a manifesto issued from Shrewsbury, he complained that the Duke of Somerset 'ever prevails and rules about the king's person', as a result of which 'the land is likely to be destroyed'; and, in the aftermath of their victory at St Albans in May 1455, the Yorkists ensured that a letter justifying their recent behaviour was entered on the Parliament roll. In the autumn of 1459 Richard Neville Earl of Warwick, by now a veritable Yorkist campaign manager, not only gave public airing to his personal grievances against the Lancastrian government but also promulgated a manifesto particularly calling for the enforcement of 'good politic laws ordained for the keeping and maintaining of the commonweal'. No doubt Warwick was responsible, as well, for a notably comprehensive recital of the shortcomings of Henry VI's regime issued from Calais shortly before the Yorkists mounted the invasion culminating in their victory at Northampton early in July 1460. Many political poems, ballads and songs, too, bear clear hallmarks of Yorkist propaganda: verses displayed on the gates of Canterbury in June 1460, for instance, not only portrayed an England divided against itself, ruled by an impoverished king dominated by incompetent ministers, and virtually on the brink of destruction, but also prayed for the return of the Yorkist lords; poems survive celebrating the Yorkist victories at Northampton and Towton and lamenting Richard of York's death at Wakefield; and, in 1462, a pro-Yorkist ballad particularly targeted Margaret of Anjou.

Not all popular poetry of the time adopted a pro-Yorkist stance. Verses written in London in 1456 condemned Richard of York in no uncertain terms, while *The Ship of State*, in 1458, both criticized the Yorkists and commended Henry VI and his ministers. Particularly significant, perhaps, is another ballad of 1458 celebrating the procession of Lancastrian and Yorkist lords to St Paul's on 25 March as a most welcome harbinger of concord and unity. Nor are government-sponsored pro-Lancastrian propaganda initiatives entirely lacking. The public oath of allegiance to Henry VI sworn by Richard of York at St Paul's on 10 March 1452, for instance, was clearly meant to highlight the legitimacy of the Lancastrian king and his regime, while the long recital of York's treacheries since 1450 that preluded the act of attainder passed by the Coventry Parliament in November 1459 has an even more overtly propagandist ring to it. In recent years, moreover, John Watts has focused a great deal of attention on the tract *Somnium Vigilantes*, a contemporary *defence* of the proscription of the Yorkists at Coventry. Perhaps written by the prominent Lancastrian polemicist Sir John Fortescue, it certainly contains a robust defence of the Lancastrian regime and a powerful condemnation of the leading Yorkists who, on account of their appalling record of conspiracy and treachery, deserve neither pardon nor mercy.[5]

Historians of Henry VI, Margaret of Anjou and the Wars of the Roses have long drawn heavily on official, semi-official and private letters. Unfortunately, although many letters bear Henry VI's name, there is a real question mark over how far he can be regarded as personally responsible for what they contain (particularly once he suffered a severe mental breakdown in 1453). Margaret of Anjou's surviving letters bear an altogether more personal imprint and they certainly show her as a vigorous, businesslike woman, very much in command of her own affairs: her good ladyship to members of her household and tenants on her estates is particularly evident, as is her willingness to canvass the support of other high-ranking women in order to achieve her ends. Since most of the letters were written during the early years of her life in England, however, their political content is regrettably thin.[6] For the historian of the Wars of the Roses, in fact, the semi-official reports contained in the *Milanese State Papers* are altogether more interesting. These ambassadorial letters – sent, mainly, by Milanese envoys in England, France and Burgundy to successive Sforza dukes of Milan – can, on occasion, prove notably unreliable, confuse rumour with fact and display a considerable degree of credulity: for instance, a despatch of 17 June 1471 reported not only that Edward IV had 'caused King Henry to be secretly assassinated in the Tower' (probably true) but also an entirely erroneous rumour that 'he has done the same' to Margaret of Anjou. Nevertheless, these letters were often written very soon after the events they reported; news of domestic developments in England was not infrequently sent by envoys in London, or by men who had only recently returned from there to the continent; and Milanese visitors to both the French and Burgundian courts often seem very well-informed on diplomatic matters. Newsletters certainly provide valuable evidence of campaigning and battles: for instance, there are reports of the first battle of St Albans in May 1455, the Yorkist campaigns culminating in success at Northampton and failure at Wakefield in 1460, the alarm in London that followed the victory of Margaret of Anjou's northern army at the second battle of St Albans in February 1461, the great Yorkist triumph at Towton a few weeks later, and Edward IV's decisive victories at Barnet and Tewkesbury in 1471. Equally important is the light thrown on Margaret of Anjou and the Lancastrians, particularly during the decade following Henry VI's deposition in 1461.[7]

Private letters and papers first appear in significant quantities in fifteenth-century England and such vernacular letters, often precisely dated and not consciously recording events for posterity, can provide valuable supplements to chronicles and records for the years 1450–71. Unfortunately, few noble letters survive but the large collection of letters and papers bequeathed by the Pastons, a Norfolk gentry family, has long been recognized as a uniquely important archive.

Many newsletters, not all of them written either by or to members of the Paston family, have certainly found their way into this rich collection: for instance, there is a graphic report of Suffolk's fate, and a harrowing account of one individual's suffering when he got caught up in Cade's rebellion, in 1450; a long and informative newsletter from London, written in January 1454, reports on Henry VI's incapacity and its dire political consequences, while another, of January 1455, contains evidence of the king's recovery; and much of the political manoeuvring and military campaigning that marked the years 1455–61 elicits comment too. Also, there are numerous letters highlighting how political and military events affected the Pastons themselves, particularly Sir John Paston (1442–79) and his brother, another John (1444–1504), culminating in both of them fighting for the Lancastrians at the battle of Barnet in April 1471.[8]

Chronicles, Annals and Lives of Henry VI

Historians of twelfth and thirteenth-century England are well served by contemporary and near-contemporary chronicles, annals and lives: William of Malmesbury, a sophisticated monastic chronicler, put together an invaluable political narrative of Henry I's reign; the *Gesta Stephani*, even if a consistently favourable life of the last Norman king, provides much insight into his turbulent times; and, in the early thirteenth century, Roger of Wendover and Matthew Paris not only penned portraits of King John as an evil tyrant that were to tarnish his reputation for hundreds of years but also established a tradition of historical writing at the monastery of St Albans that lasted until the 1460s. The fourteenth and early fifteenth centuries, too, bequeathed literary sources of real quality: the *Vita Edwardi Secundi* is a major, if hardly impartial, source for Edward II, and the *Gesta Henrici Quinti* performed a similar service for Henry V; the *Anonimalle Chronicle* covers the years 1346–81 with distinction; and Thomas Walsingham, who breathed new life into historical writing at St Albans, is indispensable for the reigns of Richard II, Henry IV and Henry V. All these, and many other, historical works were written in Latin by clerics. By the mid-fifteenth century, however, both the quality and quantity of Latin clerical sources was in serious decline: lives of Henry VI by John Capgrave and John Blacman focused almost exclusively on the man not the king; few secular clergy recorded the political events of the time; and only at St Albans and Crowland did monks show much interest in continuing earlier chronicles. The future, in fact, lay with historical composition in English for a wider and more popular audience.

C.L. Kingsford believed that 'the most popular and widely read history of England' in the fifteenth century was the *Brut*, so called because its narrative began with Brutus, legendary Trojan founder of an ancient British kingdom. A large number of manuscripts of this vernacular chronicle have survived, produced mainly in London and penned by anonymous authors, and, when

William Caxton published his *Chronicles of England* in 1480, the *Brut* became our first printed history. Entirely lacking in sophistication, firmly pro-Yorkist when recounting the last years of Lancastrian rule, and ending in 1461, the *Brut* nevertheless has great value for historians of Henry VI, Margaret of Anjou and the Wars of the Roses since its contemporary credentials are beyond question: much of it, in fact, probably reflects each particular author's knowledge of events, the reports of eyewitnesses and the content of newsletters, ballads and poems circulating in London. Two closely related versions, here dubbed the *Brut* and the *English Chronicle*, certainly have real value for the later years of Henry VI's reign. The *Brut*, significantly less detailed than the *English Chronicle*, was probably compiled between 1464 and 1470 and clearly reflects its post-1461 date of composition: for instance, while providing a splendid description of Margaret of Anjou's arrival in London in May 1445, it deplored the cession of Anjou and Maine as part of the marriage settlement, placed the blame firmly on Suffolk's shoulders, and lavished praise on his rival Humphrey Duke of Gloucester; similarly, it both sympathized with Richard of York's dilemma at Dartford in 1452 and deplored the ascendancy of Somerset. As for the Wars of the Roses, while portraying Henry VI as 'a good, simple and innocent man', the chronicler condemned the behaviour of Margaret of Anjou and the Lancastrian leadership in a robustly pro-Yorkist manner.[9] The authorship of the *English Chronicle*, too, is unknown but it seems to have been written not long after Edward IV's seizure of the throne in 1461 and, like the *Brut*, very much reflected prevailing Yorkist propaganda concerning Henry VI and his regime: indeed, J.R. Lander once dubbed its compiler a 'Yorkist pamphleteer'. Yet, for the last eleven years of Lancastrian rule, the *English Chronicle* must nonetheless be regarded as a source of major importance. The narrator provides, in particular, a detailed and independent-minded account of Cade's rebellion in 1450; much critical, but probably widely believed, comment on Somerset's behaviour in the early 1450s; and a coherent, if firmly pro-Yorkist, treatment of the political manoeuvres culminating in the first battle of St Albans in May 1455 and, later, the so-called Loveday of March 1458. Even more valuable is the chronicler's detailed and well-informed narrative of the events of 1459–61, not least his accounts of the battles fought during these years and their significance. Never are his Yorkist credentials more clearly evident, however, than when, under the year 1459, he portrayed an England 'out of all good governance', under a king who was 'simple and led by covetous counsel' and a queen who 'with such as were of her affinity ruled the realm as she liked'.[10]

The most significant development in historical writing in fifteenth-century England came in London with the compilation of a series of civic narrative histories, not infrequently continuations of the *Brut* or older city annals, known collectively as the London chronicles. More than thirty versions and fragments of the genre have come down to us, often closely connected and happily lifting material from each other, and they are probably just the survivors of a much larger class. C.L. Kingsford, whose knowledge of them has never been surpassed, remarked that these vernacular narratives are frequently 'rude and artless', often anonymous, and almost always pro-Yorkist in their perspective on later Lancastrian England. Nevertheless, he believed, London chronicles are 'perhaps the most important [of] all the original authorities for English history in the fifteenth century'. Either directly or via the *Brut*, they underpin the majority of minor chronicles of the time; many of them were contemporary with, or written very soon after, the events they record; and, particularly when covering happenings in and around London, they tend to be notably well informed. For the period 1450–69 an anonymous continuation of *Gregory's Chronicle*, perhaps compiled by a London cleric, cannot be bettered. Marked throughout by a splendidly personal tone and even humorous on occasion, the chronicler provides particularly valuable coverage of events in London and south-eastern England in 1450/1; his narrative of Henry VI's last full year as king has much material not to be found anywhere else, not least his story of Margaret of Anjou's adventures in the autumn of 1460 and very detailed treatment of the second battle of St Albans in February 1461; and, for the collapse of northern Lancastrian resistance to Edward IV in 1464, he is indispensable. Unfortunately, the narrative ends in 1469 and it breaks off so abruptly that, in all probability, one or more pages of the manuscript have been lost.[11] *Bale's Chronicle*, penned by another anonymous London annalist, provides a contemporary and, occasionally, original narrative of events during the 1450s, particularly noteworthy for its critical stance on the Lancastrian regime's failure to maintain law and order in the country.[12] The *Short English Chronicle*, ending in 1465 and probably written not long after, is essentially annalistic and adds little to what more substantial London chronicles have to offer; *London Chronicle: Gough 10* has a certain value for 1450/1 and provides an independent if clearly pro-Yorkist account of Edward IV's seizure of the throne in March 1461; *London Chronicle: Arundel 19* is not without interest for Richard of York's behaviour early in 1452; and *London Chronicle: Rawlinson B355*, a Latin fragment perhaps translated from a vernacular London original, is certainly virulently pro-Yorkist in its hostile treatment of Somerset in the early 1450s.[13] Even the *Great Chronicle of London*, although not written until the first decade of the sixteenth century, can fairly claim attention for its remarks on Towton in 1461, as well as ensuing Lancastrian resistance to Edward IV in northern England culminating in the battle of Hexham and its aftermath in 1464. For the readeption of Henry VI in 1470/1, moreover, this is a major source, containing a particularly vivid (and probably eyewitness) account of the Lancastrian king's pathetic progress through London shortly before the battle of Barnet in April 1471.[14]

Three minor English chronicles, none covering the whole period 1450–71 but all possessing characteristics peculiar to themselves, have a certain interest and value. In 1457 John Harding, a former soldier, presented a copy of the first version of his English verse chronicle to Henry VI. Much of it is chivalric in tone, recording the heroic deeds of kings like Henry V, and has little historical value, but it does contain significant stanzas highlighting the lawlessness prevailing under Henry VI and urging him to rule as his father had. The second version of *Harding's Chronicle*, this time dedicated initially to Richard of York and then his son Edward IV, was probably completed in 1464 and has an altogether more overtly pro-Yorkist tone: in particular it suggests that, even as a boy, Henry VI had dim wits and lacked judgement, while Richard of York's record in Normandy, Ireland and as protector of the realm is commended. The *Chronicle of John Warkworth*, probably penned between 1478 and 1483 by a Northumbrian cleric resident in Cambridge, covers the years 1461–71. Less partisan to the Yorkists and showing more interest in northern England than most chronicles, it should perhaps be described as critical of Edward IV rather than overtly Lancastrian. Certainly, Warkworth displays considerable sympathy for Henry VI and his plight and, when describing the king's loss of the throne in 1461, firmly blamed the 'mischievous people about the king' who were 'so covetous towards themselves' rather than Henry himself; he provides more coverage than most of resistance to Edward IV in the north during the early 1460s; and his account of events culminating in Henry VI's readeption in 1470 and Edward IV's successful campaign to regain the throne in 1471 is indispensable. Similarly, the *Arrival of Edward IV*, although very clearly an official Yorkist narrative of the 1471 campaign, provides much detail about the battles of Barnet and Tewkesbury not to be found anywhere else.[15]

Several continental chroniclers occasionally find room for events in mid-fifteenth century England, including Thomas Basin, Georges Chastellain and Philippe de Commines. None, however, provides the degree of coverage found in the pages of Jean de Waurin. A prominent Burgundian man of affairs, Waurin had a particular interest in the history of England: perhaps first fostered when, as a young man, he had fought with the English against the French, it was reinforced, later in life, by his diplomatic activities, his contacts with English exiles on the continent and, in 1467, a visit to London. Often, moreover, he writes in very considerable detail and, for the era of the Wars of the Roses, his narrative is largely independent of other sources (his discussion of Edward IV's restoration to the throne in 1471, where he relied on an abridged version of the *Arrival of Edward IV*, being the most notable exception). There is a real question mark over Waurin's reliability: he is often inaccurate, his sources of information unclear (although, presumably, he learned a lot from newsletters and visitors to Burgundy who had recently been in England) and, at times, he may have indulged in imaginative reconstruction of what he believed must have happened rather than what actually did! Nevertheless, his comments on personalities and the political scene (even if often Yorkist in sympathy) are of real value: Henry VI, for instance, he regarded as simple minded, a king 'neither intelligent enough nor experienced enough to manage a kingdom such as England'; as for Richard of York, after governing Normandy so admirably he did not deserve the treatment meted out by Margaret of Anjou and Somerset. Waurin, too, certainly had a better grasp of military matters than most chroniclers: indeed, his accounts of English campaigns and battles between 1459 and 1471 are often the fullest available.[16]

There are two Latin lives of Henry VI, both overwhelmingly concerned with the king's qualities and behaviour as a man rather than a monarch. The earlier of the two was penned by John Capgrave, an Augustinian friar from King's Lynn, about 1447, avowedly for Henry's private edification and to honour him in the eyes of his subjects. The *Liber de Illustribus Henricis*, in fact, consists of a series of eulogistic biographies of distinguished Henrys (including emperors and English royal Henrys, and culminating in a short panegyric on Henry VI himself). Since Capgrave dedicated his work to the king, and clearly wished to please him, he mainly concentrated on praising his saintly qualities yet, perhaps significantly, found little positive to say about Henry as king beyond the fact that he founded colleges: the only overt hint at criticism came in a passing regret at Henry's failure to keep the seas better.[17] John Blacman probably put together the Latin tract *Collectarium Mansuetudinum et Bonorum Morum Regis Henrici VI* (*A Compilation of the Meekness and Good Life of King Henry VI*) over a number of years between Henry VI's death in May 1471 and the transfer of his body from Chertsey abbey to St George's chapel, Windsor, in August 1484. Much of its content, no doubt, came from his own personal recollections since, until he retired from the world and entered the austere Carthusian religious order, he served the king as chaplain for a while, as an original fellow of Eton 1443–52 (founded by Henry VI) and as warden of King's Hall Cambridge 1452–8 (another royal foundation). Indeed, Blacman specifically tells us he has determined to record his reminiscences of 'the serene prince King Henry VI now deceased' because:

> . . . to praise the saints of God (in the register of whom I take that excellent king to be rightly included on account of the holy virtues by him exercised all his life long) is to praise and glorify Almighty God.

Nevertheless, Blacman is also at pains to emphasize:

> . . . of his most noble descent, how he was begotten according to the highest blood and the ancient royal stock of England, and how in the two lands of England and France he was crowned as the rightful heir of each realm, I have purposely said nothing, as of a matter plainly known to all, and not least because of that most unhappy fortune which befell him against all expectation in after-times.

And, clearly, Blacman was able to draw not only on 'such things as I have known' but also on what he had 'learned from the relation of men worthy of credit who were formerly attendant on the king'. The compilation is certainly rich in anecdotes about the king's private virtues and behaviour and, both by what it chooses to highlight and what it omits, implicitly critical of Henry VI as a ruler; it is also flawed, however, as a result of its author's personal predilections, indifference to strict accuracy and downright gullibility on occasion.[18] Yet, as Michael Hicks has emphasized, this short life is no mere 'hagiographic collection of apocryphal anecdotes'; rather, if carefully handled, it 'can be made to yield first-hand information about the king'.[19]

Although the future clearly lay with English vernacular narratives, there are several Latin chronicles, written by both secular and regular clergy, covering the era of the Wars of the Roses, particularly the last years of Lancastrian rule. Among them, *Benet's Chronicle* is the most valuable. John Benet probably transcribed the chronicle, which ends abruptly in 1462, into his commonplace book between 1462 and 1468. However, although the narrative seems to be the work of a single individual, it is unlikely to have been Benet himself, since he was rector of Harlington in Bedfordshire 1443–71 whereas the chronicle's author was probably a London-based cleric. Certainly, the account of 1450–61 occasionally displays signs of similarity with vernacular London chronicles (notably *Bale's Chronicle* and *Gregory's Chronicle*), its vantage point is very much that of London and it is at its best when dealing with events in the capital. Unusually lengthy for a mid-fifteenth-century chronicle, it also contains much information not available elsewhere, most notably on meetings of the royal council and Parliament, the movements of the king's household, and factions among (as well as disputes between) the nobility. Few narratives display so much care over chronology, moreover, but this author does take a familiarly pro-Yorkist line throughout. Richard of York is presented as the guarantor of stability in 1450/1; his behaviour early in 1452 is reported as avowedly 'for the good of the country and directed not against the king but at those who betrayed him'; and, as protector of the realm in 1454/5, he 'governed the entire kingdom of England well and honourably'. Suffolk, by contrast, is 'the wicked duke', Somerset's negligence is blamed for England losing Normandy, and Margaret of Anjou receives little sympathy either, not least since she 'greatly loathed' both York and Warwick. The chronicler vividly describes events in 1450, particularly Jack Cade's rebellion, clearly drawing on first-hand knowledge; thereafter, too, he frequently adds original detail to the narrative of political events, not least for the ill-documented later 1450s, all culminating in the deposition of Henry VI 'since he ruled tyrannously' and the coronation of the triumphant Edward IV 'with God's favour'.[20]

The *Chronicon Angliae* (often called *Giles' Chronicle* after its nineteenth-century editor), an anonymous Latin chronicle probably written by a cleric at the end of the 1450s, provides a refreshingly independent-minded account of Henry VI's reign from 1437, not least the period 1450–55. Regrettably, the narrative ends abruptly on the eve of the first battle of St Albans in May 1455: this is particularly irksome since, if we are to believe C.A.J. Armstrong, the *Chronicon Angliae* is the one contemporary chronicle unfriendly to York and not overtly hostile to Somerset.[21] Certainly, Richard of York's behaviour at Dartford in 1452 and subsequent humiliation in London elicited no sympathy from this chronicler; Somerset was accused, in the autumn of 1453, of 'betraying Normandy', and imprisoned, 'even though no charge of treason could be proved against him'; and, in March 1455, York, Salisbury and Warwick 'left the royal household and council without permission or formality, determined not to obey the king's commands' so long as their opponents enjoyed royal favour.[22] Thomas Gascoigne, an Oxford theologian whose notes were written up as *Loci e Libro Veritatem* (*Theological Dictionary*) soon after his death in 1458, was not so much independent-minded as downright sardonic, especially in his occasional comments on politics and the personalities of Henry VI's last years: the king himself he portrayed as a pathetic and gullible figure liable to blatant manipulation by his minders; Margaret of Anjou's power in the realm clearly met with his disapproval; and even Richard of York did not escape criticism.[23] The *Annales Rerum Anglicarum*, another Latin compilation, were formerly (and wrongly) attributed to the fifteenth-century antiquary William Worcester; the annals are frequently short, disconnected and not always reliable in their chronology; and the annalist was still at work as late as 1491. Nevertheless, the *Annales* do provide information about the 1450s and 1460s (they end abruptly in 1468) not to be found anywhere else and, occasionally, sound a personal note: for instance, the author tells us that 'I was present and heard' the popular acclamation of Edward IV as king in March 1461 'and afterwards I came with them immediately into the city'. When reporting Parliament's meeting in November 1450, the annalist highlighted the ensuing 'great disagreement' between York and Somerset and, in 1451, the Commons petitioning the king 'to remove several of his familiars', even if 'nothing came of it'; he regarded the onset of private war between the great northern families of Percy and Neville (specifically, events on Heworth Moor near York in August 1453) as 'the beginning of the greatest sorrows in England'; and, for the battles of Wakefield, Mortimer's Cross and second St Albans in 1460/1, he seems better informed than many sources.[24]

Although the monastic chronicle was already well on the way to extinction by 1450, the tradition still continued at St Albans and Crowland. John Whethamsted, who enjoyed a considerable contemporary reputation as a scholar and man of letters, had two spells as abbot of St Albans before his death in 1465: 1420–40 and 1452–65. During both he encouraged the compilation of *Registers* and may well, if the flowery, verbose and exuberant Latin style is anything to go by, have composed significant parts of them himself; moreover, while mainly devoted to the affairs of the abbey, the second *Register* (ending soon after Edward IV became king in 1461) is also notable for its very lengthy passages on the political and military events of the times. St Albans was well situated geographically for receiving news of political developments in London, no doubt often brought by visitors to the abbey, and, not surprisingly, the *Register* is especially informative on the two battles fought in the vicinity. The chronicle certainly provides graphic coverage of Henry VI's last years, not least the dramatic sequence of events in Parliament during the autumn of 1460 (of which John Whethamsted may well have been, in part at least, an observer) and the appalling behaviour of the northern Lancastrian army following the Yorkist defeat at Wakefield soon afterwards. Generally speaking, the chronicler's stance is sympathetic to the Yorkists but not uncritically so: for instance, although he believed Richard of York had plenty of justification for lambasting Somerset in the early 1450s, he had distinct reservations about the morality of so implacable a vendetta; similarly, while commending Yorkist efforts to avoid military confrontation at St Albans in 1455, he remarked also on the high-handedness of Richard of York's behaviour when claiming the throne in 1460.[25] The Benedictine abbey of Crowland (or Croyland) in Lincolnshire has bequeathed two chronicles (or, rather, two continuations of the spurious *Ingulph's Chronicle*) covering the Wars of the Roses era. The earlier of the two – probably written by a prior of Crowland and ending in January 1470 – is mostly devoted to the history of the abbey; as the writer approached his own time, however, the interest of the work increases, as does the amount of political content. What most moved the chronicler, clearly, was his horror of civil war and he certainly did not spare the hyperbole when recounting the sufferings it allegedly brought:

> [The] slaughter of men was immense; for besides the dukes, earls, barons and distinguished warriors who were cruelly slain, multitudes almost innumerable of the common people died of their wounds. Such was the state of the kingdom for nearly ten years.

And the depths of misery were never more plumbed than at Towton in 1461 when:

> . . . the blood of the slain, mingling with the snow which at this time covered the whole surface of the earth, afterwards ran down in the furrows and ditches along with the melted snow, in a most shocking manner, for a distance of two or three miles.

Nevertheless, despite a rather naive pro-Yorkist perspective, the first Crowland continuator is not without merit as a commentator: for instance, he had a degree of understanding of Henry VI's shortcomings and their consequences; he questioned Richard of York's wisdom in confronting the northern Lancastrian army at Wakefield; and, when that army marched south early in 1461 and seemed to threaten Crowland abbey itself, his panic-stricken reaction cannot be dismissed as mere anti-northern hysteria. The second continuator of the *Crowland Chronicle*, observing that his predecessor – out of what he calls an unworldly ignorance of secular matters – had skated over many of the political details of the 1460s, began his narrative with the rout of Ludford in October 1459. Although anonymous, the 1459–86 continuation seems to have been written by an intelligent and politically well-informed cleric, probably at Crowland abbey in April 1486. His coverage of 1459–71 is relatively slight but there is a refreshing degree of objectivity in his assessment of events and their significance, not least the Yorkist failure at Ludford and its consequences, the dramatic scenes in Parliament during October 1460 when Richard of York claimed the throne, and his son Edward IV's successful eclipsing of the Lancastrians, first in the early 1460s, and again in 1471.[26]

Polydore Vergil, an Italian cleric and Renaissance humanist historian of real quality, came to England in 1502 and, encouraged by Henry VII, began work on his comprehensive history of England about 1507. Whether the resulting *Anglica Historia* (*English History*), not completed until 1531, can be regarded as a primary source for 1450–71 is a moot point: its treatment as such can, perhaps, be tentatively justified on the grounds that, since virtually all contemporary and near-contemporary chronicles reflect a Yorkist perspective on events, Vergil at least preserved, and gave expression to, Lancastrian tradition about the Wars of the Roses. Not that he, any more than the first Crowland continuator, had any doubts about the horrors of civil war. As a result of 'intestine hatred and divisions among the noble', he declared, the state of the realm became:

> . . . most miserable, for churches and houses were everywhere spoiled, sword and fire raged all over, the realm was wholly replenished with armour and weapons, and slaughter, blood and lamentation; the fields were wasted, town and city starved for hunger, and many other mischiefs happened, which proceed commonly from the rage of wars.

When trying to explain the beginnings of such mayhem, however, Vergil put the blame firmly on Richard of York, whose 'outrageous lust of principality' for himself, and denunciation of Edmund Beaufort Duke of Somerset (a loyal and fair counsellor of the king) as 'an unjust, proud and cruel tyrant', led inexorably to the first battle of St Albans. Moreover, he believed, as a result of York's machinations 'men were so nourished by factionalism that they could not later desist from it': hence the years of civil strife that followed until, eventually, peace and stability were restored by the early Tudors, Henry VII and Henry VIII.[27]

HISTORIOGRAPHY OF HENRY VI, MARGARET OF ANJOU AND THE WARS OF THE ROSES

Henry VI

Contemporary and near-contemporary comment on Henry VI personally is not great in bulk but what there is certainly suggests a stark contrast between this king and his warrior father Henry V. Piero da Monte, a Papal official in England at the time, reported in 1437 that the young Henry VI 'avoided the sight and conversation of women', had 'resolved to have intercourse with no woman unless within the bonds of matrimony' and had a 'mild, gentle and calm' manner 'less like a king or secular prince than a monk'; a few years later, in 1447, French envoys found an opulently dressed king 'well pleased and very joyful to see them' but hardly regal in his behaviour; and in 1450 Hans Winter, a Prussian agent in London, remarked that Henry VI (although now the same age as his father had been at Agincourt in 1415!) 'is very young and inexperienced and watched over as a Carthusian'. Jean de Waurin, similarly, learned that even the adult king was 'neither intelligent enough nor experienced enough to manage a kingdom such as England' and John Capgrave, significantly, chose to portray Henry as a royal personification of conventional religious piety but remained ominously silent on his political acumen. Even before August 1453 (when the king collapsed into a condition of complete mental torpor), moreover, rumours concerning his mental shortcomings occasionally surfaced: in 1442, for instance, a Kentish yeoman was indicted in the court of King's Bench for saying that 'the king is a lunatic'; a London draper, in 1447, was alleged to have remarked not only that Henry had a child's face but also that he 'is not as steadfast of wit as other kings have been before'; in 1450, two Sussex husbandmen were charged for declaring that 'the king was a natural fool' and 'no person able to rule this land'; and, in 1453, two Southwark men apparently described Henry as 'but a sheep' who has 'lost all that his father won and would God he had died soon after he was born'. Once England dissolved into civil war, a clearly Yorkist perspective on Henry VI emerged. In 1460, for instance, Richard Neville Earl of Warwick allegedly declared that 'our king is stupid and out of his mind, he does not rule but is ruled'; Warwick's brother George Neville Bishop of Exeter, in similar vein, remarked in 1461 on 'that puppet of a king', that 'statue of a king'; and Pope Pius II (1458–64) no doubt reflected Yorkist propaganda when he described Henry, in his *Memoirs*, as 'more timorous than a woman, utterly devoid of wit or spirit', who left everything in his wife's hands. Chronicles written soon after Henry VI's deposition certainly tend to be critical: the *English Chronicle*, for instance, recorded under the year 1459 that 'the king was simple and led by covetous counsel'; *Whethamsted's Register*, although applauding the king as modest, guileless, upright and merciful, nevertheless considered him to be 'his mother's stupid offspring', a son 'greatly degenerated from the father who did not cultivate the

art of war', a pious king admittedly but 'half-witted in affairs of state'; and even
Warkworth's Chronicle, while emphasizing that the king was well meaning enough
and not personally responsible for the disasters that befell him, had to admit that
when he was 'put out of the realm by King Edward, all England, for the more
part, hated him, and were fully glad of a change'.[28]

Perhaps it is no coincidence that John Blacman finally put pen to paper not
only after Henry VI's death in May 1471 but also once popular veneration of the
king started to develop, his tomb at Chertsey abbey began to attract pilgrims and
stories spread of miracle-working there. Certainly, this is the most intimate and
detailed near-contemporary portrait we have of Henry VI's personal piety and
religious devotion: a cornucopia of the private virtues of a royal *imitator Christi*,
indeed. The king, according to Blacman, was both 'upright and just' and a man
'more given to God and devout prayer than worldly and temporal matters'; he
enthusiastically embraced the trappings of humility, even off-setting the pomp of
crown-wearing by donning 'a rough hair shirt' next to his skin; and not only was
he personally 'chaste and pure from the beginning of his days' but also sought to
ensure the chastity of his servants. Here, too, we have a charitable and
compassionate man who abhorred violence, a man who accepted his long
imprisonment in the Tower without rancour, and a man of such modesty that he
was disturbed not only by the sight of women with uncovered breasts but naked
men as well. Yet, as Roger Lovatt has convincingly argued, Blacman did not
ignore Henry VI's defects as a ruler. Rather, he redefined the king's public vices
as private virtues: thus his indiscriminate largesse, especially towards members of
his household, becomes charity; his reluctance to enforce the full rigours of the
law and readiness to issue pardons, indications of a merciful disposition; his
unwillingness to adopt an aristocratic lifestyle, symptoms of an austere and
modest piety; and his self-absorption and indifference to royal obligations,
evidence of a concern with spiritual rather than worldly affairs.[29]

Once Henry VII ascended the throne in 1485, what he wanted for propaganda
purposes was an ancestor worthy to have carried the precious blood of Lancaster:
so, if Henry VI could not be portrayed as a successful ruler (as clearly he could
not!), then he must at least be a saintly one. Even as early as April 1486, the
second Crowland continuator clearly believed the 'miracles which God has
performed in answer to the prayers of those who devoutly implored his
intercession' bore witness to Henry VI's 'life of innocence, love of God and of the
church, patience in adversity and other remarkable qualities'; the Warwick
chaplain John Rous, soon afterwards, described Henry as 'a most holy man' who
had little time for the world and worldly affairs; and James Ryman, in 1492,
celebrated the king in verse as 'full of mercy without vengeance', of 'virtue most
excellent' and 'like a second Job, steadfast of faith and mild of mode'. By the time
Polydore Vergil declared 'there was not in this world a more pure, more honest
and more holy creature', a man positively crying out for canonization indeed,

Henry VII had already petitioned more than one pope (albeit unsuccessfully) to raise his uncle to the august company of saints.[30] This portrayal rapidly became the norm as the sixteenth century progressed, culminating in William Shakespeare's 'gentle, mild and virtuous' king, 'fitter for heaven than earth'. Even in the later nineteenth century William Stubbs was still inclined to regard Henry VI, 'perhaps the most unfortunate king who ever reigned', as a man of exemplary devotion and unquestionable sincerity, 'most innocent of all the evils that befell England because of him'. James Gairdner, too, believed he was 'a pious, humane and Christian character'.[31] Yet Mabel Christie, the king's early twentieth-century biographer, considered that Henry VI, whose virtues were 'charity, long-suffering, gentleness, goodness, faith, meekness and temperance', clearly lacked the qualities required for successful kingship:

> With his inherent weakness of character, he was influenced in turn by whichever of his lords had succeeded in insinuating himself into the royal favour. . . . He had no power of self-assertion to check the turbulence of his subjects. . . . Neither did he in the least understand the spirit of his own age, for he dwelt for the most part in a dreamy realm of his own, into which he only allowed the clamour of the outside world to penetrate at necessary intervals. He showed no power either of discerning the character of those about him, or of interpreting the signs of the times.[32]

For K.B. McFarlane, what most characterized Henry VI was not saintliness but inanity, or even insanity: in this king, he declared in 1938, 'second childhood succeeded first without the usual interval and under him the medieval kingship was in abeyance'; similarly, in 1945, he remarked that the character of politics for forty years after Henry V's death largely reflected the fact that, in 1422, the crown had been placed 'upon the head of a baby who grew up an imbecile'. R.L. Storey concluded, in 1966, that accounts of friends and foes alike reveal Henry VI as 'a devout and kindly simpleton' who always inclined to leave the serious work of government to others; J.R. Lander, in 1969, believed government under Henry VI 'drifted to almost inevitable disaster in the nerveless hands of a saintly muff'; and, in 1974, J.W. McKenna found Henry VI a mixture of 'charming indifference and exasperating incompetency'. Indeed, McKenna argued, even some of his contemporaries considered him dour and puritanical: all in all, he was 'the greatest single disaster in saintly royalty since Edward the Confessor'.[33] In 1981 two major biographical studies of the king appeared: Ralph A. Griffiths, *The Reign of King Henry VI*, and Bertram Wolffe, *Henry VI*. Both Griffiths and Wolffe rejected McFarlane's contention that Henry VI progressed seamlessly from infancy to imbecility and argued that the king, for all his shortcomings, did play an active role in government from the later 1430s until 1453. Griffiths was the more cautious of the two, pointing out that, in many instances, it is not possible to be certain of Henry's *personal* intervention in politics (rather than his passive assent to measures formulated by the council): nevertheless, he believed, the king certainly rejected his father's militarism, proved himself extravagant and wasteful and, when demonstrably politically active, was also thoroughly incompetent. A well-intentioned man whose aspirations in those aspects of government that interested him – such as education, Anglo-French relations and rewarding his friends and servants – were laudable enough, he was also credulous, inappropriately compassionate to some, unnecessarily suspicious of others, and, most fatally, lacking foresight, prudence and political judgement. In particular, Griffiths argued, Henry VI:

> . . . showed little sagacity, subtlety or discrimination in his administrative
> acts, and none of the political astuteness necessary to achieve an acceptable
> balance among his subjects' competing interests – as contemporaries
> recognised who stressed his simplicity. Not that Henry was uneducated or
> unintelligent, but he was the least experienced of medieval English kings at
> his accession and never shook off his youthful dependence on others in the
> routine and detail of affairs.

B.P. Wolffe was altogether more damning in his verdict. Henry VI, he argued, was certainly no saint: rather, the suspect Blacman tract and the king's posthumous reputation as a miracle-worker have obscured the reality of a ruler who was neither so pious nor so enlightened in promoting education as traditionally supposed. Nor was he a simpleton: the impression of a king incapable of political initiative even before 1453, staple of so much Yorkist propaganda, must also be rejected. From the end of his minority in 1437 until the early 1450s, according to Wolffe, the king himself was 'the essential unique feature of the reign', actively presiding over the liquidation of the Lancastrian empire in France. Rather than the pious, non-worldly paragon of virtue depicted by Tudor historians, or even the negative tool in the hands of his favourites of Yorkist propaganda, the real Henry VI was a positive (even sinister) political menace. From the late 1430s there was truly personal rule; Henry VI's own unwise exercise of royal patronage seriously weakened the crown's financial position (as well as its political reputation); and, worst of all, from 1444 until 1453 the king took the initiative frequently and with dire consequences in foreign policy. Henry VI's own 'wilful efforts', concluded Wolffe, 'divided, demoralised and hamstrung the English war effort in France, so that it dissolved in defeat and recriminations'. Moreover, the king's conduct simultaneously led to 'creeping paralysis in home affairs and a consequent collapse of respect for law and order by the great'. Once Henry VI had suffered his mental collapse in August 1453, however, both Wolffe and Griffiths agreed that he was rarely, if ever, able to provide any kind of real political leadership again.[34]

Since 1981 there has been only one major study of Henry VI's reign: John Watts, *Henry VI and the Politics of Kingship*, published in 1996. Here, moreover, Henry VI the nullity is back with a vengeance! True, in the Public Record Office can be found:

> . . . mounds of documents, many of them bearing the royal signature, all of them claiming to be issued (one way or another) at the royal will. In addition to these, there are other sources – letters, manifestos, even narratives – which declare that the king himself was the author of particular policies or acts of government.

Yet are these documents really what they seem? Can such apparently personal expressions of opinion by the king be taken at face value? Or are they, as Watts firmly believes, merely evidence of 'institutional and conceptual conditions of kingship' which 'conspired to make Henry VI formally responsible for everything done in his name' even if, in reality, he was not. According to Watts, in fact, although Henry 'grew physically, and perhaps mentally, he never came to perform the role expected of an adult king', and there are good grounds for suspecting that the king's 'personal rule' was nothing of the kind. Even the foundation of Eton and King's College, Cambridge, derived not from Henry's personal initiative but originated in plans formulated by his advisers. Throughout the 1440s (let alone the 1450s!) 'evidence accumulates to show that the king simply lacked the independence of will to make authoritative decisions and that this frustrated all forms of government which were focused upon him'. Indeed, his lords found themselves having to cope with 'forty years of virtual minority': it is their very real commitment to doing so against the odds, rather than personal ambitions and rivalries among them, that provides the true key to understanding the politics of the time.[35]

Margaret of Anjou

No medieval English queen has been more heavily criticized than Margaret of Anjou: as the perceived manipulator of her husband Henry VI, the indomitable champion of her son Prince Edward of Lancaster's right to succeed him and, from 1456 if not before, the veritable leader of a corrupt Lancastrian regime, she was vigorously targeted in Yorkist propaganda; her supposedly manly qualities and unseemly participation in the male world of mid-fifteenth-century English politics attracted much opprobrium from Tudor commentators; and historians, too, have struggled to say much in her favour. Early criticism tended to focus on her very marriage to Henry VI and its consequences. Yet, since she was only fifteen in 1444 and very much a pawn in the Anglo-French diplomacy of the time, she can have had little say in the matter; nor can she be blamed personally for bringing virtually no dowry when she arrived in England in April 1445. Even before her husband's mental breakdown in 1453, however, there are a few indications that she may have dabbled in politics: for instance, a letter bearing Henry VI's name acknowledged that 'our most dear and well-beloved companion the queen' had 'requested us many times' to surrender Maine and Anjou to France; Margaret's close relations with William de la Pole Duke of Suffolk, who had probably done more than most to arrange her marriage, may point to a degree of political interest and involvement on the queen's part even before 1450 (although rumours of an adulterous liaison between the two were a later fabrication); and there is some suggestion that general pardons were issued to the Cade rebels early in July 1450 at her instigation. There are occasional pointers, too, to the queen's early unpopularity: in 1447, for instance, the constable of Gloucester castle is alleged to have remarked that he would be glad to see the queen drowned, as no good had resulted from her coming to England, while, in 1448, a Canterbury man asserted that Margaret should 'not be able to be queen' since 'she bore no child and because we had no prince in this land'. Most surviving evidence, including the queen's own letters written during these years, suggests, however, that Margaret of Anjou's political role prior to 1453 was negligible. Indeed, her beauty probably attracted more comment than any shortcomings as queen: the French chronicler Thomas Basin, for instance, described her, at the time of her marriage, as 'a good-looking and well-developed' girl, while a Milanese envoy reported, in 1458, that 'the queen is a most handsome woman'. She certainly seems to have spent a good deal of time with her husband in the later 1440s and early 1450s, applied herself vigorously to the management of her finances (very necessary, given her lavish expenditure) and sought to favour members of her household and tenants on her estates: in almost all respects, indeed, she probably conformed (until 1453) to contemporary expectations of queenly behaviour.[36]

What brought Margaret of Anjou into politics with a vengeance was her husband's mental collapse in August 1453 followed, in October, by the birth of her son Edward: it is from this time onwards, too, that reports of her character and behaviour become ever more critical. Early in 1454 she failed in an attempt to obtain the regency during her husband's continued illness: indeed, according to a letter written in the January of that year, she desired nothing less than 'the whole rule of this land'. In February 1456, so another letter tells us, the queen was perceived to be 'a great and strong laboured woman, for she spares no pains to pursue her objectives towards an end and conclusion favourable to her power'; the author of *Benet's Chronicle* learned that, also in February 1456, a London apprentice was 'drawn, hanged and quartered for producing bills asserting that Prince Edward was not the queen's son', while in October, although Richard of York and Warwick 'received a most gracious welcome from the king', the queen 'greatly loathed them both'; and Thomas Gascoigne recorded, before his death in 1458, 'several people' as asserting that 'almost all the affairs of the realm were conducted according to the queen's will, by fair means or foul'. Pope Pius II, writing soon afterwards, reported Warwick's alleged assertion that English government was now 'in the hands of the queen and her paramours'; the pro-Yorkist *English Chronicle*, similarly, recorded under the year 1459 that 'the queen, with such as were of her affinity, ruled the realm as she liked, gathering riches innumerable'; and a Yorkist political versifier in 1462 certainly considered it:

> . . . a right great perversion
> [For] a woman of a land to be a regent –
> Queen Margaret, I mean, that ever has meant
> To govern all England with might and power.[37]

As Patricia-Ann Lee has emphasized, Tudor writers, too, were hostile towards Margaret of Anjou and even more towards what she represented:

> Their antipathy no longer centred upon her dynastic policies nor did it spring from particular acts. . . . Instead it focused upon her behaviour as a woman.

Polydore Vergil firmly set the pattern. Although he judged the queen 'a young lady exceeding others of her time' in beauty and wisdom, he clearly did not approve of this woman 'very desirous of renown' who displayed 'all manly qualities' and determined 'to take upon herself' the rule of the realm. For Edward Hall, whose massive chronicle was published in 1548, she was a 'manly woman' who wished 'to rule and not to be ruled', ever 'desirous of glory and covetous of honour', and eventually a 'cankered crocodile and subtle serpent'. Hall's venom, in due course, filtered through to William Shakespeare, and the Margaret of Anjou of his Wars of the Roses cycle of history plays (written in the 1590s) is formidable indeed. First seeking consolation for her pathetic husband's inadequacies in Suffolk's arms, she becomes, after the birth of her son, an unbending champion of Lancaster, the 'She-wolf of France', forever railing at Henry VI, particularly once he has acquiesced in Prince Edward of Lancaster's disinheritance. Once her husband and son have been murdered, moreover, Margaret's implacability towards the house of York knows no bounds, culminating in her becoming the prophetess of vengeance against Richard III. Seventeenth- and eighteenth-century portraits of her, Ralph Griffiths tells us, 'moralized on the implications of her unhappy life', often confusing legend with fact, while, in the early nineteenth century, 'the tragic heroism of her experiences appealed particularly to those parts of western Europe with which she and her family had links'. Even in the later nineteenth century, when more serious works began appearing, 'the heavy hand of Tudor historians', and Shakespeare, still 'dictated assessments of her character and intentions'. Thus William Stubbs concluded, in 1878, that, from the very moment of her arrival in England, Margaret of Anjou came to epitomize:

> . . . the weakness and strength of the dynastic cause; its strength in her indomitable will, her steady faithfulness, her heroic defence of the rights of her husband and child; its weakness in her political position, her policy and her ministers.[38]

For much of the twentieth century – at any rate until the growing interest in women's history came to embrace even queens – Margaret of Anjou attracted very little serious attention beyond an important supporting role in books covering late Lancastrian politics and the Wars of the Roses. J.J. Bagley's 1948 biography was a noteworthy exception and, although a clearly pre-feminist work based almost entirely on printed sources, it retains considerable value as a well-informed chronological narrative of the queen's life and turbulent political career. For Bagley, Margaret was certainly a tragic figure, born out of her time and never in sympathy with her English subjects, forced into active politics and government by the circumstances in which she found herself in the early 1450s. Nevertheless, when Henry VI proved incapable of governing England, she did not shrink from the task; moreover, neither her personal unpopularity nor the strength of her opponents could deter Margaret's 'unflagging energy' and 'steadfast resolve' to fight indefatigably, and continue fighting whatever the odds, to ensure that her son (whom she loved as fiercely as she came to hate the Yorkists) secured his birthright: the succession to his father's throne. The house of Lancaster 'might have wished for a wiser and more understanding leader but nowhere could it have found a braver and more determined champion'.[39] Recently, new perspectives on Margaret of Anjou have been provided mainly by women historians. Anne Crawford, for instance, has focused our attention on the queen's household and, as far as politics are concerned, on her background as a French princess, particularly emphasizing how her husband's character 'left her to play a role she had already seen her mother and grandmother fill – as defender of her husband's and child's inheritance'; Patricia-Ann Lee has analysed contemporary, near-contemporary and Tudor sources for Margaret of Anjou in considerable detail, graphically highlighting how they reflected the perceptions and prejudices of their male authors; and Diana Dunn, after noting just how far propaganda has clouded judgements on the queen, has convincingly demonstrated that, whatever she may have done after her husband's mental breakdown and the birth of her son, before 1453 Margaret proved a dutiful young wife and an effective distributor of patronage. Clearly, however, the need for a new and detailed study of Margaret of Anjou is now urgent.[40]

Origins and Nature of the Wars of the Roses

For much of the last five hundred years the Wars of the Roses have been portrayed as dynastic wars, originating in the tragic circumstances surrounding Richard II's deposition and Henry IV's seizure of the throne in 1399. Indeed, such an interpretation is already to be found in Yorkist propaganda in the later fifteenth century, with the house of Lancaster (in the person of Henry VI) represented as rightly deprived of the throne by the Yorkist king Edward IV in 1461. The civil wars are dramatically portrayed by Yorkist apologists as God's punishment on England for the unnatural usurpation of Henry IV and the sinful murder of Richard II: when Edward IV's title to the throne was proclaimed in Parliament in November 1461, for instance, the new king and his advisers cited recent unrest, inward war and the shedding of innocent blood as God's judgement on the country for tolerating Lancastrian rule and denying rightful inheritance to the house of York for so long; while the Burgundian chronicler, Jean de Waurin, certainly reflected just such a pro-Yorkist stance that 'ill-gotten gains cannot last' when he pictured Henry VI losing the crown which his grandfather Henry IV had 'violently usurped and taken from King Richard II' and then 'caused to be shamelessly murdered'. Yet, arguably, Edward IV, after 1461, simply built on propaganda already employed by his father Richard of York in the 1450s. Most recent historians have accepted that it was only in October 1460, when Richard of York formally claimed the crown in Parliament, that the dynastic issue *actually* came to the fore: however, there is a certain amount of evidence indicating otherwise. As early as March 1450, for instance, York's chamberlain Sir William Oldhall (and others) were alleged to have been plotting 'to depose the king and put the Duke of York on the throne'; an anonymous Chancery memorandum of July 1456, alluding to York's claim to the throne via the Mortimer line, recorded that 'from the time that Jack Cade or Mortimer [in 1450] raised a rebellion in Kent, all disturbances are at the will of the Duke of York, descended from the Mortimers'; and *Whethamsted's Register*, discussing the motives of Yorkist partisans in 1459, identified a group who 'said they had risen mainly for this reason: so that the Duke of York might sit on the king's throne and rule over the kingdom'. The Lancastrian regime, as Ralph Griffiths has argued, certainly felt considerable concern about Henry VI's dynastic position so long as the king had no direct male heir: hence why, acutely conscious of Richard of York's claim to be recognised as heir-presumptive, Henry's advisers turned 'cautiously, yet unmistakably, to the wider royal family of Lancastrian blood in order to secure dynastic support', particularly the Beauforts. Even after the birth of Prince Edward of Lancaster in October 1453 the issue did not go away: Margaret of Anjou's entire political career, indeed, resulted from her indefatigable commitment to her son's right to succeed his father. Under the circumstances, and not surprisingly, Lancastrian propagandists certainly went out of their way to stress the legitimacy of Lancaster's occupation of the throne, none more so than Sir John Fortescue who, in several tracts, set out arguments in favour of Henry VI's title.[41]

The dynastic approach to fifteenth-century English history in general, and the Wars of the Roses in particular, admirably suited Tudor propaganda needs after 1485. Early Tudor writers soon took to portraying Henry VII as the agent of divine retribution at Bosworth, the man who rescued England from dynastic conflict after decades of bloodshed, and the king who, by his marriage to Elizabeth of York (Edward IV's eldest daughter), at last united the warring houses of Lancaster and York. Polydore Vergil, for instance, believed that the original cause of division was Richard II's deposition and Henry IV's seizure of the throne in 1399. The wars as such began when 'King Henry [VI], who derived his pedigree from the house of Lancaster, and Richard of York, who conveyed himself by his mother's side from Lionel, son to Edward III, contended mutually for the kingdom'; even as early as 1450, according to Vergil, York 'aspired to the sovereignty', conceiving an 'outrageous lust of principality' and never ceasing thereafter 'to plan how and by what means he might accomplish it'; as for the wars themselves, they resulted not only in the deaths of many men but also the ruin of the whole realm. Edward Hall, a lawyer who died in 1547, was very much a man of the Tudor age; he sat in the Reformation Parliament in the 1530s, strongly supporting the political and religious measures of Henry VIII (his patron); and, certainly, he rejoiced in the fact that the dynastic wars of the fifteenth century were brought to an end by Henry VII and his son. The very title of his chronicle virtually tells it all: *The Union of the two noble and illustrious families of Lancaster and York, being long in continual dissension for the crown of this noble realm . . . beginning at the time of King Henry the Fourth, the first author of this division.* Described as a 'masterpiece of Tudor propaganda', and soon proving very popular, Hall's *Chronicle* epitomized, in particular, the Tudor vision of the nature of the Wars of the Roses. 'What misery, what murder and what execrable plagues this famous region has suffered by the division and dissension of the renowned houses of Lancaster and York,' Hall declared:

> . . . my wit cannot comprehend nor my tongue declare, neither yet my pen fully set forth. For what noble man lives at this day, or what gentleman of any ancient stock or progeny is there whose lineage has not been infested and plagued with this unnatural division, [until] by the union celebrated between the high and mighty Prince Henry the Seventh and the Lady Elizabeth his most worthy queen [it] was suspended [in] the person of their most noble, puissant and mighty heir, King Henry the Eighth, and by him clearly buried and perpetually extinct.

Sir Thomas Smith, in 1561, similarly declared his commitment to the dynastic interpretation in no uncertain terms:

From the time that King Richard II was deposed . . . unto the death of King
Richard III . . . by reason of titles this poor realm had never long rest. . . .
Now this king prevailed, now the other. . . . These two blades of Lionel and
John of Gaunt never rested pursuing the one the other, till the red rose was
almost razed out and the white made all bloody. . . . They set the father
against the son, the brother against the brother, the uncle slew the nephew,
and was slain himself. So blood pursued and ensued blood, till all the realm
was brought to great confusion.[42]

The Elizabethan chronicler Raphael Holinshed, happily plagiarizing earlier
works (especially Hall), presented much the same picture and, more
importantly, became William Shakespeare's prime source in the 1590s. Thus, in
his eight-play history cycle covering the era of Plantagenet rule from 1399 to
1485, the dramatist, too, presented the deposition of Richard II by Henry IV as a
sacrilegious act, almost an original sin, for which England and her rulers
suffered decades of bloody and tumultuous civil wars until, at last, the tyrant
Richard III met his death at Bosworth and the glorious vista of Tudor rule
opened up.[43]

During the seventeenth century the origins of the Wars of the Roses
continued to be traced back to Richard II's reign and the wars themselves
portrayed as sanguinary struggles between warring dynasties. The Italian
Giovanni Francesco Biondi, whose three-volume *History of the Civil Wars of
England between the two houses of Lancaster and York* was published in Venice
between 1637 and 1644, clearly believed the wars began with Richard II and
ended with Henry VII. The succession of James II to the English throne in 1685
coincided with the appearance of *England's Happiness in a Lineal Succession; And
the Deplorable Miseries Which ever attended Doubtful Titles to the Crown, Historically
Demonstrated, By the Bloody Wars Between the Two Houses of York and Lancaster.*
Covering the history of 'that bloody, unnatural and fatal war' between York and
Lancaster which 'lasted about 106 years' from Richard II's reign to the
execution of Edward Earl of Warwick 'about 1504' (actually 1499), it certainly
did not pull its punches:

. . . it is almost incredible to believe how many bloody battles were fought,
what multitudes of men were slaughtered, how many treasons and horrid
conspiracies were carried on and perpetrated, how much noble blood was
spilt, how many families were ruined, how many barbarous executions, how
many unreasonable fines, and perpetual banishments happened, during this
unfortunate war.

Clearly, such mayhem contained an important lesson, as far as this author was
concerned, for anyone inclined to disrupt the peaceful accession of Catholic James:

[The] many miseries which attended that unfortunate quarrel may serve, at once, to show us their misery and our own happiness under the influence of the most auspicious and promising reign of our present sovereign James the Second.

In his *History of England*, first published in 1762, David Hume particularly stressed the importance of aristocratic factiousness in explaining the Wars of the Roses until its successful taming by Henry VII, while John Richard Green, whose *Short History of the English People* first appeared in 1874, believed there are:

. . . few periods of our annals from which we turn with such weariness and disgust as from the Wars of the Roses. Its thick crowd of savage battles, its ruthless executions, its shameless treasons, seem all the more terrible from the pure selfishness of the ends for which men fought, the utter want of all nobleness and chivalry in the struggle itself, of all great result in its close.

For William Stubbs, in 1878, the Wars of the Roses presented the spectacle of 'a civil war between two factions, both of which preserve certain constitutional formalities without being at all guided by constitutional principles': indeed, the period 1399–1485 saw the playing out of 'a drama of dynastic history', ending only with the battle of Bosworth, 'the last act of a long tragedy or series of tragedies' whose only unity had been provided by 'the struggle of the great houses for the crown'. As for William Denton, who penned perhaps the gloomiest survey of fifteenth-century England ever written (published posthumously in 1888), the Wars of the Roses may have had their origins in 'the rival pretensions of the houses of York and Lancaster' but, in reality, they were 'a war of the barons'; they were 'neither waged to protect national interests nor to vindicate the national honour'; and they ended 'in the destruction of almost every scion of the families of Lancaster and York', after a slaughter of people 'greater than in any former war on English soil'.[44]

During the twentieth century the Wars of the Roses have shrunk: 1399 has lost favour as the start date and 1455 received most votes as an alternative; 1485, the traditional end date, certainly saw the end of Richard III and the advent of the Tudors, although Henry VII still had to fight the battle of Stoke in 1487 and, in so far as the wars were indeed a dynastic struggle between the houses of Lancaster and York, they ended in 1471 with the deaths of both Henry VI and his only son Prince Edward. Until the 1960s, however, the Wars of the Roses attracted but scant academic attention, apart from the highly original contributions of C.L. Kingsford and K.B. McFarlane. Kingsford certainly broke the mould of Victorian doom and gloom portrayals of fifteenth-century England by arguing, in his 1923 Ford Lectures at Oxford (published, in 1925, as *Prejudice and Promise in Fifteenth Century England*), that the impact of the Wars of the Roses on most people's lives was far less than traditionally supposed. Moreover, it is a 'cardinal error' to assume the wars were a main cause of the troubles of the times, not least since the period of just over eighteen months between Blore Heath (September 1459) and Towton (March 1461) was 'the longest during which warfare was in any sense continuous or more than sporadic'. The chief ingredient lacking in the middle of the fifteenth century, he concluded, was good governance, although he also linked social disorder in the 1450s to the ignominious end of Lancastrian rule in France, economic and social change, and the political discontent which 'afforded the occasion for the beginning of the Wars of the Roses'. While in theory the issue at stake was the succession to the throne, moreover, in practice the wars 'degenerated into a fight for power between two factions'.[45] K.B. McFarlane remains the most respected of all modern historians of fifteenth-century England and a lecture on the Wars of the Roses (published in 1964) contained his final considered judgement on a subject he had very much made his own. He set the scene by clearing away what he regarded as the many misconceptions and misunderstandings surrounding the wars in general and their origins in particular. For a start, he put on one side the dynastic issue: the Wars of the Roses were not, in his opinion, primarily a dynastic struggle. Nor would he accept the idea that overmighty subjects were a fundamental cause: 'only an undermighty ruler had anything to fear from overmighty subjects', he declared, 'and if he were undermighty his personal lack of fitness was the cause not the weakness of his office and its resources'. Equally misleading, McFarlane thought, is the notion of a causal connection between the end of the Hundred Years War and the outbreak of civil strife in England soon after. In particular, he firmly rejected the suggestion that magnates 'deprived of the profits of war which had compensated them for falling rents' sought to 'escape threatened ruin in the lottery of civil war'. Surely, he argued, the fact that men like York, Salisbury, Warwick, Somerset and Buckingham were richer than their fathers had been belies any suggestion that economic difficulties drove them to political gangsterism. No less unsatisfactory, he believed, is the notion that 'the very existence of armed bands of retainers [men paid fees by, and wearing the liveries of, lords: so-called *bastard feudalism*] caused the war', especially if this involves blaming the return of 'a demoralized, unpaid and mutinous soldiery' from France. McFarlane certainly refused to accept that the existence of retainers as such was significant since, after all, such men had been around for centuries without bringing civil war. Nor could he approve the stress by some chroniclers on the importance of local disputes between families as a cause of conflict: the wars did not grow out of quarrels like that between Percy and Neville in the north or Courtenay and Bonville in the south-west. Rather, such feuds 'grew out of the paralysis at the centre induced by the struggle of Somerset and York for control'. Many lords and gentry, moreover, preferred to lie low and avoid committing themselves too strongly to either Lancaster or York.

The basic cause of the Wars of the Roses, McFarlane concluded, was simple enough: 'Henry VI's head was too small for his father's crown' and the wars were fought because 'the nobility was unable to rescue the kingdom from the consequences of Henry VI's inanity by any other means'. The king's incompetence had so divided the aristocracy that those who had profited from the crown were completely at odds with those who had not: civil war was therefore neither more nor less than 'a conflict between ins and outs', between those who had the king's ear and those who found themselves out in the cold.[46]

J.R. Lander, like K.B. McFarlane, devoted much of his career to studying fifteenth-century politics and society, especially the Wars of the Roses and their consequences. Like him, too, he believed the personality of Henry VI provided the main key to the outbreak of civil war since, as he put it in 1965, the king 'conspicuously failed' in the central task of a later medieval ruler 'to hold the balance between turbulent men too powerful to be ignored, prevent them getting undue control of his resources in land, men and money, and see that, by and large, they used their own in his and the general interest'. Like C.L. Kingsford, however, Lander felt the mayhem resulting from civil war had been much exaggerated. By modern standards, the fifteenth century was indeed turbulent but whether:

> . . . it was so much worse than the fourteenth century or the sixteenth and
> whether its disorders were due to the civil wars are other, and contentious,
> questions. . . . Most probably England was no more war-ridden in the
> fifteenth than in earlier centuries. . . . During the Wars of the Roses the total
> period of active campaigning between the first battle of St. Albans (1455)
> and the battle of Stoke (1487) amounted to little more than twelve or
> thirteen weeks – twelve or thirteen weeks in thirty-two years.

R.L. Storey, drawing heavily on unpublished records of Henry VI's reign (deposited in the Public Record Office), put forward, in 1966, what can best be called a grass roots hypothesis concerning the origins and nature of the Wars of the Roses. The outbreak of civil war, he argued, can be explained very largely in terms of an escalation of private feuds. It resulted, in fact, from the collapse of law and order in the context of the 'parasitic' and 'retrograde' urges of bastard feudalism: retaining and the lack of good governance, rather than the undermightiness of the king, eventually brought conflict to a head. Private aristocratic feuds, he declared, were very much the order of the day in the 1450s, with a strong tendency for protagonists to resort to violence, as in the clash of Thomas Courtenay Earl of Devon and William Lord Bonville in the west country. The key conflict, he thought, was that between the great northern families of Neville and Percy, at any rate once the Nevilles began backing Richard of York and the Percies Edmund of Somerset. Bastard feudalism did the rest:

Gentry, with understandable lack of confidence in the processes of law, attached themselves to lords who could give them protection against their personal enemies and in return supported their patrons in private wars with their peers. These baronial hostilities similarly resulted in the contestants aligning themselves with the major political rivals, and thus drawing their retainers into the conflict of Lancaster and York.

For Storey, then, the true causes of the wars should be sought in the shires, in the tensions of magnate and gentry society, Henry VI's personal inadequacy primarily of significance for facilitating 'a steady increase in local violence and a deterioration in men's ability to gain redress at law'. Charles Ross, writing about the Wars of the Roses a decade later in 1976, chose to follow his early mentor K.B. McFarlane rather than R.L. Storey. While declaring himself impressed by Storey's investigations of private feuds and convinced that local rivalries did help explain the eventual alignment of parties in the national struggle, he nevertheless rejected the idea that they were a prime cause. Rather, he concluded, the escalation of aristocratic feuds was a consequence of weakness at the centre: an 'adequate explanation' for civil war can be found in 'personal and political factors, especially those stemming from the weakness of the king and the impossibility of finding a political, non-violent solution to the problems which they involved'. As for the wars themselves:

> English life and civilization in general were remarkably little affected by
> thirty years of sporadic conflict. There was very little material devastation,
> little pillaging or plundering, certainly nothing to compare with the
> systematic devastation of people, buildings, stock and crops which the
> English armies had been wont to inflict on many parts of France during the
> Hundred Years War.[47]

Three further books devoted specifically to the Wars of the Roses followed in the 1980s. John Gillingham, in 1981, penned an immensely readable narrative history clearly aimed at the popular market yet containing much well-informed and astute analysis. In particular, he emphasized just how reluctant the nobility were to take up arms at all and, when they did so, they were not driven by either ideological or economic motives: in fact, they went to war simply because they could find no other way out of the political *impasse* created by Henry VI's staggering incapacity. As for the wars themselves, Gillingham believed their impact has been much exaggerated: even the nobility, who bore the brunt of the fighting, never faced the prospect of extermination (although, inevitably, many individuals met their deaths in battle or as a result of execution); as for the majority of the population, most men and women led relatively comfortable and uneventful lives, hardly touched by the quarrels of their social superiors. Anthony

Goodman, also writing in 1981, was more overtly scholarly in his approach than Gillingham and narrower in focus. Why the wars began concerned him little: rather, he aimed to show just what the Wars of the Roses were like through an analysis of the campaigns themselves, military organization and methods, and the social consequences of civil war. Certainly, Goodman regarded the wars as more significant than either Ross or Gillingham: the total period of campaigning amounted to at least a year (rather than Lander's twelve or thirteen weeks); the cost of arming, feeding and billeting soldiers was considerable, not to mention the artillery and means of transport required; and, even if campaigns tended to be brief and localized, men had to be raised, fighting had to be done, and the resulting casualties, executions and forfeitures cannot but have had palpable social as well as political effects. A.J. Pollard's short survey of the wars, published in 1988, was largely a work of synthesis but an exceptionally stimulating and illuminating one; moreover, Pollard's conclusion on the origins of the wars cannot be bettered for its masterly judiciousness:

> In the mid-fifteenth century many circumstances combined to undermine
> the authority of the Crown – growing economic and financial pressures,
> material loss and humiliation in France, the lurking doubt concerning Henry
> VI's title. They made civil war more likely. In the last resort it was Henry VI's
> incapacity after 1453 which tipped the balance. In the end, to use a metaphor
> much favoured at the time, the ship of state was without a captain and, while
> the crew fell at each other's throats, she drifted onto the rocks.[48]

What of the 1990s? A.J. Pollard, in 1995, edited a wide-ranging collection of essays on *The Wars of the Roses* for Macmillan's *Problems in Focus* series, of which two in particular broke new ground on the origins and nature of the wars. R.H. Britnell, in a review of the economic context of the struggles, emphasized that, although the onset of civil strife cannot be seen simply as a consequence of economic discontent, royal revenues were certainly falling, particularly as a result of recession in international trade; the crown's financial difficulties did help discredit the king's government and fuel the political tensions of the time; and 'something is lost in ascribing all the political problems of the 1440s and 1450s to Henry VI's inanity'. Altogether more contentious was John Watts' plea not only to allow ideas and principles back into mid-fifteenth-century politics but to give them a central role in explaining the Wars of the Roses. The wars did not occur simply because Henry VI was a disaster, Somerset corrupt and incompetent and York brimming over with resentment at his exclusion from patronage and power. On the contrary, according to Watts, vital principles concerning the commonweal and its protection were at stake, as is only too evident from so many surviving speeches, newsletters, poems, manifestos and political tracts (most notably, the *Somnium Vigilantes* of 1459). The political conflicts of the 1450s, in fact, were fought over ideological issues: York continually justified his behaviour, even the use of force, on the grounds he was seeking to promote the common good and interests of the realm; his opponents, no less vehemently, proclaimed the overriding obligation of obedience to the crowned king; and, far from being merely the stuff of cynical populist propaganda, matters of principle and constitutional propriety were regarded as central to the very functioning of political society.[49] Watts developed his thesis in much greater depth and detail in his 1996 study of *Henry VI and the Politics of Kingship*, particularly stressing the importance of Henry VI's personal shortcomings and utter incapacity to provide a satisfactory focus for the essential preservation of baronial unity. Far from seeking to profit from the confusion generated by the king's incapacity, he argued, the nobility in the 1440s and 1450s desperately sought a consensus that would enable them to govern effectively on his behalf: instead of a self-interested aristocracy pursuing financial advantage at court and territorial advancement in the provinces, Watts portrayed a mature and responsible political elite struggling, in exceptionally difficult circumstances, to maintain a unified and coherent government. Hence why the onset of full-scale civil war was so long delayed until, eventually, the king's prolonged and repeated failure to exercise will made it virtually inevitable:

> The crisis of Henry VI's reign was not brought about by overmighty subjects,
> by the misapplication of patronage, by defeat in war, by dynastic struggle, or by
> financial insolvency. Its fundamental cause was truly constitutional: the inability
> of monarchy, a means for the satisfaction of the public interest in the body
> of a single man, to adjust to one of the possible extremes of human frailty.[50]

Christine Carpenter, in the most recent survey of the Wars of the Roses era (published in 1997), had no doubts that her former postgraduate student's interpretation must supersede all others: indeed, her own account of 1437–61 is very largely based on it. Like Watts, she believed that Henry VI cannot be held responsible for any part of the rule that occurred in his name, whether at home or abroad, during the 1440s and 1450s: the consequence of the king's 'nothingness', however, was not the triumph of 'evil counsel' (as traditionally supposed) so much as 'a concerted effort' by the nobility 'to put a semblance of monarchy in the void created by the absence of an active king' until, since there was 'no impartial figure powerful enough to constrain feuding magnates', politics moved during the 1450s 'from the precarious preservation of unity under a sham king to total disunity under a king about whom there was no pretending any more'.[51] How far such an interpretation will receive general acceptance remains to be seen but, clearly, the genie of rampant revisionism, so familiar to seventeenth-century Civil War historians, is now firmly out of the bottle for the Wars of the Roses as well: turbulent and tumultuous times obviously lie ahead for fifteenth-century scholarship!

Notes

1. My discussion of the nature, scope and quality of the source material for, and the historiography of, Henry VI, Margaret of Anjou and the Wars of the Roses owes much to: C.L. Kingsford, *English Historical Literature in the Fifteenth Century* (Oxford, 1913), especially chs 4–10; V.J. Scattergood, *Politics and Poetry in the Fifteenth Century* (London, 1971), especially chs 5 and 6; M.E. Aston, 'Richard II and the Wars of the Roses', in *The Reign of Richard II*, ed. C.M. Barron and F.R.H. Du Boulay (London, 1971); C. Ross, *Edward IV* (London, 1974), especially Appendix 1: Note on Narrative Sources, and *The Wars of the Roses* (London, 1976), especially 'Introduction: The Wars of the Roses in Historical Tradition'; B.P. Wolffe, *Henry VI* (London, 1981), especially ch. 1; R.A. Griffiths, *The Reign of King Henry VI* (London, 1981), especially 'Introduction: The Making of a Reputation'; A. Goodman, *The Wars of the Roses* (London, 1981), especially 'Introduction'; A. Gransden, *Historical Writing in England II c. 1307 to the Early Sixteenth Century* (New York, 1982), especially chs 8–10, 12–14; P-A Lee, 'Reflections of Power: Margaret of Anjou and the Dark Side of Queenship', *Renaissance Quarterly*, Vol. 39 (1986); A.J. Pollard, *The Wars of the Roses* (London, 1988), especially ch. 1; M.A. Hicks, 'The Sources', in *The Wars of the Roses*, ed. A.J. Pollard (London, 1995); C. Carpenter, *The Wars of the Roses* (Cambridge, 1997), especially ch. 1. I have also drawn on editors' introductions to printed primary sources, particularly by J. Gairdner, C.L. Kingsford, R. Flenley, G.L. and M.A. Harriss and N. Pronay.

2. The Patent Rolls (PRO C66) for 1450–1471 have all been calendared and published: *C(alendar of) P(atent) R(olls), Henry VI, 1446–52, 1452–61, Edward IV, 1461–7, 1467–76*. The Pardon Rolls (PRO C67) remain largely unpublished. Most Exchequer records, too, have yet to appear in print, but historians have used them extensively, particularly Exchequer Warrants for Issue (PRO E404) and Issue Rolls (PRO E403). In recent years political and social historians have also made increasing use of unpublished King's Bench records, especially the files of King's Bench Ancient Indictments (PRO KB9).

3. *Rotuli Parliamentorum*, ed. J. Strachey and others, 6 vols (1767–77), especially Vol. 5, pp. 176–7, 224, 240–2, 284–5, 346.

4. C. Ross, 'Rumour, Propaganda and Public Opinion during the Wars of the Roses', in *Patronage, the Crown and the Provinces in Later Medieval England*, ed. R.A. Griffiths (Gloucester, 1981), p. 23.

5. J. Watts, 'Ideas, Principles and Politics', in Pollard (ed.), *Wars of the Roses*, especially pp. 128–9, and *Henry VI and the Politics of Kingship* (Cambridge, 1996), especially pp. 43–6.

6. *Letters of Queen Margaret of Anjou, Bishop Beckington and Others*, ed. C. Monro (Camden Society, 1863).

7.   *Calendar of State Papers and Manuscripts existing in the Archives and Collections of Milan,*
     Vol. 1, 1385–1618, ed. A.B. Hinds (London, 1913).

8.   *The Paston Letters,* ed. J. Gairdner, 6 vols (1904), reprinted in one volume (Gloucester,
     1983).

9.   *The Brut, or the Chronicles of England,* ed. F.W.D. Brie (Early English Texts Society,
     1908), especially pp. 489, 511–13, 519–31.

10. *An English Chronicle of the Reigns of Richard II, Henry IV, Henry V and Henry VI,* ed. J.S.
     Davies (Camden Society, 1856), especially pp. 64–8, 71–2, 77–110.

11. *Historical Collections of a Citizen of London in the Fifteenth Century,* ed. J. Gairdner
     (Camden Society, 1876), especially pp. 189–97, 207–17, 223–7.

12. *Six Town Chronicles of England,* ed. R. Flenley (Oxford, 1911), especially pp. 127–53.

13. *Three Fifteenth Century Chronicles,* ed. J. Gairdner (Camden Society, 1880), pp. 66–80;
     Flenley, especially pp. 153–7, 161–2; Kingsford, *English Historical Literature,* pp. 297–8;
     Flenley, pp. 106–8.

14. *The Great Chronicle of London,* ed. A.H. Thomas and I.D. Thornley (London, 1938),
     especially pp. 196–202, 212–20.

15. C.L. Kingsford, 'Extracts from the first version of Hardyng's Chronicle', *English
     Historical Review,* Vol. 27 (1912), especially pp. 745, 749; *Chronicle of John Hardyng,* ed.
     H. Ellis (1809), especially pp. 394, 396, 399, 401; John Warkworth, *A Chronicle of the
     First Thirteen Years of the Reign of King Edward the Fourth,* ed. J.O. Halliwell (Camden
     Society, 1839), especially pp. 1–5, 8–21; *Historie of the Arrivall of King Edward IV,* ed. J.
     Bruce (Camden Society, 1838), especially pp. 19–20, 28–31.

16. Jean de Waurin, *Recueil des Croniques et Anchiennes Istories de la Grant Bretaigne, a present
     nomme Engleterre,* ed. W. and E. Hardy, Vol. 5 1447–1471 (Rolls Series, 1891).

17. John Capgrave, *Liber de Illustribus Henricis,* ed. F.C. Hingeston (Rolls Series, 1858).

18. *Henry the Sixth: A Reprint of John Blacman's Memoir,* transl. M.R. James (Cambridge,
     1919), especially pp. 25–6.

19. Hicks, 'The Sources', p. 27. In the early 1980s Blacman's tract became the subject of
     considerable debate: Wolffe, *Henry VI,* especially ch. 1; R. Lovatt, 'John Blacman:
     biographer of Henry VI', in *The Writing of History in the Middle Ages: Essays presented to
     R.W. Southern,* ed. R.H.C. Davis and J.M. Wallace-Hadrill (Oxford, 1981), and 'A
     Collector of Apocryphal Anecdotes: John Blacman Revisited', in *Property and Politics:
     Essays in Later Medieval English History,* ed. A.J. Pollard (Gloucester, 1984). B.P. Wolffe
     was scathing in his criticisms: he questioned Blacman's authorship of the tract, argued
     that it was written not before 1485 but in the middle or later years of Henry VII's
     reign, and suggested that, as an early Tudor hagiographic collection of trivial and
     apocryphal anecdotes probably commissioned by the first Tudor king as part of a
     campaign to secure Henry VI's canonization, it 'should be discounted in any portrait
     of the living king'. Roger Lovatt, by contrast, concluded that Blacman was indeed the
     author of the tract bearing his name and argued that, although far from being an
     unbiased commentator, he was exceptionally well informed about his subject.
     Rejecting the notion that the compilation was early Tudor hagiography designed to
     advance Henry VI's claims to sainthood, Lovatt dated it at about 1480 and suggested
     that Blacman, far from presenting an artless portrait of the king's private virtues and
     devotions, actually painted 'an almost comprehensive picture of the king's defects as a
     ruler', deliberately interpreting 'public inadequacy as private rectitude'. Virtually all

historians writing since the early 1480s have rejected Wolffe's strident criticisms of Blacman and accepted Lovatt's more measured interpretation of the source.

20.   'John Benet's Chronicle for the years 1400 to 1462', ed. G.L. and M.A. Harriss, in *Camden Miscellany* (Camden Society, 1972), especially pp. 195–232.

21.   C.A.J. Armstrong, 'Politics and the battle of St Albans, 1455', *Bulletin of the Institute of Historical Research*, Vol. 33 (1960), especially pp. 6, 9, 11. M.K. Jones, too, has remarked that this is one of the few chronicles of the later 1440s and early 1450s noticeable for its lack of partisanship towards York: 'Somerset, York and the Wars of the Roses', *English Historical Review*, Vol. 14 (1989), p. 290. C.L. Kingsford, usually so reliable a guide to chronicles of the Wars of the Roses era, was uncharacteristically mistaken in judging the *Chronicon Angliae* 'strongly Yorkist' and its account of 1450–1455 reflecting 'a Yorkist point of view': *English Historical Literature*, p. 157.

22.   *Incerti Scriptoris Chronicon Angliae de Regnis Henrici IV, Henrici V et Henrici VI*, ed. J.A. Giles (London, 1848), especially pp. 34–48.

23.   *Loci e Libro Veritatem*, ed. J.E.T. Rogers (Oxford, 1881).

24.   'Annales Rerum Anglicarum', in *Letters and Papers Illustrative of the Wars of the English in France*, ed. J. Stevenson (Rolls Series, 1864), Vol. 2, part ii, especially pp. 769–70, 774–7.

25.   *Registrum Abbatiae Johannis Whethamstede*, Vol. 1, ed. H.T. Riley (Rolls Series, 1872).

26.   *Ingulph's Chronicle of the Abbey of Croyland*, ed. H.T. Riley (1854), especially pp. 418–26 (first continuation), 453–7, 465–6 (second continuation); *The Crowland Chronicle Continuations 1459–1486*, ed. N. Pronay and J. Cox (Gloucester, 1986), especially pp. 108–15, 126–31 (second continuation).

27.   *Three Books of Polydore Vergil's English History*, ed. H. Ellis (Camden Society, 1844), especially pp. 84–95, 126.

28.   Griffiths, *Reign of Henry VI*, pp. 235, 254, 491–2; Watts, *Henry VI*, p. 104; *The Chronicles of the Wars of the Roses*, ed. E. Hallam (London, 1988), pp. 192–3, 196; B. Wilkinson, *Constitutional History of England in the Fifteenth Century* (London, 1964), pp. 49–50; R.L. Storey, *The End of the House of Lancaster* (London, 1966), pp. 34–5; *English Historical Documents*, Vol. 4, 1327–1485, ed. A.R. Myers (London, 1969), p. 264; Wolffe, *Henry VI*, pp. 17–21; *Davies*, p. 79; *Whethamsted*, p. 415; *Warkworth*, pp. 11–12.

29.   *Blacman*, pp. 26–42; Lovatt, 'John Blacman Revisited' especially p. 182.

30.   *Crowland*, pp. 130–1; Wolffe, *Henry VI*, p. 5; *Historical Poems of the 14th and 15th Centuries*, ed. R.H. Robbins (New York, 1959), pp. 199–200; *Vergil*, pp. 70–1.

31.   Bishop Stubbs also remarked, however, on Henry VI's 'utter incapacity for government' since he 'never seems to have looked upon his royal character as involving the responsibility of leadership', while, for Gairdner, he was 'a well-intentioned but feeble-minded' ruler who was 'incapable of governing': W. Stubbs, *The Constitutional History of England*, Vol. 3 (Oxford, 1878), pp. 134, 155, 197, and *Paston Letters*, Vol. 1, pp. 45, 328.

32.   M. Christie, *Henry VI* (London, 1922), pp. 109, 117. Cardinal F.A. Gasquet, in *The Religious Life of Henry VI*, also published in 1922, put his faith firmly in Blacman, as the only authentic picture of Henry VI, firmly rejecting as Yorkist propaganda any notion of the king as weak minded and useless, asserting instead that Henry's rule had indeed been just and upright.

33.   K.B. McFarlane, *The Nobility of Later Medieval England* (Oxford, 1973), p. 284, and *England in the Fifteenth Century* (London, 1981), p. 42; Storey, *End of the House of*

Lancaster, pp. 33, 42; J.R. Lander, *Conflict and Stability in Fifteenth-Century England* (London, 1969), p. 68; J.W. McKenna, 'Piety and Propaganda: the Cult of Henry VI', in *Chaucer and Middle English Studies in Honour of R.H. Robbins* (Kent, Ohio, 1974), p. 79. Charles Ross, in his splendidly illustrated 1976 study of *The Wars of the Roses*, pp. 21–4, concluded that Henry VI was a peace-loving man, more merciful on occasion than most of his contemporaries; a faithful husband and a loving father, he was indeed deeply religious; however, although he did his limited best to heal the feuds among his great men, during the 1450s 'he seems to become for most purposes a political cipher'.

34. Griffiths, *Reign of Henry VI*, especially pp. 253–4; Wolffe, *Henry VI*, and 'The Personal Rule of Henry VI', in *Fifteenth-Century England 1399–1509*, ed. S.B. Chrimes, C.D. Ross and R.A. Griffiths (Manchester, 1972). Since publication in 1981 Griffiths' interpretation has stood the test of time, and further scholarship, better than Wolffe's. Anthony Goodman, when reviewing Wolffe's book, remarked that its author was 'perhaps too ready to take administrative and diplomatic evidence of Henry VI's early activity as signifying his real authorship of policy moves, and the later absence of such evidence as signifying his passivity': *The Times Higher Education Supplement*, 22/5/81, p. 15. Roger Lovatt's convincing arguments for Blacman's authorship of the tract bearing his name, and the value of the source, seriously called into question Wolffe's malign view of the king's personality: 'John Blacman: biographer of Henry VI', pp. 415–44, and 'John Blacman Revisited', pp. 172–97. Colin Richmond concluded that, in the end, 'the nasty king Wolffe wants us to believe in is less plausible than the well-intentioned duffer we have been used to, and with whom Griffiths is content'; 'After McFarlane', *History*, Vol. 68 (1983), p. 51. A.J. Pollard, in an excellent review article covering both biographies, believed Wolffe's 'attempt to discern a positively unpleasant aspect to Henry's character, although not implausible in itself, runs into the problem [of] discerning when Henry's personal initiative ends and the influence of others takes over': 'The Last of the Lancastrians', *Parliamentary History*, Vol. 2 (1983), p. 207. Pollard himself opined, in 1988, that Henry VI, 'perhaps the most unfitted to rule of all the kings of England since the Norman Conquest', was 'weak, vacillating, feckless and profligate' and, at all times, 'seems to have been like putty in the hands of those nearest to him': *Wars of the Roses*, p. 62. And, a decade later in 1997, Christine Carpenter concluded that Wolffe's 'almost deliberately provocative piece', and portrait of an 'outrageously interventionist king', has not found general acceptance by historians: *Wars of the Roses*, pp. 87–8.

35. Watts, *Henry VI*, especially pp. 105–6, 252, 364. Reactions to John Watts' important, but undoubtedly provocative, monograph have been mixed. Christine Carpenter was so convinced, in 1997, by her former pupil's 'revolutionary work' on Henry VI's reign that she based much of her own coverage of 1437–1461 on it: *Wars of the Roses*, pp. 87–155, especially p. 93. Michael K. Jones, however, while welcoming this 'highly original piece of political analysis' and emphasizing the 'many fresh insights into the politics of the period' it provides, voiced distinct reservations about Watts' portrayal of the king: *The Ricardian*, Vol. 11 (September 1998), pp. 353–6. In his recent biography of Warwick the Kingmaker, Michael Hicks certainly takes a different line on Henry VI from Watts, emphasizing that even critics of his regime accepted the king's saintliness and goodness, remarking on his capacity for mercy and abilities as a conciliator, and suggesting that,

even after 1455, he was always more than a figurehead or puppet; moreover, although he did indeed lack much inclination or capacity for government, even Henry VI was 'capable of occasional decisive action and secured obedient compliance from the political nation when he took it': *Warwick the Kingmaker* (Oxford 1998), especially p. 66.

36. Lee, 'Reflections of Power: Margaret of Anjou and the Dark Side of Queenship', especially p. 185; D. Dunn, 'Margaret of Anjou, Queen Consort of Henry VI: A Reassessment of her Role, 1445–53', in *Crown, Government and People in the Fifteenth Century*, ed. R.E. Archer (Stroud, 1995), especially pp. 110, 141–3; Griffiths, *Reign of Henry VI*, pp. 255–6; *CSPM*, p. 19; *Letters of Queen Margaret of Anjou*, pp. 89–164.

37. *Paston Letters*, Vol. 2, p. 297, Vol. 3, p. 75; *Benet*, pp. 216–7; *Wilkinson*, pp. 50, 128; *Davies*, p. 79; *Robbins*, p. 224. Among English chroniclers, only John Harding showed a degree of sympathy for this 'pitiful and lamentable lady who mourns and laments the fate and calamity of her husband', although *Warkworth's Chronicle* demonstrated no particular animus towards her and perhaps, by implication at least, sought to downgrade her political importance: Lee, 'Reflections of Power: Margaret of Anjou and the Dark Side of Queenship', pp. 199, 201. The Burgundian chronicler Philippe de Commines, an altogether more sophisticated writer, remembered in the 1490s that 'the queen supported the Duke of Somerset against the Earl of Warwick' but believed, as it turned out, 'that lady would have done much better if she had acted as a judge or mediator between the two parties, instead of saying "I will support this party"': *Memoirs: The Reign of Louis XI*, transl. M. Jones (Harmondsworth, 1972), p. 413.

38. Lee, 'Reflections of Power: Margaret of Anjou and the Dark Side of Queenship', pp. 183–4, 208–9, 215–7; *Vergil*, pp. 68, 71; Kingsford, *English Historical Literature*, p. 265; Griffiths, *Reign of Henry VI*, p. 254; Stubbs, *Constitutional History*, Vol. 3, p. 197.

39. J.J. Bagley, *Margaret of Anjou Queen of England* (London, 1948), especially pp. 8–9, 129–30. Philippe Erlanger, in what is essentially a hybrid popular biography/historical novel, was clearly captivated by the 'fabulous life' of this *femme fatale*, admirable wife, loving and devoted mother, chief of state and leader of armies, heroine and executioner, whose 'beauty was a legend' and who 'committed crimes and suffered misfortunes worthy of Greek mythology': *Margaret of Anjou Queen of England* (London, 1970), especially p. 28. Jock Haswell, rather more critically, noted that the queen was 'by nature partisan', inflexible, relentless and had 'no idea how to conciliate or how to come to terms with those who opposed her'; nevertheless, she was also clever, courageous and enterprising, the 'strong queen that England needed', and, always, motivated by maternal love for a son whose right to the throne of England must be protected and fought for whatever the cost: *The Ardent Queen: Margaret of Anjou and the Lancastrian Heritage* (London, 1976), especially pp. 58, 103.

40. A. Crawford, 'The King's Burden?: the Consequences of Royal Marriage in Fifteenth-century England', in Griffiths (ed.), *Patronage, the Crown and the Provinces*, especially p. 53, and *Letters of the Queens of England 1100–1547*, ed. A. Crawford (Stroud, 1994), especially pp. 119–24; Lee, 'Reflections of Power: Margaret of Anjou and the Dark Side of Queenship', pp. 183–217; Dunn, 'Margaret of Anjou', pp. 106–43.

41. *Rotuli Parliamentorum*, Vol. 5, p. 464; *Hallam*, p. 224; J.R. Lander, *The Wars of the Roses* (London, 1965), p. 63; *Wilkinson*, p. 128; *Whethamsted*, p. 337; R.A. Griffiths, 'The Sense of Dynasty in the Reign of Henry VI', in *Patronage, Pedigree and Power in Later Medieval England*, ed. C. Ross (Gloucester, 1979), especially p. 19.

42. *Vergil,* pp. 86, 94; E. Hall, *The Union of the Two Noble Families of Lancaster and York* (1548); Aston, 'Richard II and the Wars of the Roses', especially pp. 282–3. The Elizabethan Jesuit Robert Parsons, too, traced the 'bloody division' of the houses of Lancaster and York back to Richard II's deposition, believed these 'most pernicious wars' continued for almost a hundred years, and resulted not only in the ruin of the royal house of Lancaster but also the overthrow of many other noble princes: Ibid., p. 299.

43. W. Shakespeare, *Richard II, Henry IV Parts 1 and 2, Henry V, Henry VI Parts 1, 2 and 3* and *Richard III.*

44. Aston, 'Richard II and the Wars of the Roses', pp. 286–8; D. Hume, *The History of England,* Vol. 3 (London, 1762), especially pp. 307–8; J.R. Green, *A Short History of the English People* (London, 1874), p. 288; Stubbs, *Constitutional History,* Vol. 3, pp. 5, 177; W. Denton, *England in the Fifteenth Century* (London, 1888), pp. 115–16.

45. C.L. Kingsford, *Prejudice and Promise in Fifteenth Century England* (Oxford, 1925), especially 'Social Life and the Wars of the Roses', pp. 48–77. The eminent economic historian Michael Postan concluded, in 1939, that the dwindling resources of landlords in an era of agricultural depression contributed to the 'political gangsterism' of the times; while, in 1953, C.D. Ross and T.B. Pugh suggested not only that financial crisis made lords increasingly desperate to obtain royal patronage but also that the Wars of the Roses were probably fought 'not because magnates could afford to hire armies of retainers to fight their battles but rather because they could no longer afford to pay them': 'The Fifteenth Century', *Economic History Review,* Vol. 9 (1939); 'The English Baronage and the Income Tax of 1436', *Bulletin of the Institute of Historical Research,* Vol. 26 (1953), especially pp. 1–2.

46. K.B. McFarlane, 'The Wars of the Roses', Raleigh Lecture on History, *Proceedings of the British Academy,* Vol. 50 (1964), pp. 87–119, reprinted in McFarlane, *England in the Fifteenth Century,* pp. 231–61. Whereas McFarlane (who died in 1966) has achieved almost legendary status among fifteenth-century historians, Kingsford's work has been unduly neglected since his death in 1926, although Christine Carpenter has recently (and rightly) reminded us of its importance: *Kingsford's Stonor Letters and Papers 1290–1483* (Cambridge, 1996), new introduction by Carpenter, pp. 10–15, and *Wars of the Roses,* pp. 15, 16, 19.

47. *Lander,* especially pp. 20–1, 29; Storey, *End of the House of Lancaster,* especially p. 27; Ross, *Wars of the Roses,* especially pp. 37–42, 163.

48. J. Gillingham, *The Wars of the Roses* (London, 1981); Goodman, *Wars of the Roses;* Pollard, *Wars of the Roses,* especially pp. 65–6. The 1980s also saw several other important contributions to the debate on the origins and nature of the Wars of the Roses, most notably from the pens of Bertram Wolffe and Michael K. Jones. B.P. Wolffe particularly sought to emphasize, in 1981, the central importance of the fall of Lancastrian France in explaining the decline of the king's authority in England: apportioning blame for the disasters in France *circa* 1449–53, he argued, was a major issue in domestic politics for the rest of the reign and must certainly figure in any explanation of the outbreak of civil war: *Henry VI,* especially pp. 133–4. For M.K. Jones in 1989 the real key to the onset of the Wars of the Roses should be sought in the quarrel of Edmund Beaufort Duke of Somerset and Richard Plantagenet Duke of York. The origins of their mutual hostility, he believed, can be found in Lancastrian

France in the 1440s: York could never forgive Somerset's role in easing him out of his command there, a resentment accentuated by Beaufort's dismal record of failure as his replacement. Then, in the early 1450s, he found himself thwarted again and again at home, as Somerset not only turned the king against him personally but also helped deprive him of the fruits of royal patronage. Eventually, finding himself increasingly isolated and fired by an ever more intense animosity towards his rival, he resorted to armed force: 'Somerset, York and the Wars of the Roses', pp. 285–307.

49. R.H. Britnell, 'The Economic Context', pp. 41–64, and J. Watts, 'Ideas, Principles and Politics', pp. 110–33. In another paper Rosemary Horrox highlighted notions of allegiance and service underpinning the behaviour and actions of individuals in the mid-fifteenth century, particularly noting how, following his father's death at Wakefield, his son Edward deliberately projected himself as the man most able to unite a shattered political community, a role Richard of York himself could not plausibly play since, in contemporary eyes, he had been 'the begetter of faction': 'Personalities and Politics', pp. 89–109.

50. Watts, *Henry VI*, especially pp. 363–6; see also Watts' paper 'Polemic and Politics in the 1450s', in *The Politics of Fifteenth Century England: John Vale's Book*, ed. M.L. Kekewich and others (Stroud, 1995), pp. 3–42.

51. Carpenter, *Wars of the Roses*, especially pp. 93, 115, 128.

Henry VI

Henry VI, only son of Henry V and Catherine of Valois, daughter of the French king Charles VI, was born at Windsor on 6 December 1421; nine months later, following his father's premature death on 31 August 1422, he became the youngest English prince to succeed to the throne and the only one to be crowned twice as dual monarch of England and France (at Westminster in 1429 and Paris in 1431). Although evidence for the young king's upbringing and early interests is sparse, the instructions to his tutor Richard Beauchamp Earl of Warwick in 1428 suggest a conventional royal/aristocratic training was envisaged (1a): by 1432, however, warning bells about his shortcomings were already being sounded (1b) and, according to John Harding, Warwick had so despaired of his great innocence, simplicity and inability to distinguish good from evil by 1436 that he sought release from his role as guardian (1c). Clearly, the young Henry soon displayed his lack of aptitude for, or interest in, military – and perhaps political – matters; he proved prone, from an early age, to give credence to ill-judged, unsuitable advice and counsel; and, by the time he declared his minority at an end in 1437 (perhaps at the urging of those around him), he had probably already become the obsessionally religious and morally censorious cleric-in-king's-clothing he was to remain for the rest of his life (2).

Since Henry VI learned to speak French fluently and read Latin, he cannot have been the complete simpleton of contemporary rumour and later Yorkist propaganda (3, 7, 10, 12); moreover when, as an adult, his interest was engaged, he may well have made his personal mark: his pivotal role in the foundation of Eton in September 1440 and King's College, Cambridge, in February 1441 is too well documented to be discounted (5, 13, 15); he managed, on occasion, to fulfil the courtly duties required of him (4); and he certainly supported, even if he did not initiate, efforts to bring about a permanent peace between England and France in the 1440s. Yet it is difficult to accept B.P. Wolffe's picture of a politically hands-on king not only pursuing clear objectives of his own but also prepared to ride roughshod over opponents to his plans. Rather, those commentators who remarked on his susceptibility to management by those around him, and their determination to do so, probably had it about right. Perhaps they controlled Henry VI, as John Watts and Christine Carpenter would have us believe, out of genuine concern for the well-being of the commonweal. Yet too many contemporaries and near-contemporaries remark on self-interested, even evil, counsellors playing on the king's gullible nature when it came to patronage and contributing to the collapse of law and order in the country for their testimony to be dismissed as mere Yorkist propaganda (3, 8, 9, 12). As an anointed and crowned king whose piety was widely admired, Henry VI, whatever his political shortcomings, was above overt contemporary criticism. Not so those around him: in 1450, indeed, his chief minister, William de la Pole Duke of Suffolk, was impeached by Parliament and executed while sailing into exile; his keeper of the Privy Seal, Adam Moleyns Bishop of Chichester, was murdered at Portsmouth; and his former treasurer, James Fiennes Lord Saye and Sele, was seized and beheaded in London. Manifestos circulating during Jack Cade's rebellion in June/July 1450 particularly highlighted the reprehensible behaviour of the 'false traitors' around the king, while Richard Duke of York, in the autumn of the same year, deliberately projected himself as the saviour of the commonweal from the corruption and oppression of a discredited court clique. Yet Henry VI's right to reign remained unchallenged and, by the summer of 1453, even his 'familiars' (such as Edmund Beaufort Duke of Somerset) had apparently become politically unassailable.

Everything was thrown into turmoil when the king suffered a complete mental collapse at the end of July 1453. Until then, for all his political naivety and gullibility, Henry VI's personal wishes could not be ignored. His misplaced generosity to some, and failure to capitalize on the abilities of others, in the 1440s helped fuel the political crisis of 1449/1450: yet the fact that, in the early 1450s, full-scale civil war was nevertheless averted may also be partly down to him. Similarly, the king's abhorrence of warfare and desire for a permanent settlement with France may well underpin, in part at least, the diplomatic manoeuvrings of 1444 to 1449; yet Henry's pursuit of peace at any price may also explain why, once war was resumed in 1449, English possessions in France were so rapidly lost. Why Henry VI collapsed into a condition of complete mental torpor in the summer of 1453, accompanied by severe physical incapacity, has been much debated, as has the nature of his illness and the extent to which he ever really recovered. Perhaps it was partly hereditary: his grandfather, Charles VI of France, had certainly suffered prolonged bouts of insanity for at least thirty years. Or perhaps the shock of England's recent defeat at Castillon in July 1453, and the resulting loss of Gascony, was too much for him, especially if he was already finding his wife's one and only pregnancy difficult to handle. As for his symptoms, they seem only too consistent with what we now call catatonic schizophrenia: John Blacman later remembered how, for a time, the king was 'not conscious of himself, or of those around him, as if he were in a trance' (although, for Blacman, this was not so much insanity as spiritual rapture!), while *Whethamsted's Register* provides a particularly graphic description of Henry's utter mental and physical prostration (10). Certainly, the king was completely incapable of governing the country now, whatever the situation before, and he was destined to remain in this condition until the end of 1454. Even then, his recovery may only have been partial and, following the battle of St Albans in May 1455 (where he somehow managed to sustain a slight arrow wound), he almost certainly suffered what may well have been but the first of a series of mental and physical relapses. In the later 1450s, apart from very occasional glimpses of renewed activity (for instance, as a conciliator between rival factions in the spring of 1458), Henry VI became so withdrawn into himself, and so overwhelmingly preoccupied with private religious observance and silent contemplation of matters spiritual, as to be no more than a political cipher, entirely under the control of those around him: such is the king who visited Crowland abbey during Lent 1460 (11) and perhaps wrote the prayer often attributed to him (6). Such, too, is the king who, after he fell into Edward IV's hands in 1465, accepted his imprisonment in the Tower without complaint, began to experience visions (perhaps another symptom of his schizoid personality) and eventually provided a convenient puppet for Warwick the Kingmaker in 1470/1 (12). No wonder, following his probable murder on Edward IV's orders in May 1471, his obscure grave in Chertsey abbey soon began to attract pilgrims; by the time Richard III moved his remains to St George's chapel, Windsor, in August 1484, the cult of Henry VI, as a saintly man in life and a miracle-worker in death, was well-established; and early Tudor writers – indeed, Henry VII himself – certainly gave an enthusiastic seal of approval to such hagiography (14, 15).

1) The Minority of Henry VI (1422–37)

a) Instructions to Richard Beauchamp Earl of Warwick, as Guardian and Tutor of Henry VI, 1428
(Christie, *Henry VI*, p. 47)
[The earl was urged by the council] to remain about the king's person, to do his utmost in teaching him good manners, literature, languages, nurture and courtesy and other studies necessary for so great a prince; to exhort him to love, honour and fear the Creator; and to draw himself to virtues and eschew vice; to chastise him reasonably from time to time as occasion shall require; [also to lay before him] mirrors and examples of times passed of the good grace, prosperity and well-being that have fallen to virtuous kings.

b) Richard Beauchamp Earl of Warwick: on the Tutoring of Henry VI, 1432
(*Paston Letters*, Vol. 2, pp. 36–7)
Considering how the king is grown in years, in the stature of his person and in knowledge of his high and royal authority, causing him more and more to begrudge and loath chastisement, [the Earl of Warwick requests the council] assist him in the exercise of his authority over the king's person.

[Since the king] has been distracted by some from his learning, and spoken to about unsuitable matters, the earl, fearing the harm that may befall the king if such contacts be allowed, desires that, in all conversation men may have with the king, he [or his assignees] be present and privy to it.

c) Harding's Chronicle
(*Chronicle of John Harding*, ed. H. Ellis, pp. 394, 396)

> The Earl Richard of Warwick kept the king
> During all this time [1428–36] . . .
> The Earl Richard, in much worthyhead,
> Informed him; but of his simplehead
> He could little within his breast conceive,
> For good from evil he could scarce perceive . . .
> The Earl of Warwick then conceived
> Of the simpleness and great innocence
> Of King Henry, as he it well perceived,
> Desired to be discharged of his diligence
> About the king . . .

2) Piero da Monte, November 1437
(Griffiths, *Reign of Henry VI*, p. 235)

[Henry VI at the age of sixteen] avoided the sight and conversation of women, affirming these to be the work of the devil and quoting from the Gospel, 'He who casts his eyes on a woman so as to lust after her has already committed adultery with her in his heart.' Those who knew him intimately said that he had preserved his virginity of mind and body to this present time, and that he was firmly resolved to have intercourse with no woman unless within the bonds of matrimony.

3) Jean de Waurin
(*Hallam*, p. 196; *Wilkinson*, p. 50)

[Richard of York's recall from France in 1445] and other changes that took place in the kingdom were due to the simple-mindedness of the king who was neither intelligent enough nor experienced enough to manage a kingdom such as England. . . . For it is a true proverb which says, 'Very afflicted is the land whose prince is a child or rules like one'. . . . For, because the king, Henry VI, has not in his time been such a man as is needful to govern such a realm, each one who has had power with him has wished to strengthen himself by getting control over the king.

4) Henry VI's Meeting with French Envoys, July 1446
(Griffiths, *Reign of Henry VI*, pp. 491–2)

[The envoys] found the king [in Westminster hall] seated upon a high chair [and] clothed in a rich robe down to the ground, of red cloth of gold. . . . As soon as the Count of Vendôme and the Archbishop of Rheims entered the hall, and the king perceived them, he came down and stood exactly in front of his chair, [took] by the hand all those of the king [of France's] party, taking off his hat a little to the count and the archbishop . . . [Later] the king gave a very good appearance of being well pleased and very joyful, [came] towards the ambassadors and, putting his hand to his hat and raising it from his head, [he] patted each one on the back and gave very many indications of joy . . .

5) *John Capgrave, circa 1447*
(*Hallam*, pp. 192–3; *Wilkinson*, p. 49)

In 1441 the most pious King Henry founded two splendid colleges and devoted great care and expense to their buildings. He graced the laying of the foundation stones with his presence and with great devotion offered his foundations to Almighty God. The first is at Eton near Windsor, dedicated to the Blessed Virgin; the other, King's College at Cambridge, in honour of St Nicholas . . .

Would that his subjects were inclined towards the example of our king. With what reverence he adores the sign of the cross when his priests meet him. For I know how many men of more robust life, who did not have the cross in great reverence, were turned by the example of our most devoted king to a greater fervour of faith and to a most faithful embracing of the glorious sign of our Lord. It would be most highly pleasing to our lord [the king] if his subjects should be reformed by his good example.

6) *Henry VI: A Devout Prayer of His*
(*Blacman*, p. 24)

O Lord Jesu Christ, who didst create me, redeem me, and foreordain me unto that which I now am: Thou knowest what Thou will do with me: deal with me according to Thy most compassionate will. I know and confess in sincerity that in Thy hand all things are set, and there is none that can withstand Thee: Thou art Lord of all. Thou therefore, God Almighty, compassionate and pitiful, in whose power are all realms and lordships, and unto whom all our thoughts, words, and works, such as have been, are, and shall be, are continually open and known, who only has wisdom and knowledge incomprehensible: Thou knowest, Lord, what is profitable for me poor sinner: be it so done with me as pleaseth Thee and as seemeth good in the eyes of Thy divine Majesty.

Receive, O compassionate Father and merciful God Almighty, the prayer of me Thy most unworthy servant; and let my supplications, which I offer before Thee and Thy saints, come unto the ears of Thy mercy. Amen.

7) *King's Bench Ancient Indictments, 1450*
(*EHD*, p. 264)

It is to enquired for our sovereign lord the king whether John Merfeld of Brightling in the shire of Sussex, husbandman, and William Merfeld, [at] Brightling in the open market [on 26 July 1450], falsely said that the king was a natural fool and would often hold a staff in his hands with a bird on the end, playing therewith as a fool, and that another king must be ordained to rule the land, saying that the king was no person able to rule the land.

8) Thomas Gascoigne
(*Wilkinson*, p. 50)
Lord Saye, with other persons around Henry VI, would not permit anybody to preach before the king unless they had first seen the sermon in writing, or unless the preacher would swear and promise that he would not preach anything against those who were around the king, or against the actions of the king, or against the king, or against the actions of his privy – or more truly his evil – council.

9) Gregory's Chronicle
(*Gregory*, p. 203)
During all the holy time of Lent [in 1458] no man could preach before the king unless he showed his sermon in writing, whether he be doctor or other, [to] the lords ABC [so they] could determine what he might say on anything concerning the commonwealth. . . .

10) Whethamsted's Register
(*Whethamsted*, pp. 163, 415; Gransden, *Historical Writing in England*, 11, p. 384; Wolffe, *Henry VI*, p. 19)
A disease and disorder of such a sort overcame the king [in 1453] that he lost his wits and memory for a time, and nearly all his body was so unco-ordinated and out of control that he could neither walk, nor hold his head upright, nor easily move from where he sat. . . .

[Henry VI was] his mother's stupid offspring, not his father's, a son greatly degenerated from the father, who did not cultivate the art of war . . . a mild-spoken, pious king, but half-witted in affairs of state.

11) Crowland Chronicle: First (Prior's) Continuation
(*Ingulph*, pp. 420, 424)
[During Lent 1460] King Henry, being inspired by feelings of devotion, came to Crowland in order to present his humble offerings at the tomb of our holy father Guthlac. . . . Here he stayed, in the full enjoyment of tranquillity, three days and as many nights, taking the greatest pleasure in the observance of his religious duties, and most urgently praying that he might be admitted into the brotherhood of our monastery, a request accordingly granted. Shortly after, desiring to present us with a due return, of his royal liberality he graciously granted and confirmed to us the whole village of Crowland, so that its inhabitants might be exempted from all demands by servants and tax-gatherers of the king . . .

[In 1461] the nobles of the realm, and all the people who inhabited the midland counties of England, as well as those who lived in the eastern and western parts, or in any way bordered upon the midland district, seeing that they were despised and abandoned by King Henry, who, at the instigation of the queen, had taken himself to the north, utterly deserted him: [for] their hearts were now no longer with him, nor would they any more allow of his being king. Besides, in consequence of an illness increasingly afflicting him for many years, he had fallen into a weak state of mind, and had for a time remained in a condition of imbecility and held the government of the realm in name only.

12) *Earl of Warwick, circa 1460*
(*Wilkinson*, p. 50)
Our king is stupid and out of his mind; he does not rule but is ruled. The government is in the hands of the queen and her paramours.

13) *John Blacman*
(*Blacman*, pp. 26–30, 32, 34, 36–9, 41–2)
[Henry VI] was, like a second Job, a man simple and upright, altogether fearing God and eschewing evil. He was a simple man, without any craftiness or untruth, as is plain to all. With none did he deal craftily, nor ever would say an untrue word to any, but framed his speech always to speak truth.

He was both upright and just, [never] consciously inflicting injustice on anyone. To Almighty God he rendered most faithfully that which was His, [showing] most painstaking devotion, so that even when wearing kingly ornaments and crowned with the royal diadem, he made it a duty to bow before the Lord as deep in prayer as any young monk . . .

[That] this prince cherished a son's fear towards the Lord is plain from many of his acts and devotions. [A] certain reverend prelate of England used to relate that, during the ten years he served as confessor to King Henry, no blemish of mortal sin touched his soul . . .

A diligent and sincere worshipper of God was this king, more given to God and devout prayer than worldly and temporal matters, or practising vain sports and pursuits: these he despised as trivial, and was continually occupied either in prayer or the reading of the scriptures . . .

[Wherever] this king was, he always showed himself a venerator and most devout adorer of the Holy Cross and other symbols of the Christian religion. . . . Moreover, he would never allow hawks, swords or daggers to be brought into church, or commercial agreements or conferences to happen there: even his great men and nobles he urged to give themselves frequently to prayer . . .

This King Henry was chaste and pure from the beginning of his days. He eschewed all licentiousness in word and deed while he was young; until he was of marriageable age, when he espoused Lady Margaret [by] whom he fathered but one son Prince Edward; and he kept his marriage vow to her wholly and sincerely, even during her sometimes very lengthy absences, never dealing unchastely with any other woman . . . [Indeed] it happened once that, at Christmas time, a certain great lord brought before him a dance or show of young ladies with bared bosoms who were to dance in that mode before the king, perhaps to prove him, or to entice his youthful mind. But the king . . . very angrily averted his eyes, turned his back upon them, and went out to his chamber, saying: 'Fy, fy, for shame, forsooth ye be to blame'. At another time, riding by Bath, [the] king, looking into the baths [there], saw in them men wholly naked, [at] which he was displeased, and went away quickly, abhorring such nudity as a great offence. . . . Moreover, he took great precautions to preserve not only his own chastity but that of his servants, for, before he was married, being as a youth a pupil of chastity, he would keep careful watch through hidden windows of his chamber, lest any foolish impertinence of women coming into the house grow to a head and cause the downfall of any of his household . . .

[When] the executors of his uncle [Cardinal Beaufort] Bishop of Winchester came to the king with a very great sum [£2000] to relieve the financial burdens of the realm, he resolutely refused the gift. . . . The executors [then urged him to] accept the gift for the endowment of his newly founded colleges at Cambridge and Eton. This petition and gift the king gladly accepted . . . [He] founded these two noble colleges, and endowed them with large lands and revenues, for the maintenance of poor scholars. . . .

[At] the principal feasts of the year, especially those where by custom he wore his crown, he would always have put on his bare body a rough hair shirt, so that by its roughness his body might be restrained from excess, or more truly so that all pride and vainglory, apt to be encouraged by pomp, might be repressed. . . .

[Concerning the behaviour] of the king and how he passed his days, it is well known to many who are still alive that he used to devote high days and Sundays entirely to hearing the divine office and to devout prayer on his own behalf and his people's, [and] he was earnest in seeking to induce others to do the same. Indeed, some who once attended on him declare that all his joy and pleasure lay in the praise of God and performance of divine service. Even days of less solemnity he passed, not in sloth and vanities, not in banquetings and drunkenness, not in vain talk or other mischievous speech and chatter, [but] in transacting government business with his council or in reading the scriptures . . . [The] king himself once complained heavily to me in his chamber at Eltham, when I was alone there with him studying his holy books, and giving ear to his wholesome advice and the sighs of his most deep devotion, [concerning] a knock on his door by a certain mighty duke of the realm: the king said, 'They so interrupt me that, whether by day or night, I can hardly snatch a moment for reading holy scripture without disturbance'. . . .

Once, when he was journeying from St Albans to London via Cripplegate, he saw over the gate there the quarter of a man on a tall stake, and asked what it was. When his lords answered that it was the quarter of a traitor, who had been false to the king's majesty, he said: 'Take it away. I will not have any Christian man so cruelly handled for my sake'. And the quarter was removed immediately. . . . Again, four nobles of high birth were convicted of treason [and] condemned by the judges to suffer a shameful death, [but] he compassionately released and delivered them from such a bitter death. . . .

Furthermore, I think it not well to pass over the miracles shown to this king. When he was imprisoned in the Tower of London, his chaplain asked him, about Eastertime, how his soul coped at so holy a season with the troubles pressing upon him and impossible to avoid. The king answered in these words: 'The Kingdom of Heaven, unto which I have devoted myself always from a child, do I call and cry for. For this kingdom, which is transitory and of the earth, I do not greatly care. Our kinsman of March [Edward IV] throws himself into it as is his pleasure. The only thing I require is to receive the sacrament at Easter, and the rites of the church on Maundy Thursday, with the rest of Christendom, as I am accustomed'. And for the great devotion he always had to God and His sacraments, it is apt he was so frequently comforted in his afflictions by miracles. He is reported [to] have often seen the Lord Jesus held in the hands of the celebrant and appearing to him in human form at the time of the Eucharist, [as well as] a vision of the assumption of the Blessed Mary, both corporal and spiritual.

14) James Ryman: A Remembrance of Henry VI, 1492
(Robbins, pp. 199–200)

> O good Harry, the sixth by name,
> Both of England and of France,
> A king you were of royal fame,
> And of full worthy governance,
> Full of mercy without vengeance . . .
> A king you were of great renown
> And of virtue most excellent . . .
> As a true knight, both day and night,
> Our Saviour you did honour
> With heart and mind, with will and might . . .
> A prince you were meek and benign,
> Patient in adversity . . .
> In your gesture you were like Job
> Steadfast of faith and mild of mode . . .

15) Polydore Vergil
(Vergil, pp. 70–1, 156–7)

King Henry [VI] was a man of mild and plain dealing disposition who preferred peace before wars, quietness before troubles, honesty before utility, and leisure before business; and, to be short, there was not in this world a more pure, more honest and more holy creature. There was in him honest reproachfulness, modesty, innocence, and perfect patience, taking all human chances, miseries, and all afflictions of this life in so good part as though he had justly by some offence deserved the same. He ruled his own affections so that he might more easily rule his own subjects; he hungered not after riches, nor thirsted for honour and worldly estimation, but was careful only for his soul's health. . . .

[Henry VI] was tall of stature, slender of body [and] of comely visage. . . . He did of his own natural inclination abhor all vices both of body and mind, by reason whereof he was of honest conversation even from a child, pure and clean, partaking of no evil, ready to conceive all that was good, a condemner of all those things which commonly corrupt the minds of men; so patient also in suffering injuries, received now and then, as if he coveted in his heart no revenge but, for the very same, gave God most humble thanks because he thought his sins to be washed away; yes, what shall we say, since this good, gracious, holy, sober and wise man would affirm all these miseries happened to him both for his own and his ancestors' manifold offences. Wherefore he did not much account what dignity, what honour, what state of life, what son, what friends he had lost, nor showed much sorrow for the same; but if in any thing he had offended God, that he had regard of, that did he mourn for, that was he sorry for. These and similar actions and offices of perfect holiness made, so that, for his cause, God showed many miracles in his lifetime. By reason whereof King Henry VII, not without desert, began a few years past to petition to [Pope] Julius [11] that he might be canonized for a saint. . . . Moreover, this Henry VI was of liberal mind; he had great learning in great reverence [and] helped his own people so that they might be instructed: for he founded a sumptous school at Eton, a town near Windsor, in which he placed a college of priests, and children in great number, there to be brought up and taught their grammar freely and without cost. The same man was also founder of King's College at Cambridge. . . .

Margaret of Anjou

Born in 1430, Margaret of Anjou was the younger daughter of Réné Duke of Anjou and titular King of Sicily, Naples, Hungary and Jerusalem, and his strong-minded wife Isabella, heiress of Charles Duke of Lorraine. A good-looking and vivacious girl (2, 3), who revelled in French courtly romances and loved the chase, she was raised as a princess. However, although well-endowed with titles, her father possessed virtually no land beyond Anjou and little money: consequently, when her marriage to Henry VI was arranged in 1444, it was very much a political match (England gained a much-needed two-year truce with France) and she brought no dowry (3). Margaret arrived in England early in April 1445 and, if we are to believe a Milanese correspondent writing over a decade later, her first meeting with her new husband was extraordinary to say the least (3); the two were married later in the month; and, following a ceremonial entry into London, the queen was crowned at Westminster at the end of May (1). Although later criticized for her closeness to William de la Pole Duke of Suffolk and her advocacy of peace with France at any price in the later 1440s (particularly the surrender of Maine and Anjou to the Valois king Charles VII), at most she merely jumped aboard a bandwagon already rolling before her marriage. Nor, in all probability, did she play any significant role in determining the eventual outcome of Cade's rebellion in 1450. Rather, as Diana Dunn has argued, Margaret's actions during her first eight years as England's queen 'deserve to be judged as those of a dutiful young wife and effective distributor of patronage' to her dependants, certainly not those of the 'imperious and passionate power-seeker' she may later have become.

1453, in fact, was a clear turning-point in Margaret of Anjou's life, for two very obvious reasons; first, her husband's mental collapse at the beginning of August and, second, the birth of her son Edward of Lancaster on 13 October. The king's breakdown clearly meant that, whatever the situation before, there was now a veritable power vacuum at the heart of the body politic. Initially, every effort was made to conceal the reality of Henry VI's condition but, by the autumn of 1453, the need for firm measures to deal with this unprecedented situation was becoming ever more urgent. What brought Margaret of Anjou on to the political stage with a vengeance was the birth of her son and her determination to safeguard his position; moreover, since she came from a family where women had been accustomed to exercise authority when their husbands were incapacitated or absent, it is not surprising that, in January 1454, she sought to obtain power for herself as regent (4).

The fact that she failed probably reflects not so much widespread support in political circles for Richard of York becoming protector as deep-rooted resistance to the very notion of a woman regent (10). Nevertheless, once launched into the world of politics, Margaret proved indefatigable in pursuit of her objectives, developing an ever deeper loathing for Richard of York (6) and becoming a firm ally of his rival Edmund Beaufort Duke of Somerset. Following Somerset's death at St Albans in May 1455, she probably kept a low profile during the few months of York's ascendancy but, by the autumn of 1456, she had become virtually the leader of a Lancastrian faction. Thereafter, although both her husband (in so far as he was politically active at all) and the Yorkist lords may have sought to avoid political conflict and promote reconciliation, Margaret of Anjou concentrated on consolidating her own position and that of her son, by securing the advancement of men close to her and building up support in the country (especially in the midlands and north-west). By 1459, as a result, she had become a prime target for anti-government propaganda and, although pro-Yorkist commentators probably exaggerated the degree of power she exercised (5, 7), her credentials as a formidable and determined champion of the Lancastrian dynasty must have been clear to all (8).

During 1459 Margaret of Anjou certainly played a major role in the political manoeuvring and military preparation that culminated in the battle of Blore Heath in September, the rout at Ludford in October and the subsequent flight of the Yorkist leaders into exile. No doubt her hand can be detected, too, in the strongly worded condemnation of Richard of York by the Coventry Parliament in November 1459. Following the Yorkist victory at Northampton in July 1460, when Henry VI fell into the hands of her enemies, the queen herself fled to Wales. According to *Gregory's Chronicle*, the Yorkist lords, in the months that followed, would very much 'have liked to have got her to London, for they knew well that all the arts that were done were encouraged by her, for she was more intelligent than the king'. However, she managed to evade capture and, when news reached her of the so-called Act of Accord in October 1460 (cutting out Edward of Lancaster from the succession to the throne in favour of Richard of York and his heirs), she very much took the intiative in rallying Lancastrian opposition to the settlement, especially in the north of England. This paid off handsomely. While in Scotland, where she had journeyed shortly before in search of Scottish backing for her cause, she learned that York had been defeated and killed at the battle of Wakefield on 30 December 1460: not that this prevented her condemning him once more, in notably colourful terms, in a letter sent to the city of London soon afterwards (9). Fortunately for the Yorkists, Margaret and her military advisers (reunited at York early in January 1461) entirely failed to reap the benefits of the great Lancastrian success at Wakefield. Nor did a further convincing victory at the second battle of St Albans on 17 February 1461 bring the rewards it might have done (although the queen did recover control of her husband!) Part of the problem, clearly, lay in the appalling behaviour of the Lancastrian army during its march south in the early weeks of 1461. London, sympathetic to the Yorkists anyway, found the prospect of such a force within its walls terrifyingly unpalatable. The queen, perhaps foolishly, rejected the option of storming the city and, instead, retreated back to the north. Early in March 1461 Richard of York's eldest son was proclaimed king in London as Edward IV and, before the month was out, he had inflicted a massive (and, as it turned out, decisive) defeat on the Lancastrians at the battle of Towton.

Margaret of Anjou, Henry VI and Edward of Lancaster, after narrowly avoiding capture in York, now fled to Scotland. From there, for the next two years, the queen valiantly struggled to sustain Lancastrian resistance to Edward IV in northern England, even sailing to France in the spring of 1462 to enlist the backing of the new French king, Louis XI: so lukewarm was his response, however, that an attempted invasion of north-eastern England in the autumn of 1462 failed dismally and, in the summer of 1463, Margaret of Anjou, her son (but not her husband!) and a band of hangers-on left Scotland to become exiles on the continent. The Burgundian chronicler Georges Chastellain penned a compelling portrait of her destitute condition on arrival (11) while Sir John Fortescue, a member of her shadowy court-in-exile, recorded that, living in Koeur castle on a tiny income and small estate at St Mihiel-en-Bar provided by the queen's father Réné of Anjou, 'we are all in great poverty' but, since 'the queen sustains us in meat and drink, we are not in extreme necessity'. Over the next few years Margaret regularly lobbied Louis XI to back resistance to Edward IV but elicited little response until, in the summer of 1470 and for political objectives of his own, he engineered a reconciliation between Margaret and Warwick the Kingmaker. The outcome was the marriage of Edward of Lancaster to Warwick's daughter Anne and, in October, the restoration of Henry VI to the English throne. By the time the queen and her son reached England again in April 1471, however, Edward IV had won the battle of Barnet and, early in May, he triumphed at Tewkesbury as well: Edward of Lancaster lost his life on the field, Henry VI was murdered in the Tower soon after, and Margaret of Anjou herself was captured. For a few months the queen was closely confined, first in the Tower and subsequently in Windsor castle until, at the end of 1471, she passed into the custody of her former companion Alice Duchess of Suffolk, with whom she remained for the next four years. Then, under the terms of the Anglo-French treaty of Picquigny in 1475, she was ransomed by Louis XI for 50,000 crowns and permitted to return to France: in exchange, however, she had to renounce both her rights to dower in England and entitlement to any Angevin estates. Consequently, her last few years were spent in poverty and isolation until, on 25 August 1482, she died (12).

1) Brut Chronicle
(*Brut*, p. 489)
[On Friday 26 May 1445] the mayor of London, with the aldermen, sheriffs and commons of the city, rode to Blackheath in Kent, where they remained on horseback until the queen's coming. Then they came with her [to] the Tower of

London, where she rested all night. The king, in honour of the queen and her first coming, made forty-six knights of the Bath. On the morrow, in the afternoon, the queen came from the Tower in a horse-bier, with two steeds decorated all in white damask powdered with gold, as was the clothing she had on; [her] hair was combed down about her shoulders, with a coronel of gold, rich pearls and precious stones; [and there were] nineteen chariots of ladies and their gentlewomen, [as well as] all the crafts of the city of London [who proceeded] on foot in their best array to St Paul's. On the way, as she came through the city, many devices were displayed and stories told, with angels and other heavenly figures, and songs and melodies heard in several places. The conduits ran with wine, both white and red, for all the people who wished to drink. . . . On the morrow, which was Sunday, the coronation and feast were royally and worthily held at Westminster in the king's palace.

2) Polydore Vergil
(*Vergil,* pp. 68, 71, 102, 147–8)
[Henry VI] took to wife Margaret, daughter of Réné Duke of Anjou and King of Sicily, a young lady exceeding others of her time, as well in beauty as wisdom, imbued with a high courage above the nature of her sex, as her noble acts have manifestly declared. . . .

[Margaret of Anjou was] a woman of sufficient forecast, very desirous of renown, full of policy, counsel, comely behaviour, and all manly qualities, in whom appeared great wit, great diligence, great heed and carefulness: but she was of the kind of other women, who commonly are much given [to] mutability and change. This woman, when she perceived the king her husband to do nothing of his own head [following her marriage in 1445] but to rule wholly by [Humphrey] Duke of Gloucester's advice, [determined] to take upon herself that charge and, little by little, deprive the duke of his great authority. [For she feared] she also might be reported to have little wit if she allowed her husband, now of mature years, to remain under another man's government. . . .

[In 1459] the queen [who was], for diligence, circumspection and speedy execution of causes, comparable to a man, believed for certain that [there was a malignant enterprise] whereby the Duke of York [might] attain the sovereignty. Wherefore this wise woman [called] together the council to provide remedy for the disordered state of things. . . .

[When Margaret of Anjou landed at Weymouth in April 1471, she learned] that King Henry her husband was deserted and taken, that the Earl of Warwick and his brother were killed, and that his forces were partly destroyed, partly scattered. . . . When she heard these things the miserable woman swooned for fear; she was distraught, dismayed and tormented with sorrow; she lamented the calamity of the time, the adversity of fortune, her own toil and misery; she bewailed the unhappy end of King Henry, which she believed assuredly to be at hand; and, to be short, she behaved as one more desirous to die than live. . . .

3) Milanese State Papers: Report to Bianca Maria Visconti Duchess of Milan, 24 October 1458
(*CSPM*, pp. 18–19)
I am writing to report what an Englishman told me about the magnificence of the Queen of England and how she was brought to England. I will also tell you something of the King of England. First of all the Englishman told me that the King of England took her without any dowry, and he even restored some lands which he held to her father. When the queen landed in England the king dressed himself as a squire, the Duke of Suffolk doing the same, and took her a letter which he said the King of England had written. While the queen read the letter the king took stock of her, saying that a woman may be seen very well when she reads a letter, and the queen never found out it was the king because she was so engrossed in reading the letter, and she never looked at the king in his squire's dress, who remained on his knees all the time. After the king had gone the Duke of Suffolk said: 'Most serene queen, what do you think of the squire who brought the letter?' The queen replied: 'I did not notice him, as I was occupied in reading the letter he brought.' The duke remarked: 'Most serene queen, the person dressed as a squire was the most serene King of England,' and the queen was vexed at not having known it, because she had kept him on his knees. . . .

The Englishman told me that the queen is a most handsome woman, though somewhat dark and not so beautiful as your serenity. He told me that his mistress is wise and charitable. . . . He said that his queen had an income of 80,000 gold crowns. She has a most handsome boy, six years old. . . .

4) Paston Letters
(*Paston Letters*, Vol. 2, p. 297)
John Stodeley, in London, to the Duke of Norfolk, 19 January 1454
. . . the queen has made a bill of five articles, desiring them to be granted, the first of which is that she desires the whole rule of this land; the second is that she may appoint the chancellor, treasurer, [keeper of the] privy seal, and all other officers of this land, with sheriffs and all other officers, that the king should make; the third is that she may give all the bishoprics of this land, and all other benefices belonging to the king's gift; the fourth is that she may have sufficient livelihood assigned to her for the king, the prince and herself. As for the fifth article, I cannot yet find out what it is.

5) Thomas Gascoigne
(*Wilkinson*, p. 128)
Almost all the affairs of the realm were conducted according to the queen's will, by fair means or foul, as was said by several people. What will be the result of all this, God knows.

6) Benet's Chronicle
(*Benet*, pp. 216–17)
[In February 1456] John Helton, an apprentice at court and formerly of Gray's

Inn, was drawn, hanged and quartered for producing bills asserting that Prince Edward was not the queen's son; however, before his death, he retracted all such statements. . . .

[In October 1456] the king sent for the Earl of Warwick and the Duke of York, who came and received a most gracious welcome from him; however, the queen greatly loathed them both.

7) *English Chronicle*
(*Davies*, pp. 79–80)
[In 1459] the queen, with such as were of her affinity, ruled the realm as she liked, gathering riches innumerable. The officers of the realm, especially the Earl of Wiltshire, treasurer of England, to enrich himself, fleeced the poor people, disinherited rightful heirs and did many wrongs. The queen was defamed and denounced, that he who was called prince was not her son but a bastard conceived in adultery; wherefore she, dreading that he should not succeed his father in the crown of England, sought the alliance of all the knights and squires of Cheshire, to have their goodwill, and held open household among them. And she made her son, called the prince, give a livery of swans to all the gentlemen of the countryside and to many others throughout the land, trusting through their strength to make her son king, and making secret approaches to some of the lords of England to stir the king that he should resign the crown to her son; but she could not bring her purpose about.

8) *Pope Pius II's Commentaries: An Anecdotal Report of a Speech by Margaret of Anjou to Her Captains, and Their Reactions*
(P.-A. Lee, 'Reflections of Power: Margaret of Anjou and the Dark Side of Queenship', *Renaissance Quarterly*, Vol. 39, pp. 198–9)
'I have often broken their [the English] battle line. I have mowed down ranks far more stubborn than theirs are now. You who once followed a peasant girl [Joan of Arc] now follow a queen. . . . I will either conquer or be conquered with you.' All marvelled at such boldness in a woman, at a man's courage in a woman's breast, and at her reasonable arguments. They said that the spirit of the Maid, who had raised Charles [VII of France] to the throne, was renewed in the queen.

9) *Margaret of Anjou to the Citizens of London, 1461*
(*Letters of the Queens of England*, ed. A. Crawford, p. 129)
. . . whereas the late Duke of York, of extreme malice long hid under colours, plotted by many ways and means the destruction of my lord's [Henry VI's] good grace, whom God of his mercy ever preserve, has now of late, on an untrue pretence, feigned a title to my lord's crown, royal estate and pre-eminence, contrary to his allegiance and several solemn oaths freely sworn by him, [and] fully proposed to have deposed him of his regality, had it not been for the wise, unchangeable and true disposition of you and others, his true liegemen. And howbeit that [he], of very pure malice, proposed to continue in his cruelness, to

our utter undoing and that of our son, the prince, [has promulgated] several untrue and feigned matters and surmises, especially that we [intend to] draw towards you with an unseen power of strangers, disposed to rob and despoil you of your goods and property, we desire that you know for certain [that] none of you shall be robbed, despoiled nor wronged by any person [in our company].

10) Pro-Yorkist Ballad, 1462
(*Robbins*, p. 224)

> [As] scripture says, 'Woe be to that region
> Where is a king unwise or innocent'.
> Moreover it is a right great perversion
> [For] a woman of a land to be a regent –
> Queen Margaret, I mean, that ever has meant
> To govern all England with might and power,
> And to destroy the right line was her intent. . . .

11) Georges Chastellain
(*Lander,* p. 147)

[Margaret of Anjou arrived in Burgundy in 1463] poor and alone, destitute of all goods and all desolate. [She] had neither credence, nor money, nor goods, nor jewels to pledge. [She] had her son, no royal robes, nor estate, and her person without adornment befitting a queen. Her body was clad in one single robe, with no change of clothing. [She] had no more than seven women for her retinue, whose apparel was like that of their mistress, formerly one of the most splendid women of the world and now the poorest. And finally she had no other provision, not even bread to eat, except from the purse of her knight Sir Pierre de Brézé. . . . It was a thing piteous to see, truly, this high princess so cast down and laid low in such great danger, dying of hunger and hardship. . . .

12) Margaret of Anjou's Will, 2 August 1482
(Bagley, *Margaret of Anjou,* p. 240)

I, Margaret of Anjou, sound of mind, reason and thought, however weak and feeble of body, make and declare this my last will and testament in the manner following. First I give and recommend my soul to God . . . my body also I give to God . . . and it is my will and desire that it be buried and interred in holy ground according to the goodwill and pleasure of the king [Louis XI], and, if it pleases him, I elect and choose to be buried in the cathedral church of Saint Maurice d'Angers. . . . My will is [that] the few goods which God and he [Louis XI] have given and lent to me be used for this purpose and for the paying of my debts as much to my poor servants [as] to other creditors to whom I am indebted. . . . And should my few goods be insufficient to do this, as I believe they are, I implore the king [to] meet and pay the outstanding debts as the sole heir of the wealth which I inherited through my father and mother and my other relatives and ancestors. . . .

Richard of York

Born in 1411, Richard Plantagenet Duke of York, son of Richard Earl of Cambridge (executed for treason in 1415), and Anne Mortimer, was a direct descendant of Edward III: his grandfather Edmund of Langley Duke of York was the king's fourth son, while his mother's great-grandfather Lionel of Antwerp Duke of Clarence was his second. Arguably, the Mortimer claim to the throne, although via the female line, was superior to Henry VI's own, since he descended from John of Gaunt Duke of Lancaster, Edward III's third son. At the very least, as a man of such exalted ancestry and, indeed, vast estates (particularly in Wales, the Welsh marches and Ireland), Richard of York could reasonably expect a prominent role in Henry VI's council and even, perhaps, formal recognition as the king's heir (at any rate until the birth of Edward of Lancaster in 1453). Certainly, York believed he deserved better treatment than he received in the later 1440s and 1450s, putting out a series of documents reciting both his personal grievances and his perceived obligation, by virtue of birth and social status, to represent the public good and the needs of the commonweal: when writing to Henry VI in October 1450, for instance, he proclaimed his concern for 'the welfare of your most noble realm' and 'the preservation of good tranquility and peaceable rule' (7c); his Shrewsbury manifesto of February 1452 highlighted his desire 'to promote the ease, peace, tranquillity and safeguard of this land'; and, on the eve of the first battle of St Albans in May 1455, he claimed to be acting on behalf of 'the honour, prosperity and welfare of our sovereign lord, his land and people'. Pro-Yorkist chroniclers, predictably, portray Richard of York as admirably altruistic in his objectives, only to be frustrated, again and again, by the corrupt clique surrounding the king, especially (in the early 1450s) Edmund Beaufort Duke of Somerset: the *English Chronicle*, for instance, recorded that the common people hated Somerset but loved York 'because he loved the commons and preserved the common profit of this land' (8); *Benet's Chronicle* remarked that, when York resigned as protector in 1455, he did so 'with great honour and love of all' (9); and *Whethamsted's Register*, although occasionally prepared to criticize York, nevertheless believed his hostility to Somerset in the early 1450s was well justified, noted with approval his willingness to negotiate with the Lancastrians in 1455, and reported that, when York fled to Ireland following Ludford in 1459, he was received there 'as though another Messiah had descended'. Richard of York's contemporary critics, by contrast, tended to condemn him as a man motivated by personal self-interest rather than concern for the public good who, eventually, became an out-and-out traitor: a Chancery memorandum of 1456 recorded that all disturbances since Cade's rebellion in 1450 had been 'at the will of the Duke of York, descended from the Mortimers' (5); the Coventry Parliament in 1459 set out a dismal catalogue of his alleged treacheries (6); and the tract *Somnium Vigilantes*, similarly, judged the behaviour of York and his principal allies 'subversive to the commonwealth' over many years. Not every chronicle, moreover, was pro-Yorkist: the *Chronicon Angliae*, for instance, showed little sympathy for York's behaviour in the early 1450s, while Polydore Vergil, writing in early Tudor times, was notably critical of the factionalism he promoted. Not surprisingly, historians have brought in contrasting verdicts. The Victorian James Gairdner believed Richard of York 'protested by every loyal means against misgovernment, and exhausted every peaceable remonstrance, before he advanced his title to the throne', while, more recently, Ralph Griffiths has argued that York's concern for better government did indeed lead to practical reformist efforts (if not lasting achievements) during his two periods as protector in 1454/5 and 1455/6. Yet, for J. R. Lander, the duke was an ambitious, opportunist and self-interested magnate who failed to win much committed support from his peers; his modern biographer P. A. Johnson, in 1988, brought in a decidedly mixed verdict on a man who, although capable of exercising high office effectively, proved lacking in political judgement; and Christine Carpenter has suggested that, even if York cannot and should not be portrayed as merely greedy and self-seeking, his sense of his own self-importance may well have 'led him to believe he must be the natural and only arbiter of the nation's destinies'.

Richard of York secured early political and military prominence when, in 1436/7 and, again, between 1440 and 1445, he served as king's lieutenant (commander-in-chief) in France. Pro-Yorkist chroniclers, predictably, praised his achievements there (1, 2) and, although recent historians have been more circumspect when judging his record, he did at least restore English authority in Normandy. Perhaps, therefore, York had every reason to resent his replacement by Somerset (1), especially if his own new appointment as lieutenant of Ireland (2, 3a) constituted a deliberate snub designed to get him out of the way. Indeed, if we are to believe *Whethamsted's Register*, York had ruled Normandy so well that not only did the council thank him for his efforts when he returned to England (in September 1445) but also, initially, secured his reappointment for a further five years; Somerset, in collusion with Suffolk, engineered a reversal of this decision in his own favour (in December 1446); and here, according to this chronicler, lay the real origins of the bitter York/Somerset feud of the early 1450s. Historians, too, have often regarded York as very much a victim of the machinations of the court clique surrounding Henry VI, deliberately exiled to Ireland as a man unsympathetic to current government policies respecting France. Only recently has the notion of York the ambitious but admirably well-meaning political outsider of the later 1440s, the natural heir to Humphrey Duke of Gloucester's mantle maliciously ostracized by the ruling faction as a result, been seriously called into question, as altogether too reliant on later Yorkist propaganda. Rather, it has been suggested, considerable efforts were made to placate him for his loss of office in France; he did not actually depart for Ireland until June 1449; and, anyway, his absence from the centre of political decision-making for so many months thereafter carried a positive bonus since no blame could attach to him for the disastrous English defeat at Formigny in April 1450 and the ensuing loss of Normandy. Certainly, York reacted strongly to news of events in France following the foolhardy attack on Fougères in March 1449, particularly the fall of Rouen (in October 1449) and the loss of his own Norman estates, for which he regarded Somerset as primarily responsible (4). He resented, too, the lack of government support he felt he had received, and the financial losses he had incurred, while on the king's service both in France and Ireland. Moreover, although charges of his complicity in Cade's rebellion in the summer of 1450 are almost certainly a later fabrication (5, 6a), the rebels did highlight his credentials as the best potential saviour of England from its current corrupt and partisan rulers and, later in the year, he himself began pressing for many of the reforms so strongly demanded in rebel manifestos (7b). What probably led him to return from Ireland early in September, however, was Somerset's continued high profile in the king's entourage (3b) and fear concerning his own reputation and interests in England (7a). Following his arrival, in the colourful language of *Whethamsted's Register*, he 'sharpened as lightning his sword' and, 'taking justice into his own hands', made for London. Initially, his main concern was to counter rumours of his disloyalty to Henry VI but, before long, he was also presenting himself as the man best able to restore justice, law and order in the realm (7a, c). The king's response, although conciliatory, clearly did not satisfy him (7b, d) and, over the next few months, he spearheaded a campaign, both in Parliament and outside it, to secure the removal from power of Somerset and other men close to the king. When this failed, York resorted to armed force at Dartford early in 1452, the first of a series of miscalculations that were eventually to culminate in his defeat and death at the battle of Wakefield in December 1460. Most of the nobility remained firmly loyal to Henry VI, as they had been in 1450 and 1451, and, whatever their opinions of Somerset and his friends, they were not prepared to back York's attempted *coup d'etat*. Consequently, however much popular support he may have enjoyed, he was forced to surrender at Dartford, suffer the humiliation of seeing Somerset triumphant, and retire to his estates: yet, although lucky to have avoided charges of treason, York was in no way chastened, regarding events in March 1452 as an unjustified slur on his honour and more determined than ever to bring Somerset down. Nevertheless, by the summer of 1453, the victory of Henry VI and the court seemed complete, while York appeared hopelessly isolated and thoroughly discredited.

Everything was thrown into the political melting pot when Henry VI suffered his mental breakdown at the end of July 1453. During the faction-ridden months that followed Richard of York was determined, at all costs, to prevent either Somerset or Margaret of Anjou gaining the upper hand. Initially, his wife Cicely (no doubt with his connivance) put out feelers concerning the possible rehabilitation and reconciliation of her husband with the royal household: perhaps this helps explain why Somerset not only failed to ensure York's absence from a council meeting in November 1453 but also soon found himself a prisoner in the Tower of London (8). Not until the spring of 1454, however, did York become protector of the realm. Perhaps, as pro-Yorkist chroniclers later emphasized (2, 9), he provided better government during the next few months than had prevailed before. Throughout, though, his position was far from secure, not least because, as Ralph Griffiths has argued, the protectorate had been 'unenthusiastically established, partly to forestall a regency by the queen, and the supporting council preserved a strong element of men who had served Henry VI well before he became ill'. Certainly, once the king recovered at the end of 1454, it did not take long for Somerset to be released from prison and York's protectorate terminated. When York and his new Neville allies retreated to their estates and proceeded to arm, and Somerset and his friends responded, the result was the first battle of St Albans in May 1455 (8): moreover, as *Whethamsted's Register* later emphasized, this armed confrontation was, in a very real sense, a culmination of the personal quarrel of Somerset and York. Somerset lost his life during the fighting and, a few months later, a second short-lived Yorkist protectorate ensued (November 1455 to February 1456). By the autumn of 1456, however, York was once more firmly excluded from the inner circle of politics. Even more than before, during the later 1450s, he came to be perceived as very much a faction-leader and, in all probability, only the reluctance of most lords to become involved prevented a rapid resumption of military conflict. When it came, in the autumn of 1459, York's abject failure at Ludford Bridge forced him into exile in Ireland and, at the Coventry Parliament, he was pronounced a traitor and both his life and property declared forfeit. Just when he decided to claim the throne for himself is far from clear but, in the wake of the Neville victory at Northampton a few weeks earlier, claim it he certainly did in October 1460 (6b). This proved another political miscalculation: the best York could get from Parliament, and that reluctantly, was the promise of the succession after Henry VI's demise. His own death at Wakefield on 30 December 1460, in a battle he should never have fought, finally put paid even to this ambition.

1) Jean de Waurin
(*Hallam*, pp. 194, 196)
[As] governor-general of the duchy of Normandy and consequently of all the conquered territories [in France, Richard of York's] duty was to guard and

protect this country from the French, our enemies, and during this time in office he governed admirably and had many honourable and notable successes over the French. . . . Everything he did was highly commendable not only for himself but also for the honour and furtherance of the crown of England, and for the exaltation of his master the king, whom he served with due reverence and loyalty. . . . Nevertheless, [envy] reared its head among the princes and barons of the kingdom of England, and was directed at the Duke of York, who was gaining in honour and prosperity. . . . Above all, envy prompted the Duke of Somerset, who despised the Duke of York and who found a way to harm him. He was well liked by the Queen of England, Margaret of Anjou, [who] worked on King Henry, her husband, on the advice and support of the Duke of Somerset and other lords and barons of his following, so that the Duke of York was recalled from France to England. There he was totally stripped of his authority to govern Normandy. . . . In York's place, the Duke of Somerset was appointed due to the solicitation and exhortation of the queen and some of the barons who, at that time, were in positions of power in the kingdom.

2) Harding's Chronicle
(*Chronicle of John Hardyng*, ed. H. Ellis, pp. 399, 401)

> [To France] was sent [the Duke of York], with great power royal,
> And regent was he of all that belonged to the king,
> And kept full well Normandy in especial;
> But France was gone afore in general:
> And home he came at seven year end again . . .
> The Duke of York sent was then to Ireland,
> Lieutenant then he was there many a day,
> And great thanks there and love of all the land
> He had among the Irish always,
> And [all the Irish] began him to obey;
> He ruled that land full well and worthily . . .
> The Duke of York then was made protector,
> And governed well, but two year not endured,
> Discharged he was with passing great murmur
> Of commons whole, among them there ensued,
> To help him so, with power adventured;
> For he was set the commonweal to quail,
> By his labour and his whole counsel.

3) Chancery Patent Rolls
(*Calendar of Patent Rolls*, 1446–52, pp. 185, 401)

a) *9 December 1447*: appointment of Richard Duke of York as lieutenant of Ireland for ten years.

b) *11 September 1450*: appointment of Edmund Duke of Somerset as constable of England.

4) *Richard of York's Condemnation of Somerset's Record in France*
(*Flemming*, pp. 122–3)
. . . Edmund Duke of Somerset has been the means, consenter, occasioner, cause and mediator [of] the loss [of] your duchy of Normandy. . . .

[Edmund] Duke of Somerset was the cause and voluntary consenter of the breaking of the truce and peace, for a time prevailing between your highness and your uncle of France, which was well understood at the taking of Fougères in Brittany by Francis [de Surienne] through his advice, consent and counsel. . . . [He] diminished several garrisons and other strong places, in your duchy of Normandy, of soldiers and men of war accustomed to maintain their security and safeguard, [and] would give no counsel, aid nor help to the captains of several strong places and garrisons which, at that time, constrained by need, desired provision and relief from him. . . .

5) *Chancery Memorandum, July 1456*
(*Wilkinson*, p. 128)
From the time that Jack Cade or Mortimer, called captain of Kent, raised a rebellion in Kent [in 1450], all disturbances are at the will of the Duke of York, descended from the Mortimers.

6) *Rolls of Parliament*

a) *Indictment of Richard of York, Coventry Parliament, 1459*
(*Rotuli Parliamentorum*, Vol. 5, p. 346)
May it please your highness [Henry VI] to recall how you had Richard of York in his youth in your most high presence and noble court [before he turned traitor]. When he was in Ireland, as your lieutenant there, John Cade, otherwise called Jack Cade, your great traitor, led a large insurrection against your highness in Kent [in 1450]. Some of his adherents, when on the point of death, confessed their intentions and on whose behalf they acted. They intended to have exalted the Duke of York, against all reason, law and truth, to the estate [crown of England] which God and nature have ordained that you and your successors should be born.

b) *Richard of York's Claim to the Throne, October 1460*
(*Rotuli Parliamentorum*, Vol. 5, p. 375)
To Richard Duke of York, as son to Anne, daughter to Roger Mortimer Earl of March, son and heir to Philippa, daughter and heir to Lionel, third son of King Edward III, the right, title, royal dignity and estate of the crowns of the realms of England and France, and the lordship of Ireland, of right, law and custom

appertains and belongs, before any issue of John of Gaunt, fourth son of the same King Edward.

7) Richard of York's Grievances and Henry VI's Responses, September/October 1450 (Wilkinson, pp. 110–13)

a) Richard of York to Henry VI, September 1450
. . . since my departure out of your realm by your command, and being in your service in your land of Ireland, I have been informed that language has been used about me in your presence [to] my dishonour and reproach. . . . In spite of this, I have been, and ever shall be, your true liegeman and servant. If there be any man who dare say the contrary, or will charge that I am otherwise, I beseech you to call him to your high presence, and I will clear myself, as a true knight ought to do. And if I do not (though I doubt not that I shall), I beseech you to punish me as the poorest man in your land. And if he be found untrue in his suggestion and information, I beseech your highness that he be punished according to his deserts, as an example to all others.

May it please your excellency to know that, both before my departure from your realm to Ireland in your full noble service and since, certain persons have been charged, so I am informed, to take me and put me into your castle of Conway [and juries have been impanelled to indict me of treason]. . . .

I beseech your royal majesty [to] examine these matters and do such justice [as] the case requires. For my intention is fully to sue before your highness for the conclusion of these matters.

b) Henry VI to Richard of York, September 1450
[For] a long time now there have been, amongst the people, many strange reports in regard to you [particularly the rumour] that you intended to [come and] take upon yourself that which you ought [not] to take. . . . Wherefore we sent [several persons to] listen and take heed if there was any such manner of coming and, if there were, to resist it. But since you came to our land, as you did, as our true subject, our intention was not [that you] should be prevented [but rather] be received in goodly manner (although, perhaps, your sudden arrival, without certain warning, caused our servants to do as they did). . . . [For] the easing of your heart in all such matters, we declare, repute and admit you as our true and faithful subject and as our faithful cousin.

c) Richard of York to Henry VI, October 1450
May it please your highness to consider indulgently the great complaining and rumour that is universal throughout this realm, to the effect that justice is not duly administered to such as trespass and offend against your laws, especially [regarding] those who are indicted of treason and others who have been openly

cused of the same. On account of this great troubles have befallen, and are likely to
fall hereafter, your realm, unless suitable provision is made by your highness for
.e reformation and punishment in this matter.

Wherefore I, your humble subject and liegeman Richard Duke of York, desiring the
'ety and prosperity of your most royal person and the welfare of your noble realm,
• counsel and advise your excellency, for the preservation of good tranquillity and
aceable rule among all true subjects, to ordain and provide that due justice be had
ainst all so indicted or openly so accused. Wherein I offer [to] execute your
mmands in these matters, in respect of such offenders, and to redress such
sgoverning according to my might and power. . . .

Henry VI to Richard of York, October 1450

. touching your bill recently presented to us, we understand well that you counsel
d advise us from the goodness of your heart regarding the setting up of justice and
e speedy punishment of certain people who have been indicted or accused, and
at you have offered your services [in this] matter. Since, for many reasons moving
, we have determined in our soul to establish a responsible and substantial council,
'ing it more ample authority and power than we ever did before this, in which we
ve appointed you to be one. But since it is not customary, safe or expedient to
rive at a conclusion and behaviour by the advice and counsel of one person by
mself, [we] have determined to send for our chancellor and other lords of our
uncil, and all others [of the council], so that they may ripely commune together
thin a short time concerning these and other great matters. . . .

English Chronicle
avies, pp. 78, 99–100)

ne of the causes of trouble between the Duke of York and the Duke of Somerset
s this. During the king's sickness the Duke of York was made protector of England,
a result of which the Duke of Somerset was greatly indignant, and always maligned
m and stirred the king against him. Nevertheless, many of the lords of the council
oured the Duke of York more than him. As a result of certain articles laid against
m, the Duke of Somerset was committed to the Tower of London by the king's
uncil: however, thanks to the mediation of his friends he was soon delivered, on
ndition that he never after sought the governance of the realm or came within
enty miles of the king; moreover, he swore upon a book to observe these
nditions. [Yet] once he was released from the Tower, he took upon himself even
ore than before, stirring the king daily and maliciously against the Duke of York
d the Earls [of Salisbury and Warwick], plotting how he might destroy them:
wever, at St Albans, he fell into the same snare he had ordained for them. . . .

[In the autumn of 1460 Richard of York], remembering the great wrongs, exiles
d villainies he had suffered at the hands of King Harry, and how he had been
ongfully and unjustly deprived of his rightful inheritance of the realm and crown

of England by the violent intrusion of King Harry IV, who wrongfully and tyrannously usurped the crown after the death of King Richard [II], now claimed, as rightful heir of King Richard by lineal descent, the very realm and crown of England [for himself].

9) Benet's Chronicle
(*Benet*, p. 212; *Hallam*, p. 214)
[In 1454/5 Richard Duke of York] governed the entire kingdom of England well and honourably for a whole year, and miraculously pacified all rebels and malefactors, in accordance with his oath and without great severity. And then, with great honour and the love of all, he resigned his office.

Origins of the
Wars of the Roses

Contemporary and near-contemporary sources provide a range of indications as to why civil strife broke out in the 1450s and, although many are critical of late Lancastrian government at best (particularly chronicles written after Henry VI was deposed in 1461) or overtly propagandist in the Yorkist interest at worst, they do pioneer in microcosm virtually every avenue of causation since pursued by historians. Most obviously, there is the dynastic issue and the political theorist Sir John Fortescue, for one, certainly found the existence of rival claims to the throne in the mid-fifteenth century both fascinating and challenging: indeed, he composed no fewer than four tracts on the dynastic question, as well as devoting a great deal of attention to it in his major work *De Natura Legis Naturae*. In three of these tracts, and in the *De Natura Legis Naturae*, he set out arguments in favour of the Lancastrian title, rejecting Richard of York's main line of descent from Edward III on the grounds that, transmitted as it was via female blood, it was invalid under the Law of Nature. Only after Edward IV's restoration to the throne in 1471 did he pen a fourth tract refuting his own earlier arguments. John Blacman, interestingly, recorded Henry VI's personal conviction, even after he had been deposed by Edward IV and imprisoned in the Tower, that he had ruled by hereditary right (13), while pro-Yorkist chroniclers drew attention to both the justification of Yorkist, and the invalidity of Lancastrian, claims to the throne (6, 11). As for Polydore Vergil, he had no doubts at all that the Wars of the Roses were indeed dynastic in origin (14).

Many historians have put much stress on the importance of Henry VI's shortcomings in explaining the onset of civil war, both before and since they were so strongly urged by K.B. McFarlane. Contemporaries and near-contemporaries were reluctant to criticize the king personally but, by implication at least, even John Blacman had distinct reservations about his willingness to forgive even the most unworthy of men (13); *Benet's Chronicle* was certainly critical of his rule; and it is surely no coincidence that Polydore Vergil specifically drew attention to Richard of York's conviction that Henry was 'unsuitable in all respects for the right government of a commonwealth' (14).

Clearly, too, the perceived personal inadequacies of Henry VI lie behind the stress in several contemporary sources on the importance during the 1450s of growing resentment at the power, wealth and influence of those around the king. Yorkist manifestos certainly made much of this (8, 9); so did pro-Yorkist chronicles (1, 5, 6); and even John Warkworth, while sympathetic towards Henry's plight, had no time for the 'false lords' who undermined men's loyalty to him (12).

Aristocratic feuds and escalating lawlessness, central to R.L. Storey's explanation of the outbreak of the Wars of the Roses, did not escape the attention of contemporaries. The chronicler John Harding, for instance, contrasted the ineffectual leadership of Henry VI with that of his father Henry V, resulting, so he believed, in increasing lawlessness and misrule in the shires (especially the development of feuds between neighbouring magnates) and a notable failure of the legal processes to cope (3); the *English Chronicle* declared that, by 1459, England was 'out of all good governance, as it had been many days before' (5); Yorkist manifestos issued in 1459 and 1460, similarly, put a great deal of stress on the lack of justice prevailing in the realm and its consequences (8, 9); and Sir John Fortescue was certainly much exercised by 'the perils that may come to the king by overmighty subjects'. Richard of York in his own propaganda, and chroniclers of a pro-Yorkist bent thereafter, frequently headlined the bitter personal feud between himself and Edmund Beaufort Duke of Somerset. York certainly blamed Somerset for the collapse of English power in France, while the *English Chronicle*, reviewing the political situation on the eve of St Albans in 1455, remarked that Somerset, by whom 'the king was principally guided and governed', invariably 'kept near the king, and dared not depart from his presence, dreading always the power' of York and his Neville allies. Even the early Tudor historian, Polydore Vergil, while firmly putting the alternative view of York as the aggressor and Somerset as the 'good councillor' of the king, recognized the vital importance of the powerful personal antagonism between the two men (14). Nor was the York/Somerset feud the only aristocratic confrontation seen as feeding into burgeoning civil war. In the west country, for instance, the rivalry between Thomas Courtenay Earl of Devon and William Lord Bonville clearly did much to influence their response to national developments in the 1450s, while the mutual antagonism of Henry Holland Duke of Exeter and Ralph Lord Cromwell, similarly, helped determine their political affiliations. Most importantly, bitter dispute raged between the great northern families of Neville and Percy from at least 1453, resulting in the Middleham Nevilles forging an alliance with York in the winter of 1453/4, while the Percies threw in their lot with the Lancastrian regime: indeed, according to the *Annales Rerum Anglicarum*, the onset of private war between Percies and Nevilles at Heworth Moor in August 1453 marked 'the beginning of the greatest sorrows in England' (4).

Contemporary chroniclers clearly believed there was a link between the loss of English possessions in France in the early 1450s and the outbreak of civil strife at home (2, 11). Richard of York certainly made much of this, stressing, in particular, Edmund Beaufort Duke of Somerset's dismal record in Normandy compared with his own period of service there in the early 1440s. In his Shrewsbury manifesto of February 1452, for instance, he remarked on the 'derogation, loss of merchandise, damaging of honour and villainy' resulting from the loss of Normandy, putting the blame firmly on Somerset's shoulders; York's early ally John Mowbray Duke of Norfolk, in a petition to the council in 1453, castigated Somerset no less vigorously for 'the great dishonour' suffered by the realm as a result of 'the loss of two so noble duchies as Normandy and Guienne'; and, in a manifesto issued from Calais in 1460, the Yorkist lords were still attacking those 'enemies of the commonweal' who 'have allowed all the old possessions which the king had in France [to] be shamefully lost and sold' (9). As for Polydore Vergil, in the early sixteenth century, the connection between English failure abroad and the onset of civil war at home was only too abundantly clear (14).

Another area of failure by late Lancastrian government often commented on by contemporaries in the context of the slide towards civil strife was the chronic condition of the royal finances in the 1440s and 1450s. The cost of defending the Lancastrian empire in France in the 1440s, the disruption of English shipping once Anglo-French warfare resumed in 1449 and the eventual loss of all the king's continental possessions (apart from Calais) by the summer of 1453 obviously had serious implications for government income and expenditure. Economic recession, too, had a real impact on the crown's revenues from both land and customs duties. For the government's critics, however, the sheer wastefulness of Henry VI's regime and its apparent inability to manage its financial affairs effectively was the heart of the problem. The Cade rebels in 1450, for instance, declared that Henry was 'so placed that he may not pay for his meat and drink', while a Paston correspondent reported, at the beginning of 1451, that the king had been forced to borrow his expenses for Christmas! A Yorkist manifesto of 1459 asserted that the crown had been 'immeasurably and outrageously spoiled of its livelihood and possessions' (8); another, of 1460, remarked on 'the poverty and misery in which the king finds himself' (9); and, according to the pro-Yorkist *English Chronicle*, Henry VI's debts 'increased daily' in the later 1450s 'but payment there was none' and, since he had given away 'all the possessions and lordships' pertaining to the crown, by 1459 'he had almost nothing to live on' (5). Even John Blacman commented, pointedly, on the king's liberality in granting 'great gifts and offices' (13). For Sir John Fortescue, moreover, regal poverty was a fundamental weakness of mid-fifteenth-century government. If a king be poor, he remarked in his treatise on *The Governance of England*, this can only be highly prejudicial to his prestige and

power; worse still, it is 'most to his insecurity' since 'his subjects will rather go
with a lord that is rich and may pay their wages and expenses' than a king who
'has nought in his purse'.

Nor, if we are to believe John Watts and Christine Carpenter, can we afford to
dismiss as mere political propaganda the very real concern for the
commonwealth's health and prosperity found in letters, proclamations and
manifestos promulgated by both Lancastrian and Yorkist partisans. The
Lancastrian tract *Somnium Vigilantes*, for instance, vigorously argued that the
common good can only be served by maintaining obedience to the king and his
laws; the pure malice and long-premeditated wickedness of the Yorkists, only too
evident in their willingness to resort to violence and treachery, proved the
falseness of their professed concern for the commonwealth; and, 'as for the
favour of the people' (which the Yorkist lords claimed to have), it cannot be
relied upon since 'it is so variable' and, for the most part, the product of
'opinionable conceit and not of truth' (7). Yorkist proclamations certainly did
dwell very much on the public good and the needs of the commonweal as
justification for the behaviour of Richard of York and his aristocratic backers:
Richard Neville Earl of Warwick's manifesto of 1459, for instance, claimed the
Yorkist lords were motivated by 'the tender love that we bear to the
commonwealth and prosperity of this realm and pride in the king's estate' (8),
while, in 1460, they again professed to be true liegemen of the king, devoted to
the prosperity, welfare and commonweal of the land (9). How far high-minded
principles like these, rather than perceived self-interest, really did inspire the
mid-fifteenth-century English nobility remains an open question but what cannot
be disputed is that such ideas were indeed much debated during these turbulent
years.

Clearly, the origins of the Wars of the Roses are nothing if not complex.
Dynastic considerations cannot be ignored: there was an enormous reluctance to
remove Henry VI from the throne in the 1450s (for all his manifold
shortcomings as a ruler) on the grounds that he was England's rightful and
anointed king; yet there is evidence, as well, that the house of Lancaster was only
too conscious of its dynastic weakness when faced by Richard of York's claim to
be, first, heir-presumptive and, ultimately, king in his own right. Even if
Lancastrians and Yorkists were not, in practice, out-and-out devotees of
principle, the political crises of these years certainly did spawn considerable
ideological argument and controversy. Neither can economic considerations be
set on one side: the Lancastrian government's financial situation was chronically
weak by the early 1450s, while Henry VI's exercise of royal patronage, partisan
and divisive as it was, did help foster jealousy and rivalry between great men.
Aristocratic feuds, often both personal and political in derivation, have their role
to play in explaining the wars, as does failure by government adequately to
maintain law and order. Equally clearly, apportioning blame for the disasters in

France was a major issue in domestic politics in the 1450s, fuelling York's mounting hatred of Somerset in particular. Yet, in the end, all avenues of investigation lead back to the king and it is difficult to avoid the conclusion that, if Henry VI had not been the man he was and if his government had not developed along the lines it did, the Wars of the Roses might never have happened.

1) Crowland Chronicle: First (Prior's) Continuation
(Ingulph, pp. 418–19)
In these recent times sprang up between our lord, King Henry VI and Richard, the most illustrious Duke of York, those divisions, never sufficiently to be regretted, and never henceforth to be allayed: dissensions, indeed, which were only to be atoned for by the deaths of nearly all the nobles of the realm. For there were certain persons enjoying the royal intimacy, who were rivals of the duke, and who brought serious accusations of treason against him, and made him to stink in the king's nostrils even unto death; as they insisted that he was endeavouring to gain the kingdom into his own hands, and was planning how to secure the sceptre of the realm for himself and his successors. For this reason he was often summoned by threatening letters to appear in the royal presence, and was so often prevented by his rivals, as he was never allowed to gain admission to the royal presence, nor yet so much as to gain a sight of the king. At last, a solemn oath was demanded of him upon the sacrament at the altar, to the effect that, so long as he should live he would never aspire to the rule of the kingdom, nor in any way attempt to usurp the same. Without any further delay, he was forbidden all intercourse with his adherents, and was most strictly ordered not to presume publicly to go beyond his own estates, or to pass the boundaries of his castles. Upon this, many of the nobles of the realm, who held the duke in some degree of honour, took it very much to heart that injuries so monstrous and so great should be inflicted upon an innocent man: [indeed], unable to bear this state of things any longer, [they] determined to watch for an opportunity to inflict due vengeance for their malice upon their malignant rivals, in case they could find any means of removing them from the side of the king, in whose presence they were in continual attendance.

2) Brut Chronicle
(Brut, p. 512)
[As a result of Henry VI's] breaking his promises, and because of his marriage to Queen Margaret, what losses has the realm of England had, by losing Normandy and Guienne, by division of the realm, and the rebelling by the commons against their princes and lords. What division among the lords, what murder and slaying of them! What fields fought and made! In conclusion, so many that many

a man has lost his life. And, in the end, the king deposed and the queen with her son forced to flee to Scotland, and from thence to France, and so to Lorraine, the place from where she first came.

3) Harding's Chronicle
(*EHD*, pp. 274–5; *Wilkinson*, p. 356; *Flemming*, p. 135)

> The peace at home and law so well maintained
> Were root and head of all his [Henry V's] great conquest,
> Which exiled is away and foully now [mid-1450s] disdained
> In such degree that north and south and west
> And east also enjoys now little rest,
> But day and night in every shire throughout
> With salets [helmets] bright and jack[et]s make fearful rout . . .
> In every shire with jacks and salets clean,
> Misrule does rise, and makes the neighbours war.
> The weaker goes beneath, as oft is seen,
> The mightiest his quarrel will prefer
> That poor men's causes are set back too far,
> Which if the peace and law were well conserved
> Might be amended, and thanks of God deserved.

> They kill your men always one by one,
> And he who shall say ought shall be crushed doubtless;
> For in your realm is no just peace; there are none
> That dare ought now the quarrellers suppress.
> Such sickness now has taken them and excess,
> They will naught heed of riot or debate,
> So common is it now in each estate.

> Withstand, good lord, the outbreak of debates,
> And chastise well also the rioters.
> Who in each shire are now confederates
> Against your peace, and all their maintainers;
> For truly else will fall the fairest flowers
> Of your great crown and noble monarchy,
> Which God defend and keep through his mercy.

4) Annales Rerum Anglicarum
(*Annales*, p. 770)

In August [1453] Thomas Neville, son of the Earl of Salisbury, married [Maud Stanhope Lady Willoughby], niece of Lord Cromwell, at Tattershall in

Lincolnshire. After the wedding, when returning home, there was a very great division between Thomas Percy Lord Egremont and the Earl [of Salisbury] near York. This was the beginning of the greatest sorrows in England.

5) English Chronicle
(*Davies*, p. 79)

[In 1459] the realm of England was out of all good governance, as it had been many days before, for the king was simple and led by covetous counsel, and owed more than he was worth. His debts increased daily but payment there was none. All the possessions and lordships that pertained to the crown the king had given away, some to lords and some to other simple persons, so that he had almost nothing to live on. And of the impositions that were imposed on the people, such as taxes, tallages and fifteenths, all that came from them was spent in vain, for he maintained no household and waged no wars. For these misgovernances and many others, the hearts of the people were turned away from those who governed the land, and their blessing was turned into cursing.

6) Whethamsted's Register
(*Whethamsted*, p. 337; *Wilkinson*, p. 131)

Three of the greater lords of this realm, namely the Duke of York, the Earl of Warwick and the Earl of Salisbury, confederated together [in 1459]. They gathered together in one body, containing many common folk. Though they were by no means against the Lord, they were nevertheless against his Christ, namely the most serene king. They did this for several reasons, reasons differing from one to another, for they held varying opinions concerning their assembly or insurrection. Some said they had risen against the king because the more powerful members of his council had ousted them from their places and exalted others. . . . Others said that, for this reason, did they stiffen their necks: in order to chastise with rods of iron those familiars of the king who daily called these lords false and betrayers of the king and put in their place men of greater wisdom. A third group said they had risen mainly for this reason: so that the Duke of York might sit on the king's throne and rule over his kingdom, and that [possession of the throne] should be vested in him and his heirs by hereditary succession, now and for ever.

7) Somnium Vigilantes: A Contemporary Defence of the Proscription of the Yorkists at the Coventry Parliament, 1459
(*Flemming*, pp. 143–5)

Listen well to me now. I remember that, among many things by which the commonwealth of a realm stands, the principal is this: a due subjection, with faithful and voluntary honour, to the sovereign of the kingdom and no incompatible rank usurped by any person; also, they who have, under the king, a governance of his people, should be diligent in keeping the king's laws, and all controversies and debates, civil or criminal, regal or personal, ought to be decided by the king's laws without any wilful interruption of the course of justice; and, if any matters cannot be resolved by common law, the prince must be asked, and resolution determined by his authority and the prudence of his council. . . .

Lord God, what reasonable answer may be given by the [Yorkist] lords if they are questioned about why they came against the king, first at Blackheath, afterwards at St Albans? [That] their intention was subversive to the commonwealth may be expressly proved by their behaviour towards the king's people. . . . Everyone knows well what extortions, what injuries and oppressions, what faction making and division, they caused, how their behaviour has subverted many men and resulted in the king's people being daily slain and murdered. . . . If the public good of this realm has been deficient in any way and in peril of decay, what authority and power had they to reform it without the king's commission? . . .

[There] is no need to give them [the Yorkist lords] pardon or mercy; rather, exercise all rigour against them conducive to their irreparable destruction. . . .

8) Yorkist Manifesto Promulgated by the Earl of Warwick, on His Way from Calais to Ludlow, 1459

(*Flemming*, pp. 139–41)

[The] commonweal and the good politic laws ordained for the keeping and maintaining of the commonweal, the rest and peace of the realm, the cause of merchandise, the due and even administering of justice, have been piteously overturned. . . .

[The] mighty crown of our sovereign lord is immeasurably and outrageously spoiled of its livelihood and possessions [and there has been] great hurt to merchants and great extortion of the goods and chattels of poor people by ministers of the king's household. . . .

[Great and] abominable murders, robberies, perjuries and extortions [are] openly used and practised in the realm, while great violence is not punished but favoured and cherished. . . .

[Although] our sovereign lord [has] as graciously applied himself to the commonweal [as] any Christian prince, yet certain people for their own covetousness [have] shown their utter malice against those who, as God knows, have been the very lovers of the commonweal. . . .

[No] Christian land may long endure in prosperity where the prince is so robbed of his livelihood and knows not the wretchedness of his land and subjects, the overthrowing of his laws and good rules, the exile of justice out of it, the great hurt to merchandise, the continual murders, robberies, perjuries and extortions, [and] the violent malice of certain people, [so much so that] it must fall to ruin [unless] sufficient and convenient remedies be hastily found. . . .

We, therefore, seeing these mischiefs so perilous and known by our enemies out of this land [who] enterprise the subduing and loss of all the land, for the tender love that we bear to the commonwealth and prosperity of this realm and pride in the king's estate, are disposed [to] go into the presence of our sovereign lord and, as true subjects, liegemen and lovers of the commonweal, and lovers of the honour of his estate, [to] beg his good grace as respectfully as we can [to] redeem his land and subjects from the jeopardy of these mischiefs and, by the advice of the great lords of his blood, [redress] them. . . .

9) Yorkist Manifesto Soliciting the Support of Thomas Bourchier Archbishop of Canterbury and the Commons of England, Calais, 1460
(Davies, pp. 86–90)

. . . we, the Duke of York, and the Earls of March, Warwick and Salisbury, offered to come to the king our sovereign lord's most noble presence, to have declared before him, in accordance with our duty to God and his highness, and to the prosperity and welfare of his most noble estate, and to the commonweal of all this land, as true liegemen, the following matters: First, the great oppression, extortion, robbery, murder and other violence done to God's church and to its ministers. Also, the poverty and misery in which the king our sovereign lord finds himself, to our great distress, not having any livelihood from the crown of England by which to keep his honourable household, which livelihood is now in the hands of those who have been destroyers of his estate and the commonweal. This causes the despoiling of his liegemen by the purveyors of his household.

Also, his laws have been directed with partiality, and those who should most love and cherish his laws have most favoured oppression and extortion. In general, all righteousness and justice are exiled from the land, and no man is afraid to offend against the law.

Also, they ask that it will please his good grace to live upon his own livelihood. . . . Nor should he suffer the destroyers of the land, and of his true subjects, to live upon it, since, as a result, he lacks the income which should sustain him [and] has to sustain his household upon his poor commons. . . .

Also, the commons have often been greatly and astonishingly charged with taxes and tallages, to their great impoverishment. Out of this, little good has accrued either to the king or to the land. With regard to most of his substance, the king has not retained half to his own use. The other part has been taken by other lords and persons, enemies to the commonweal, who have allowed all the old possessions which the king had in France and Normandy, Anjou and

Maine, Gascony and Guienne, won and gained by his father of most noble memory, and his other noble ancestors, to be shamefully lost or sold. . . .

Also, continually, since the piteous and shameful murder at Bury of that noble, worthy and Christian prince Humphrey Duke of Gloucester, the king's true uncle, there have been activities, plots and conspiracies to destroy and murder the Duke of York and the issue which it pleased God to send me of the royal blood, and the same against us, the Earls of Warwick and Salisbury. There was no other reason [since as] God knows we have ever borne, and bear, a true heart for the profit of the king's estate, the commonweal of the realm, and its defence.

Also, the Earls of Shrewsbury and Wiltshire, and Lord Beaumont, our mortal and extreme enemies, now and for a long time past, have had governance over the most noble person of our sovereign lord, whom they have restrained and kept from the liberty and freedom that belong to his estate. Nor would the supporters and favourers of all the above allow the king's good grace to receive and accept us into his presence, as he might have done of his own will, dreading the charge that would have been laid against them concerning their responsibility for the misery, destruction and wretchedness of the realm. They are the cause of this and not the king: he is, himself, as noble, virtuous, righteous and blessed of disposition as any earthly prince.

Also, the Earls of Wiltshire and Shrewsbury, and Lord Beaumont, not satisfied with the king's possessions and goods, have moved and excited his highness to hold his parliament at Coventry. There an act was made, by their provocation and instigation, against us the Duke of York, my sons March and Rutland, the Earls of Warwick and Salisbury, the sons of the Earl of Salisbury, and many other knights and squires, containing various matters falsely and untruly conceived, [for] the destruction of us and our issue so they might have our livelihood and goods.

We therefore offer yet again, with God's grace, to come to the presence of our sovereign lord. . . .

10) Benet's Chronicle
(*Benet*, p. 230; *Hallam*, p. 224)
[In 1461] Henry VI, since he had ruled tyrannously like his grandfather and father, was deposed from the crowns of England and France.

11) Jean de Waurin
(*Hallam*, p. 224)
[In 1461] King Henry himself and his wife Queen Margaret were overthrown and lost that crown which his grandfather Henry IV had violently usurped and taken from King Richard II, his first cousin, whom he caused to be shamelessly murdered. . . . Men say that ill-gotten gains cannot last.

12) *Warkworth's Chronicle*
(*Warkworth*, pp. 11–12)

[When Henry VI] was put out of his realm by King Edward, all England, for the more part, hated him, and were fully glad to have a change. The cause was that the good Duke of Gloucester was put to death, John Holland Duke of Exeter poisoned, and the Duke of Suffolk, Lord Saye [and] other mischievous people about the king were so covetous towards themselves, and had no care for the king's honour, welfare or the commonweal of the land. [Also] France, Normandy, Gascony and Guienne were lost in his time. These were the causes, with others, that made the people grudge against him, and all because of his false lords, and never of him; and the common people said, if they might have another king, he should get all again, and amend all manner of things that were amiss, and bring the realm of England to great prosperity and rest.

13) *John Blacman*
(*Blacman*, pp. 31, 33, 39, 40–1, 44)

Against the pest of avarice [King Henry VI] was most wary and alert. For neither by the splendid presents given to him nor by the ample wealth which he possessed was he ever entrapped into the unlawful love of them, but was most liberal to the poor in lightening of their wants and enriched very many others with great gifts and offices. . . . Never did he oppress his subjects with unreasonable exactions as do other rulers and princes but, behaving himself among them like a kind father, relieved them from his own resources in a most comely manner and, contenting himself with what he had, preferred to live uprightly among them, rather than that they should suffer in poverty, trodden down by his harshness. . . . The same prince when, in the end, he lost both England and France, which he had ruled before, along with all his wealth and goods, endured it with no broken spirit but with a calm mind, making light of all temporal things, if he might but gain Christ and things eternal. . . .

[When] three great lords of the realm conspired the death of the king [and] assembled an innumerable host of armed men, aiming ambitiously to secure the kingly power, [he] forgave all, both the leaders and the men under them, what they had maliciously designed against him, provided they submitted themselves to him. . . .

[Yet] the men among whom and towards whom the king was so kind and merciful proved at the last wholly ungrateful to him, as the Jews to Christ. For whereas God's right hand had raised him to so glorious a place [they], conspiring together with savage rage, deprived even this most merciful king of his royal power, and drove him from his realm and governance.

[When] this King Henry was asked, during his imprisonment in the Tower, why he had unjustly claimed and possessed the crown of England for so many years, he would answer thus: 'My father was King of England and peaceably possessed the crown of England for the whole of his reign. And his father and my grandfather were kings of the same realm. And I, a child in the cradle, was peaceably and without any protest crowned and approved as king by the whole realm, and wore the crown of England some forty years, and each and all of my lords did me royal homage and plighted me their faith, as was also done to my predecessors.'

14) Polydore Vergil
(*Vergil*, pp. 83–4, 86–7, 89, 93–4)
[When] William Duke of Suffolk was dead, peace could not the better be preserved, by reason of civil dissension, the beginning of which sprang from the contention of factions, [which] always have been and ever will be more harmful to commonwealths than foreign war, famine or sickness; whereunto the Kentish people were most prone, as well for that they can hardly bear injuries as for that they are desirous of novelties. For, whether it were by instigation of Richard Duke of York, who, aspiring to the crown, sought to make innovations, his policy tending to this end, that by occasion of discord amongst the commons he might procure himself authority and become head of some one faction, or else that they were desirous to revenge injuries done to them, especially by the king's officers, so it was they took weapons in hand [in 1450], made one John, by surname Cade, their captain, and, gathering a great power together, marched towards London. . . .

When this insurrection in Kent was pacified, [Richard] Duke of York, who aspired to the sovereignty, [began] to attempt and practise greater matters, [and] the Duke of Somerset [believed] for certain that the Duke of York aspired to the kingdom and had determined the destruction both of him and also King Henry. . . .

[The battle of Castillon and the fall of Bordeaux in 1453 were] the end of foreign war and also the renewing of civil calamity: for when the fear of outward enemy [was] gone from the nobility, such was the contention among them for glory and sovereignty that even then the people were apparently divided into two factions, according as it fell out afterwards, when these two, that is to say King Henry, who derived his pedigree from the house of Lancaster, and Richard Duke of York, who conveyed himself by his mother's side from Lionel, son to Edward III, contended mutually for the kingdom. By such means these two factions soon grew so great throughout the whole realm [that] many men were utterly destroyed and the whole realm brought to ruin and decay. . . . But the source of all this stir [arose] from Richard Duke of York: for he had conceived an outrageous lust of principality, and never ceased to plan how and by what means he might accomplish it; thinking nothing better for his purpose than to stir up the hatred of noble men against the Duke of Somerset; [for] it grieved him much that the realm was ruled on his terms. Therefore he daily reported everywhere to all the nobility that the state of the commonwealth was most miserable [and] ascribed the cause [to] the Duke of Somerset alone, whom he denounced as an unjust, proud and cruel tyrant. He found much fault also with King Henry, saying that he was a man of soft and feeble spirit, of little wit, and unsuitable in all respects for the right government of a commonwealth. . . .

Jack Cade's Rebellion, 1450

For pro-Yorkist chronicles such as the *Brut* the dramatic events of 1450 resulted from mounting political corruption at home and military failure abroad during the later 1440s, years when fortune turned against Henry VI on all sides: the king's marriage to Margaret of Anjou in 1445, for instance, not only brought the ceding of Anjou and Maine to the French but also paved the way for the loss of Normandy at the end of the decade; as for Humphrey Duke of Gloucester, 'a noble man and a great scholar' who had devoted his life to defending his brother Henry V's political ideals and military legacy, he became a tragic victim, in 1447, of the envy and fear of Henry VI's closest associates when he was humiliated, arrested and, so rumour had it, murdered (1). Even the more independent-minded *Chronicon Angliae* reported the widespread belief that 'men known to enjoy the king's particular favour', most notably William de la Pole Duke of Suffolk, William Aiscough Bishop of Salisbury and James Fiennes Lord Saye and Sele, were responsible for Humphrey Duke of Gloucester's death, while Suffolk and Edmund Beaufort Duke of Somerset were 'held in contempt by the Duke of York' (2). Historians, too, have traditionally portrayed political life in the later 1440s as dominated by Suffolk, Somerset, Saye and a group of corrupt and greedy councillors who manipulated a naive and gullible Henry VI as they saw fit and presided over ill-judged and unsuccessful policies both at home and abroad, culminating in their sanctioning, in 1449, the misguided assault on Fougères in Brittany that rapidly precipitated a full-scale renewal of Anglo-French warfare, the fall of Rouen and the complete collapse of English power in Normandy. Only recently have serious modifications to this picture been suggested. B.P. Wolffe, in 1981, chose to emphasize Henry VI's personal impact on policy and decision-making, particularly the pursuit of peace with France and its implications once warfare did resume. John Watts and Christine Carpenter, by contrast, have portrayed a responsible and mature nobility (apart, perhaps, from Gloucester) struggling to maintain unity and coherence when confronted by exceptionally difficult problems, both at home and abroad, and a king incapable of performing the executive role required of him: Suffolk, on this interpretation, becomes very much the front man for policies widely supported by the ruling elite and, as Carpenter put it in 1997, 'should be rescued from opprobrium and given credit for taking on an impossible job'.

The year 1450, irrespective of whether Suffolk became a scapegoat for hitherto well-supported but now clearly failing policies or the victim of his own well-deserved unpopularity, certainly did prove an *annus horribilis* for the Lancastrian regime. Early in the year there is evidence of seditious bills, anti-government propaganda and rioting in London; Henry VI's keeper of the Privy Seal, Adam Moleyns Bishop of Chichester, was seized and murdered at Portsmouth by an enraged mob of unpaid soldiers and sailors (7); and, at the end of January, Thomas Cheyne, a Surrey labourer who adopted the pseudonym Bluebeard, helped engineer a minor rising in Kent: the rebels demanded the heads of traitors around the king (Suffolk's and Saye's in particular) but, after a week, the rebellion's end was marked by Cheyne's capture in Canterbury and execution soon afterwards at Tyburn (3, 4). Then, in February 1450, mounting discontent at failure in France and misgovernment at home resulted in the impeachment of Suffolk by the Commons in Parliament and, although many of the charges against him cannot stand the test of close examination, he was duly condemned (2, 4, 11a). Indeed, he was only saved from almost certain execution by the king hastily sentencing him to five years' banishment instead (4). While in the very act of sailing into exile at the beginning of May, however, Suffolk's ship was intercepted, the duke seized, and his head peremptorily lopped off 'by one of the most ignorant of the ship's company' (4, 10a). Soon afterwards, as rumour spread through the county that, at Saye's suggestion, Kent was to be turned into a 'wild forest' in retaliation for Suffolk's death, rebellion once more broke out there.

Jack Cade's rebellion, the most formidable popular uprising in England since the Peasants' Revolt of 1381, began in the Weald of Kent at the end of May 1450; unrest spread rapidly throughout south-eastern England and, indeed, as far west at Wiltshire, where William Aiscough Bishop of Salisbury, a member of Henry VI's inner circle, was murdered at the end of June (2, 7); and, as its most recent historian Isobel Harvey put it in 1991, the rebellion provides a 'mirror in which is caught a reflection of the disastrous failure' of Henry VI's kingship. Jack Cade, mysterious leader of the insurrection, apparently adopted the pseudonym John Mortimer and claimed to be Richard of York's cousin (6, 7, 11b); rebel propaganda laid particular stress on York's 'true blood' and demanded that he be given a prominent place on the royal council (9); and, if we are to believe later allegations, York's chamberlain Sir William Oldhall and others had already, for some time, been plotting 'to depose the king and put the Duke of York on the throne' (5). There is no reliable evidence, however, of any direct (or even indirect) involvement of Richard of York personally in Cade's rebellion: anyway, he was still in Ireland in the spring and summer of 1450. Its origins, in fact, lay primarily in local Kentish concerns: the burdens on the county occasioned by the renewal of Anglo-French warfare, particularly supplying the Calais garrison; the vulnerability of the south-east to French raids, recently exemplified by an attack on Queenborough castle (4); the depressed condition of the cloth industry (felt most heavily in the Weald); and, above all, the oppressive and deeply resented rule of the county by a narrow faction led by James Fiennes Lord Saye and Sele (7, 9).

Before long, however, national political issues had become prominent, as is only too evident in a rebel manifesto of June 1450 (9). Chronicles tell the story of the rebellion in considerable detail although, more often than not, adopting a hostile stance, particularly when describing the unruly behaviour of Cade's men in London (2, 3, 6, 7). Early June saw the rebels firmly encamped on Blackheath but, soon after a successful confrontation with royal troops at Sevenoaks, they made for London (2, 3, 6, 10b). Henry VI and many of his ministers hastily retreated to Kenilworth towards the end of the month; a few days later Cade and his men entered the capital where, initially, they seem to have been greeted with some enthusiasm; and, before long, the hated Lord Saye (abandoned by the king when he left London) had been seized, condemned and beheaded, as had his son-in-law, accomplice and former sheriff of Kent, William Crowmer (2, 3, 6, 7). Once violence and looting began in earnest, despite Cade's strict orders to the contrary, even sympathetic Londoners became alienated and, following a skirmish on London Bridge during the night of 5 July, most of the rebels, when offered a general pardon, dispersed (2, 3, 7). Jack Cade himself fled but, on 12 July, he was seized in Sussex, sustaining fatal wounds in the process: even so, his dead body was beheaded, his head set on London Bridge and, in 1451, he was posthumously attainted for treason (3, 7, 8, 11b).

1) Brut Chronicle
(*Brut*, pp. 511–13, 515)

[After 1445] King Henry never profited nor went forward; but fortune began to turn from him on all sides, as well in France, Normandy and Guienne as in England . . . [The king] wedded Queen Margaret, [a] dear marriage for the realm of England, for it is well known that, in order to have her, he delivered the duchy of Anjou and the county of Maine, which was the key of Normandy, to the French. And, above this, the Marquis of Suffolk asked Parliament for a fifteenth and a half in order to fetch her out of France. See now, what a marriage was this: [for] so much gold should have been given with her that all England should have been enriched thereby; but the contrary befell. . . .

[In 1447] a Parliament met at Bury St Edmunds, to which were summoned all the commons of the country in their most defensible array to await upon the king. To this Parliament came Humphrey Duke of Gloucester, the king's uncle, who had been protector of England during the minority of the king. After he had reached his lodging, he was arrested by Viscount Beaumont, constable of England, accompanied by the Duke of Buckingham and many other lords; all his servants were commanded to leave him; and thirty-two of them were arrested and sent to several prisons. On the morning after his arrest, the duke was found dead: on whose soul God have mercy, Amen! The certainty of how he died, and in what manner, is not known to me. Some said he died of sorrow; some said he was murdered between two feather beds; and others said that a hot spit was put in his fundament. . . . When he was dead he was exposed, so that all men might see him. Then lords, knights of the shire and burgesses came and saw him dead, but they could not see any wound or evidence of how he died. . . . This duke was a noble man and a great scholar, and had honourably ruled this realm to the king's advantage. No fault could ever be found in him. However, the envy of those who were governors, and had promised the duchy of Anjou and the county of Maine, caused [his] destruction, [for] they feared that he would have prevented their deliverance [to the French].

[In 1449], despite the truce prevailing between England and France, an English knight Francis de Surienne took a town in Normandy called Fougères, against the truce, [and this provided the opportunity] by which the French got all Normandy.

2) Chronicon Angliae
(*Giles*, pp. 34–5, 38–41)
[Humphrey Duke of Gloucester's death in 1447] was everywhere regretted and mourned by the English people, who voiced their discontent against the Earl of Suffolk, William Aiscough Bishop of Salisbury and James Fiennes Lord Saye, men known to enjoy the king's particular favour. . . .

[In 1447/8] Edmund Beaufort became Duke of Somerset and governor of Normandy [but], as a result of his behaviour there, both he and the recently created Duke of Suffolk were held in contempt by the Duke of York. Since Suffolk so enjoyed royal favour, York's scorn hardly affected him, especially since, soon afterwards, York became lieutenant of Ireland, far from the king's presence. . . .

[In 1450] men began to protest about the sudden and complete loss of all the king's lands in France. . . . The Commons in Parliament [particularly complained of] the Duke of Suffolk, blaming him for all these failures since it was as a result of his advice [that these disasters had occurred]. . . . Before long the men of Kent rebelled contrary to the peace and tranquillity of the realm, selecting as their captain an Irishman John Cade, who gathered a great mob [and] marched towards London. . . . [Once] the evil John Cade realized [the people of London] were angry, he became even more impudent than before, [entered] the city, issued proclamations, robbed some of the citizens, and beheaded James Fiennes [Lord Saye] at the standard in Cheapside without due process of law, as well as many other innocent men. Eventually the more prominent London citizens, concluding that his evil behaviour reflected not zeal for justice, as he claimed, but destruction, took measures to resist him. . . .

[Meanwhile] rebellion had spread into several parts of England, common folk attacking and robbing their lords. . . . Then William Aiscough Bishop of Salisbury was violently seized while celebrating mass at Edington in his own diocese, and needlessly robbed and killed, with no respect or reverence for the sacrament of the altar. This pitiless murder made him a martyr. . . .

3) *Benet's Chronicle*
(*Benet*, pp. 196–202; *Hallam*, pp. 202–5)
[In the autumn of 1449] the French king captured Rouen by storm after it had been betrayed by its inhabitants. . . . The Duke of Somerset fled to Caen. . . . [Also] the French king took Harfleur, the lands of Anjou and Maine, and all Normandy this side of the Seine. . . .

[On 31 January 1450] Thomas Cheyne, who called himself Bluebeard, was captured in Kent, where he had gathered many men together to rise up against those whom they called traitors, namely the evil Duke of Suffolk, the Bishop of Salisbury and Sir James Fiennes, lately made Lord Saye. . . . On 9 February, at Tyburn, he was drawn, hanged and his entrails ripped out and burnt. He was then beheaded and quartered. . . .

[Early in June 1450] 50,000 men of Kent rose in rebellion, choosing as their captain a most impudent and clever man calling himself John Mortimer. [On Thursday 11 June] the Kentishmen came to Blackheath [where Cade] made it clear by proclamation that he had no wish to hurt or plunder anyone. . . . [On Thursday 2 July] the captain came to Southwark with 20,000 men [and on the following day] entered London, where he was enthusiastically welcomed by the people. . . . [On Saturday 4 July] he came into London again, riding through the city flourishing his sword. [William] Crowmer, sheriff of Kent, he removed from the Fleet prison, carried him to Tower Hill, and then to Mile End, where he beheaded him and another man, impaling their heads on stakes and carrying them to Cheapside. . . . [Lesser] captains and the men of Kent took [Lord Saye] to the standard in Cheapside where he was beheaded without delay. Then the captain himself, carrying the two heads impaled on spears, placed Lord Saye's head on a longer spear, stripped the body of its clothing, tied the feet to the saddle of a horse, and dragged it naked, with arms outstretched, from Newgate via the Old Bailey, Watling Street and Candlewick Street to the bridge. There he rode round [London] stone and struck it with his sword. . . . When the Londoners saw how the captain had so infringed his own proclamation they turned against him. On the following night, about 10 o'clock, Lord Scales, Matthew Gough and several London aldermen engaged the men of Kent on London Bridge, and fighting continued until 8 o'clock on Monday [6 July]. Many on both sides were killed, among them Matthew Gough [and] about forty Londoners, as well as 200 Kentishmen. This persuaded the men of Kent to accept a general pardon, [after which] they and the men of Essex dispersed to their own counties. The new sheriff of Kent and many others followed and, on 12 July, killed the captain on the seashore. Next day his body was brought to London and, on 15 July, he was quartered and beheaded. . . .

At this time all the towns and castles of Normandy were lost, apart from the town and castle of Cherbourg. [Consequently] all the common folk of Kent, Essex and Wiltshire [once more] rose against the evil governance in the realm. The king, hearing this, sent the Archbishop of York, the Duke of Buckingham and others to Rochester in Kent, together with a newly appointed justice since all existing justices, conscious of their earlier extortions, absented themselves: sitting as a commission of oyer and terminer they sought to placate the Kentishmen and contain their insurrection. [About 15 August] Cherbourg surrendered to the King of France, [as a result of which] the Duke of Somerset returned to England, having completely lost Normandy.

4) Bale's Chronicle
(*Flenley*, pp. 127–9)

[In January 1450] an individual calling himself Queen of the Fairies rode into Kent and Essex [but did no] harm to anyone. . . . [On 9 February] a man calling himself William Bluebeard, who had laboured to raise a great fellowship aspiring to have had rule among the lords, was drawn through the city and hanged. . . . Then all Englishmen driven out of France, Normandy and Anjou came home in great misery and poverty, [and] rode into several parts of the land [hoping to] live upon the alms of the people: however, many gave themselves over to theft and misrule, sorely annoying the commonalty of the land, [of whom many were] afterwards hanged. . . .

[In] Parliament the Commons appealed to the king's highness against the Duke of Suffolk alleging various points of treason, the duke then being a prisoner in the Tower. Notwithstanding this appeal, the king, using his prerogative powers, sanctioned the duke's release from the Tower. [On 15 March] the duke secretly stole away from Westminster and rode no one knew where. The commons of the land were angered at this and several of the duke's men were seized by watchmen of the city during the night, only to be freed again soon after. [On 29 March] one John Ramsey, servant to a vintner in London, was drawn, hanged and quartered because he had said London should put the king from his crown, and, on the Monday following, Parliament moved to Leicester. [On 21 April] Queenborough castle was assaulted by Frenchmen and almost seized. In the meantime the Duke of Suffolk, who had taken up residence at East Thorp near Bury St Edmunds, rode to the sea, [but] when he was at sea between Dover and Calais [he was] taken and beheaded, his body cast upon the sands at Dover and his head put upon a stake [on 1 May].

5) King's Bench Ancient Indictments
(*Lander*, pp. 63–4)

[According to an Ipswich jury Sir William Oldhall and others], proposing to depose the king and put the Duke of York on the throne and realising they could not do this while he remained powerful with his lords about him, plotted his [Henry VI's] death and destruction at Bury St Edmund's on 6 March [1450]. . . . [Several bills were posted] on men's doors and windows [alleging] that the king [following the] counsel of the late Duke of Suffolk, the Bishops of Salisbury and Chichester, Lord Saye and others around his person, had sold the kingdoms of England and France. . . . All this [was intended to remove] the love of the king's subjects from him and promote the Duke of York's claim to the realm and crown of England. Moreover, they sent letters to several English counties, especially Kent and Sussex, urging rebellion against the king, on account of which the Duke of Suffolk was murdered. . . .

6) *London Chronicle: Gough 10*
(*Flenley*, pp. 153–4)

[On 11 June 1450] the commons of Kent arose with great power and came to Blackheath where they remained seven days, surrounded by stakes and ditches. When the king heard this [at Leicester] he made all the lords gather as many armed men as they could to go with him against the Kentishmen, and so they did and came to London, [from where he] sent several lords to Blackheath to discover what was afoot. [The Kentishmen] said they were petitioners, and requested the king to amend their grievances, but the king would not grant their request. Their captain they called John Mortimer. . . .

[On 17 June] the king took all his lords, with all their men in good array in manner of war, and rode to Blackheath: however, the captain and his men had left the night before, and no man knew where. [Soon afterwards] Sir Humphrey Stafford, William Stafford Esquire [and] all their company met with the Kentishmen near Sevenoaks, where Sir Humphrey, William and many of their men were slain in a skirmish. [On] the Friday after, a number of lords' men gathered together on Blackheath, saying they had seen their friends slain and that they were likely to be slain also if they followed the king and his traitors. When the Duke of Buckingham heard this he went to the king at Greenwich and told him that his people would forsake him unless he performed execution on his traitors. Wherefore, the king at once caused Lord Saye to be arrested and brought to the Tower of London by the Duke of Exeter and, on the morning after Midsummer's Day, the king left Westminster for the castle of Kenilworth: however, before he went, he was told that the Kentishmen would return. Wherefore, he sent for the mayor, aldermen and council of London, and commanded them to keep [the Kentishmen] out of the city.

7) *English Chronicle*
(*Davies*, pp. 64–8)

[On 9 January 1450] Adam Moleyns, Bishop of Chichester and keeper of the king's privy seal, was sent to Portsmouth to make payment of money to certain soldiers and shipmen for their wages; [however], they fell on him and cruelly killed him. [On 29 June] William Aiscough Bishop of Salisbury was slain by his own parishioners and people at Edington after he had said mass; he was taken from the altar and led to a hill nearby, in his alb and with his stole around his neck; and there they slew him horribly, their father and their bishop, despoiled him to the naked skin, rent his bloody shirt in pieces and bore them away, boasting of their wickedness. [Also], the day before his death, [he was] robbed of a huge store of treasure to the value of 10,000 marks by men of the same county, as those who knew it said. These two bishops were amazingly covetous men, much disliked by the common people and suspected of many faults, who had willingly assented to the death of the Duke of Gloucester, as it was said. . . .

[In late May/June 1450] the men of Kent arose and chose themselves a captain, a ribald, an Irishman, called John Cade, who at the beginning took upon him the name of a gentleman and called himself Mortimer so as to have more favour of the people; and he also called himself John Amend-All, since then and long before the realm of England had been ruled by untrue counsel, as a result of which [all] the common people, oppressed with taxes and tallages, could not live by their handiwork and husbandry, and so complained bitterly against those who had governance of the land. . . .

When the Kentishmen heard that the king had gone from London [to Kenilworth], they came to Southwark [from Blackheath] and their captain was lodged at the [White] Hart. The Thursday after, by favour of some of the men of London, he came into the city, but soon after they repented, for they were divided amongst themselves: the keys of the city were delivered to the captain and he kept them two days and two nights. When he had entered the city [on 3 July], he and his men at once fell to robbery. . . . The captain rode about the city bearing a naked sword in his hand, armed in a coat of mail, wearing a pair of gilt spurs and a gilt helmet, and a gown of blue velvet, as if he had been a lord or a knight – and yet he was but a knave – and had his sword borne before him. . . .

[On Saturday 4 July] the captain commanded that Lord Saye be brought out of the Tower of London to the Guildhall, where certain justices sat at that time. However, when he arrived the Kentishmen would not allow him to bide by the law but led him to the Standard in Cheap, and there his head was struck off, and his body was drawn naked at a horse's tail upon the pavement so that the flesh cleaved to the stones from Cheap to the captain's inn in Southwark. Also a squire called [William] Crowmer, formerly sheriff of Kent, who had married Lord Saye's daughter, was brought out of the Fleet by command of the captain, and led to Mile End outside London where, without any other judgement, his head was struck off. Then the Lord Saye's head, and Crowmer's also, were borne upon two long shafts to London Bridge, and there set up, and Lord Saye's body was quartered.

[On Sunday 5 July] the men of London, having seen the tyranny and robbery of the cursed captain and his men, laid hands, when it was night, on those who were dispersed about the city, and shut the gates. When the captain, who was in his inn in Southwark, saw this, at once he and his men made an assault on

London Bridge, and would have come in and despoiled the city. However, Lord Scales, with his own men and men of the city, fought with them from 9 o'clock in the evening until 10 o'clock on the morrow, and many men were slain on both sides. . . . This skirmish lasted until the wooden bridge was set on fire, [after which] the Kentishmen withdrew little by little. Their captain put all his pillage and the goods he had stolen into a barge and sent it to Rochester by water, [while] he went by land and would have gone into the castle of Queenborough, with the few men who were left with him, had he not been prevented from achieving his purpose. At once he fled into the wooded country near Lewes, the sheriff of Kent pursued him and there he was mortally wounded, taken and carried in a cart towards London, and on the way he died. Then his head was struck off and set on London Bridge, and his body quartered and sent to several towns of England, [and] thus ended this captain of mischief.

In this same year the commons arose in several parts of England, such as Sussex, Salisbury, Wiltshire and other places, and [they] did much harm to many people.

8) Gregory's Chronicle
(*Gregory*, p. 194)

[On 12 July 1450] the captain was proclaimed traitor, by the name of John Cade, in various parts of London and also in Southwark, along with many others, [and it was further proclaimed that any man who] might or would bring John Cade to the king, alive or dead, should receive 1000 marks; also, whoever might or would bring any of his chief counsellors or affinity, who had kept any rule or governance under the false captain John Cade, should have as his reward of the king 500 marks. And that day was the false traitor, the captain of Kent, taken and slain in the Weald in the county of Sussex and, upon the morrow, he was brought in a cart all naked [to the White Hart in Southwark where] the cart was made to stand still so that the wife of the house might see if it were the same man or no who had lodged in her house during the time of his misrule and rising. Thereafter he was brought to the King's Bench, where he lay from Monday to Thursday evening [when] he was beheaded. On the same day he was drawn on a hurdle in pieces, with the head between his breast, from King's Bench through Southwark, over London Bridge, and then through London to Newgate; then his head was taken and set upon London Bridge.

9) Proclamation of Jack Cade, June 1450
(*Wilkinson*, pp. 82–6; *EHD*, pp. 266–7)

These are the points, causes and discontents, relating to the gathering and assembling of us, the king's liegemen of Kent, on the fourth day of June [1450]. . . .

We believe the king our sovereign lord is betrayed by the insatiable covetousness and malicious purpose of certain false and unsuitable persons who are around his highness, day and night, and daily inform him that good is evil and evil is good. . . .

[They] assert that at his pleasure our sovereign lord is above his laws, and that he may make them and break them as he pleases. . . . The contrary is true. . . .

[They] say that the commons of England would first destroy the king's friends and afterwards the king himself, and then raise the Duke of York to be king, so that by their false means and lies they make him hate and destroy his friends and cherish his false traitors. . . .

[They] say that the king should live upon his commons, and that their bodies and goods are the king's. . . .

[They] say that it would be a great cause of reproof for the king to take back what he has once given away, so they will not permit him to have his own livelihood, neither goods, lands nor forfeitures.

We seek remedy for this: that the false traitors will allow no man to come to the king's presence for any reason, unless there is a bribe such as ought not to be. . . .

[It] is a grievous thing that the good Duke of Gloucester was impeached of treason by one false traitor alone and was then so soon murdered that he might never answer the charges. But the false traitor [William de la] Pole [Duke of Suffolk] was impeached by all the commons of England. . . .

[The] law serves for no other purpose in these days but to do wrong, for almost no cause is heard except dishonest ones, as a result of bribery, fear and favour. . . .

[The king's] false council has lost his law, his merchandise is lost, his common people are destroyed, the sea is lost, France is lost, the king himself is so placed that he may not pay for his meat and drink, and he owes more than ever any King of England ought, for daily his traitors about him, when anything should come to him by his laws, at once they ask it from him. . . .

[We] will have it known we will not rob, thieve or steal but, when these wrongs have been amended, then we will go home. . . .

[The king's true commons] desire that he will dismiss all the false progeny and affinity of the Duke of Suffolk, who are openly known, and that they be punished according to the law of the land. Moreover, the king should take about his noble person men of his true blood from his royal realm, that is to say, the high and mighty prince the Duke of York, exiled from our sovereign lord's presence by the machinations of the false traitor the Duke of Suffolk and his affinity. He should also take about his person those mighty princes the Dukes of Buckingham and Norfolk, together with the true earls and barons of this land. Then shall he be the richest Christian king.

[The king's] true commons desire the punishment of the false traitors who plotted and planned the death of the high, mighty and excellent prince the Duke of Gloucester. . . . By these traitors the realm of France was lost, the duchy of Normandy, Gascony, Guienne and Anjou. . . .

[They] desire that all extortions be laid low; [the] taking of wheat and other grains, beef, mutton and other victuals, which is an intolerable burden on the commons [be outlawed]; [the] Statute of Labourers, and the great extortioners of Kent, that is to say [Stephen] Slegg [sheriff of Kent 1448/9], [William] Crowmer [sheriff of Kent 1444/5 and 1449], [William] Isle [MP for Kent] and Robert Est.

[We] move and desire that true lords and knights be sent into Kent to enquire of all traitors and bribers, and bring true justice [to the county].

10) Paston Letters
(*Paston Letters*, Vol. 2, pp. 146–7, 153–5)

a) William Lomner to John Paston, 5 May 1450
[On 30 April 1450] the Duke of Suffolk came to the coast of Kent near Dover with two ships and a little pinnace [but], from those who were in the pinnace, the master of a ship called the *Nicholas of the Tower* had knowledge of the duke's coming. When he sighted the duke's ships he sent a boat to know who they were. The duke himself spoke to them and said he was, by the king's command, sent to Calais. They said he must speak with their master and so he, with two or three of his men, went with them in their boat to the *Nicholas*. When he came there, the master bade him 'Welcome traitor', as men say. After this the master desired to know if the shipmen wished to support the duke, and they sent word that they would not in any way; and so he was on the *Nicholas* until the following Saturday. Some say he wrote many things to be delivered to the king, but that is not truly known. He had his confessor with him. Some say he was arraigned on the ship, in their way, upon the articles of impeachment and found guilty.
[Then] in the sight of all his men he was taken out of the great ship into a boat; there was an axe and a block; one of the most ignorant of the ship's company bade him lay down his head, so he should be fairly treated and die by a sword; and the man took a rusty sword and struck off his head with half a dozen strokes, took away his russet gown and mailed velvet doublet, and laid his body on the sands of Dover. And some say that his head was set on a pole by it. . . .

b) John Payn to John Paston, 1465
. . . please it your good and gracious mastership to consider the great losses and hurts your poor petitioner has endured ever since the commons of Kent came to Blackheath fifteen years ago, when my master Sir John Fastolfe commanded me to take a man, and two of the best horses in his stable, to ride to the commons of Kent to get the articles [demands for reform] that they came for. So I did and, as soon as I came to Blackheath, the captain had the commons seize me, and I was brought before him. The captain demanded of me, what was the cause of my coming, and I said that I came to have cheer with my wife's brother and others present there who were my allies and gossips. Then one of those present said to the captain that I was one of Sir John Fastolfe's men, and the captain let the cry of treason be pronounced throughout the field, [saying] plainly that I should lose

my head. Forthwith I was taken and led to the captain's tent, where an axe and a block were brought forward to have struck off my head. Then Master Poynings, with others of my friends, came, saying plainly that a hundred or two should die if I died; so by that means my life was saved at that time. And then I was made to swear to the captain and commons that I would go to Southwark, and come again to help them; and so I got the articles and brought them to my master, and that day amongst the commons cost me more than 27s. . . . [Later] the captain put me into the battle at London Bridge, where I was wounded and hurt nearly to death. . . .

11) Rolls of Parliament

a) Impeachment of Suffolk, 1450
(*Rotuli Parliamentorum*, Vol. 5, pp. 176–7)
[In February 1450] the Commons [in Parliament], through William Tresham their Speaker, accused and impeached William de la Pole Duke of Suffolk of certain high treasons, offences and misprisions committed by him against the royal majesty, as appear more clearly in a bill which the Commons handed to the chancellor and Lords through their Speaker. They begged him that he would ask the king on their behalf that this bill might be produced in the present Parliament, and that there should be proceedings against the duke on the articles it contains, according to the law and custom of this realm of England.

b) Attainder of Jack Cade, 1451
(*Rotuli Parliamentorum*, Vol. 5, p. 224)
. . . the false traitor John Cade, naming himself John Mortimer, lately called captain of Kent, on 8 July [1450] at Southwark in Surrey, and on 9 July at Dartford and Rochester in Kent, and at Rochester on 10 and 11 July, falsely and traitorously plotted your [Henry VI's] death, destruction and subversion of this your realm, by gathering and raising a great number of your people, stirring them to rise against you [and] falsely and traitorously levied war against you and your highness, and, although he is dead and beheaded, yet by the law of your land not punished.

[The Commons], by the advice of the Lords temporal and spiritual in this Parliament, [request] that he be attainted of all these treasons [and] forfeit all his goods, lands, tenements, rents and possessions.

Dartford, 1452

When Richard of York suddenly returned from Ireland early in September 1450, he clearly felt resentful at his recent treatment and fearful for his future: his claim to be Henry VI's heir-presumptive had remained unrecognized; his efforts in Ireland had elicited little backing from London; his name had figured prominently in rebel propaganda during the summer and rumours had spread that, in pursuit of the crown for himself, he had urged his agents to promote discontent; and, most galling to him of all, Edmund Beaufort Duke of Somerset, despite his responsibility for recent disasters in France, had now become the most favoured man in the king's entourage. Evading attempts at interception in Anglesey, he made his way to London via his Welsh estates, arriving there with a considerable retinue and determined to make his presence felt (1, 2). Perhaps, as was alleged when York was condemned by the Coventry Parliament in 1459, he forced his way into the king's presence (12a) where, if we are to believe the *Chronicon Angliae*, he was 'not very sociably' greeted by the king (2); *Benet's Chronicle*, by contrast, suggests he was 'most graciously received' (1). Initially, York's personal grievances were paramount in his mind but, no doubt reflecting the mood he found in the capital, by early October he was presenting himself as the champion of 'many things which are much after the desire of the common people': as a result, moreover, it was reported that 'all the king's household was, and is, right sore afraid' (9). When Parliament met in November York's chamberlain Sir William Oldhall was elected Speaker of the Commons (4); there were vigorous criticisms of the king's government and its failures (1); and, seemingly, the bitter personal rivalry of York and Somerset soon manifested itself as well (5). London, much to the alarm of the city authorities, was awash with aristocratic retainers, particularly York's men and supporters of his ally John Mowbray Duke of Norfolk (2, 4). At the end of November serious disturbances erupted on the streets and, on 1 December, Somerset's house was attacked and plundered (4, 5, 6). Just what was going on is variously reported: the *Chronicon Angliae*, for instance, suggests Somerset was the victim of an unprovoked attack by servants of the Dukes of York and Norfolk (2) and Jean de Waurin, too, recorded that the assault, a product of York's desire to see his rival incarcerated in the Tower, was indeed perpetrated by his men; *Benet's Chronicle*, however, would have us believe that, at York's request, Somerset was rescued by Thomas Courtenay Earl of Devon, 'discreetly arrested', and conveyed to the Tower for his own safety (1), while the *Annales Rerum Anglicarum*, similarly, recorded that he was 'nearly killed but saved by a barge belonging to the Earl of Devon' (5). Pro-Yorkist chroniclers, not surprisingly, also highlight York's commitment to the restoration of law and order at this time and the fact that, on 3 December, he joined Henry VI and 'the most prominent lords of the land' in a solemn public display of baronial unity in the face of adversity (1, 6).

At the end of 1450 York appeared nicely positioned to become the main political beneficiary of all the shattering setbacks recently suffered by Henry VI and his apparently discredited regime. Was this merely a fleeting illusion? Or did everything change in 1451? Perhaps, as Michael K. Jones has argued, the sheer violence of York's attacks on Somerset in the autumn of 1450, and his clumsy attempts to manipulate the political situation in his own interests, only served to alienate many of the aristocracy and negate all his efforts to elicit popular sympathy. Somerset, whose sojourn in the Tower in December 1450 was short indeed, clearly continued to enjoy the king's complete confidence, so much so that, in April 1451, he was appointed captain of Calais. According to the *Annales*, indeed, he was not only 'most familiar with the king' but 'controlled everything, both within the royal household and outside it'; nothing came of a petition in Parliament to remove several 'familiars' from the king's presence; and when, in May 1451, one of York's councillors Thomas Young proposed in the Commons that his patron be formally recognized as heir-presumptive, he was peremptorily imprisoned for his pains (5). Earlier in the year, moreover, a judicial commission into Kent, headed by Henry VI himself, Somerset and other prominent members of the king's inner circle, resulted in such savage reprisals on the county for the events of 1450 and so many executions that, according to *Gregory's Chronicle*, the men of Kent dubbed its proceedings 'the harvest of heads' (6). Even more significantly, as Somerset and his friends established an ever tighter control at the centre, York, despite the king's declared intention in October 1450 to establish a 'responsible and substantial council [in] which we have appointed you to be one', remained very much a political outsider: indeed, if we are to believe *Benet's Chronicle*, even when, in the autumn of 1451, he 'despatched 2000 men to prevent hostility and harm' in the west country during a flare-up of the Courtenay/Bonville feud there, his efforts were deliberately misconstrued (1).

Early in 1452, having failed to make progress by constitutional means and even more bitter than he had been in 1450, Richard of York resorted to armed force and, once more, Edmund Beaufort Duke of Somerset was clearly his prime target, as is only too evident in his Shrewsbury manifesto of 3 February (8). Once he had raised a force from his estates in Wales and the Welsh marches, and enjoying support, too, from Thomas Courtenay Earl of Devon and Edward Lord Cobbam (both, no doubt, resentful at the outcome of events in the south-west in the autumn of 1451), York marched towards London (1, 2, 7, 9). Denied entry to the capital on the king's orders, he made for his estates in north Kent and, at the beginning of March, drew up his army at Brent Heath, near Dartford, only a few miles from an altogether larger and better equipped royal force encamped at Blackheath (1, 2, 7, 9). Probably realizing he was seriously outnumbered and aware, in particular, of how little aristocratic support he had (most of the nobility remained firmly loyal to Henry VI), York promptly entered into negotiations and, apparently believing Somerset would now be committed to custody and required to answer charges of incompetence and misgovernance in both France and England, came to the king's tent and surrendered: however, not only did Somerset remain at liberty but York, finding himself virtually a prisoner, had to swear a solemn and public oath of allegiance to Henry VI at St Paul's on 10 March, promising never again to 'make any assembly of your people without your command or licence', even in his own defence (1, 2, 7, 9, 10). Chronicles variously interpreted the significance of Dartford, very much reflecting the political stance of their individual authors: *Benet's Chronicle* clearly sympathized with York's claim that 'his actions were for the good of the country and directed not against the king but at those who had betrayed him' (1), while the *Brut* believed he had been duped into submission and, had not a rumour spread that 'the Earl of March, his son, was coming with 20,000 men towards London', he would have remained a prisoner (7); the *Chronicon Angliae*, by contrast, offered no criticism of the king's behaviour (2) and, indeed, there is a strong case for arguing that York was fortunate to get off so lightly for actions that could all too easily have been interpreted as out-and-out treason. Certainly, Somerset and his friends were now even more firmly entrenched in power around the king and, seemingly, determined to demonstrate the fact (2, 7, 11). Pro-Yorkist chronicles suggest there was considerable hostility towards Somerset and sympathy for York in the months that followed (6, 7, 11) and, when Parliament met at Reading in March 1453, the Commons petitioned once more for 'a responsible and wise council' (12b): the same assembly also demanded, however, that York's prominent servant Sir William Oldhall be 'reputed and held a traitor, and a person attainted of high treason' (12c). By the summer of 1453, in fact, Somerset's supremacy, and York's permanent exclusion from power, appeared set in concrete, while Queen Margaret of Anjou's pregnancy clearly offered the prospect of Lancastrian dynastic security as well.

1) Benet's Chronicle
(*Benet*, pp. 202–7; *Hallam*, pp. 205–10)
[About 8 September 1450] the Duke of York returned from Ireland to England and landed in Wales. . . . [On 27 September he] arrived in London with 5000 men and was most graciously received by the king at Westminster. . . .

The king opened Parliament at Westminster [on 6 November 1450 and] all the dukes, earls and barons came with considerable bodies of well-armed men. [On 30 November] when they realized that neither the king nor his counsellors were addressing the correction of those who were being accused of treason throughout England, particularly the Duke of Somerset who had so carelessly and ignominiously lost Normandy, the lords' men called upon the king three times, before all the dukes, earls and barons in Westminster Hall, to 'provide justice against the traitors and punish them'. This greatly disturbed the king and his lords. The following afternoon, almost 1000 well-armed men attacked the Duke of Somerset without warning, and would have slain him, had not the Earl of Devon, at the Duke of York's request, pacified them and discreetly arrested Somerset, brought him [from] Blackfriars to the Thames, and thence to the Tower of London, leaving the rioters at Blackfriars to pillage. Next day the Duke of York seized one of the looters and sent him to the king: he ordered the Earl of Salisbury to have him beheaded at the standard in Cheapside and so it was done. On Thursday 3 December the king, accompanied by his dukes, earls, barons, knights and squires [and others], all in full armour and about 10,000 in number, marched in solemn procession through London. The Duke of Norfolk and the Earl of Devon, with 3000 men, provided the vanguard; the king, the Duke of York, the Earl of Salisbury, the Earl of Arundel, the Earl of Oxford, the Earl of Wiltshire, the Earl of Worcester and others, with 4000 men, followed; and the Duke of Buckingham, the Earl of Warwick and others, with 3000 men, brought up the rear. . . .

[On 17 September 1451] the Earl of Devon, Lord Moleyns and Lord Cobham on one side, and the Earl of Wiltshire and Lord Bonville on the other, with many men, threatened to do battle. The Duke of York, however, despatched 2000 men to prevent hostilities and harm. The king, nevertheless, much angered by these disturbances, sent for the participants, imprisoned the Earl of Wiltshire and Lord Bonville in Berkhamstead castle, and the Lords Moleyns and Cobham in Wallingford castle, even if only for a month. York and Devon, despite several summonses, failed to respond. . . .

When the king heard [in February 1452] that the Duke of York, the Earl of Devon and Lord Cobham were approaching London with 20,000 men, he rode to Northampton, sending the Bishop of Winchester [and others] to the duke, ordering him not to take up arms against the crown. The duke responded that he would never do so and remained as obedient as ever: his actions were for the good of the country and directed not against the king but at those who had betrayed him. The king, however, ordered the mayor of London to prevent the duke entering the city and, when he was refused admission, [Richard Duke of York] went to Kingston, where he remained for three days. Then [on 29 February], accompanied by 20,000 very heavily armed men, he rode to Dartford, took up a position strongly fortified for his own safety with posts, ditches and guns, and awaited the opportunity to enter the king's presence so he could warn him against men threatening the destruction of his kingdom, particularly Edmund Duke of Somerset (who had shamefully lost Normandy) and Cardinal

[Kemp] Archbishop of York and chancellor of England. [On 1 March] the king, with 24,000 men, rode to Blackheath and then to Welling. The Bishops of Winchester and Ely, the Earls of Salisbury and Warwick, [and others], meanwhile, sought to negotiate a settlement between the king and the duke [and, as a result, on 2 March] the king granted the duke's petition and they were reconciled on Blackheath. The Duke of York, the Earl of Devon and Lord Cobham knelt before the king. Then the Duke [of York] promulgated his complaints against Somerset, charging him with the loss of Normandy and Gascony. Thereafter, the king with all his lords returned to London. Later the Duke of York swore an oath before the king at the high altar of St Paul's, declaring that he had never rebelled against the king and promising never to take up arms against him in the future.

2) *Chronicon Angliae*
(*Giles*, pp. 42–4; *Wilkinson*, pp. 116–17)

[In September 1450] Richard Duke of York returned from Ireland. The king, worried by his return when there was so much disturbance, determined to prevent his progress. . . . [Nevertheless] the duke journeyed to London, with a considerable following and, in the royal presence, declared he had come to offer the king assistance against rebels and traitors. The king, not very sociably, responded that, 'We will seek your aid when occasion demands and its need is apparent.' When Parliament met in November [1450], the Duke of York came with considerable numbers of knights and other armed men, as did the Duke of Norfolk. When these lords had been in London about a fortnight, their servants attacked the Duke of Somerset as he, with a few men but no fear of violence, dined at Blackfriars. Then, embarrassed by these occurrences, the lords left, nothing having been achieved in Parliament. . . .

After Candlemas [2 February 1452] the king ordered Richard Duke of York to join him in Coventry but the duke refused to come and marched vigorously towards London. When the king heard of this he too made his way towards the capital, accompanied by such forces as he had managed hastily to muster. The Duke of York and his men camped near Dartford in Kent and, in company with the Earl of Devon and Lord Cobham, awaited developments. However, when the king took the field against them, the duke and the other lords submitted to him, through the gracious mediation of lords spiritual and temporal, and begged for mercy which was freely given. Afterwards, they were brought to London with the royal army and, not long after, the Duke of York swore an oath on the Gospel before the high altar of St Paul's that he was, had been and would be in the future loyal to the king as his principal liege lord and would never again rise against him. . . . He was then given a general pardon. . . .

[Following Dartford] the king visited various parts of the realm and, wherever he found men who had committed crimes despite receiving pardons, sentenced large numbers of them to death in Kent, Sussex and Essex.

3) Paston Letters
(*Paston Letters*, Vol. 2, p. 174)
William Wayte to John Paston, 6 October 1450
. . . I was in my Lord of York's house and I heard many things [there and in] Fleet Street. Sir, my Lord [of York] was with the king, and he so presented the matter [of his grievances] that all the king's household was, and is, right sore afraid; and my lord has presented a bill to the king and desired many things which are much after the desire of the common people. . . .

4) Bale's Chronicle
(*Flenley*, pp. 136–7)
[On 6 November 1450] Parliament began at Westminster, and the Commons chose Sir William Oldhall, knight with the Duke of York, as Speaker. . . . At the same time it was ordained in various parts of the city that chains should be drawn across the ways to keep the city safe, for people stood in great fear and doubt on account of discord between lords, and a proclamation was made [in] the king's name that no one should speak or meddle with any matters done in Parliament or by lords. . . .

[On 23 November] the Duke of York, with 3000 men and more, came riding through the city, his sword borne before him, and rode to Parliament and to the king. And, on the following morning, came riding through the city the Duke of Norfolk with a great crowd of men in body armour, and six trumpets blowing before him. Then, on the following morning, the Earl of Warwick came through the city with a great company arrayed for war, and [on 30 November] there was a dreadful storming and noise of the commons, crying and saying to the lords: 'Do justice upon the false traitors or let us be avenged.' [On the morning of 1 December] the lords' men assaulted the Duke of Somerset's house at Blackfriars in London, and there plundered many of his goods, but the mayor and commons of the city gathered a force together and remedied it at once; otherwise the duke would have been taken or slain.

5) Annales Rerum Anglicarum
(*Annales*, pp. 769–70; *Wilkinson*, p. 114; *Lander*, p. 66)
In November [1450] Parliament met. During it, a great disagreement arose between the Dukes of York and Somerset and, not long afterwards, Somerset was robbed in the house of the London Friars Preachers. The same day Somerset was nearly killed but saved by a barge belonging to the Earl of Devon. . . .

[After Christmas 1450] the Duke of Somerset became captain of Calais and most familiar with the king, so that he controlled everything, both within the royal household and outside it.

In this same Parliament [1451] the Commons petitioned the king to remove several of his familiars but nothing came of it. . . . [Also, in May 1451] Thomas

Young of Bristol, apprentice in law, moved that, because the king as yet had no offspring, it would promote the security of the kingdom if he openly established who was his heir apparent. And he nominated the Duke of York. For this reason he was afterwards committed to the Tower of London.

6) Gregory's Chronicle
(*Gregory*, pp. 195–8)

[On 2 December 1450] the Duke of Somerset was attacked in the Friars Preachers in London, robbed of all his goods, and his jewels taken and borne away by lords' men and, on the morrow, they plundered the houses and belongings of several lords, bearing away all the goods that were in them. . . . [On] the same day a member of this fellowship, who had been at the plundering and robbing of the Friars Preachers, was beheaded at the standard in Cheap, as an example to all others; [however, this] caused even more ill-will against the Duke [of Somerset].

On the same day, in the afternoon, the Duke of York rode through London, proclaiming in several places that any man who robbed or rifled any person should receive speedy justice. And, on the Thursday next following, the king came from Westminster, riding through London, accompanied by the Duke of York and the most powerful lords of the land, with their retinues of armed men: a gay and glorious sight if it had been in France, but not in England, for it so emboldened some men's hearts as to cause many men's deaths in the future. . . .

[On 2 February 1451] the king was at Canterbury, accompanied by the Duke of Exeter, the Duke of Somerset, Lord Shrewsbury, many other lords and many justices, where they held [judicial] sessions for four days: there were condemned many of the captain's [Jack Cade's] men for their rising, and for speaking against the king, having more favour towards the Duke of York than to the king, and the condemned men were drawn, hanged and quartered. Nine men were beheaded, at the same time, at Rochester, their heads sent to London by the king's command, and all set upon London Bridge; and, at another time, twelve heads were similarly brought to London by the king's command. Men in Kent call it the harvest of heads. . . .

[In 1452/3] every man was in charity but the hearts of the people sorrowed somewhat for the dead Duke of Gloucester, while some said the Duke of York had suffered great wrongs: what wrongs no man dared say. . . .

7) Brut Chronicle
(*Brut*, pp. 520–1)

[In 1452] the Duke of York came out of the Welsh marches, with the Earl of Devonshire and Lord Cobham, and many men, for the reform of certain injuries and wrongs, and also to obtain justice against certain lords about the king, and took a field at Blackheath beside Dartford in Kent, which was a strong field. As a result of this the king, with all the lords of the land, went to Blackheath with a great and strong multitude of people, armed and prepared for war in the best manner. When they had mustered on Blackheath, certain lords were sent to [the duke] to negotiate terms with him, namely the Bishops of Ely and Winchester and the Earls of Salisbury and Warwick. They concluded that the Duke of Somerset should be [required] to answer such charges as the Duke of York should put to him; and then the Duke of York should break his field and come to the king, which was promised by the king. And so the king commanded that the Duke of Somerset should be put in ward [confined]; and then the Duke of York should break his field, and come to the king. But when he was come, contrary to the promises before made, the Duke of Somerset was present in the field, awaiting and chief about the king, and made the Duke of York ride as a prisoner through London; and after they would have put him in hold [prison]. But a rumour arose that the Earl of March, his son, was coming with 20,000 men towards London, whereof the king and his council feared. And then they concluded that the Duke of York should depart at his will. . . .

You have well understood before how, contrary to the promise of the king and also the conclusions negotiated between the king and the Duke of York at Blackheath, the Duke of Somerset was not in ward but abode about the king, and had great rule. Afterwards he was made captain of Calais, and ruled the king and his realm as he would: as a result the great lords of the realm, and also the commons, were not pleased. . . .

8) Richard of York's Manifesto, Addressed to the Burgesses of Shrewsbury, Ludlow, 3 February 1452
(*Wilkinson*, pp. 114–16; *EHD*, pp. 269–70; *Flemming*, pp. 120–1; *Lander*, pp. 66–7)
. . . I suppose it is well known to you . . . what praise, dignity, honour and manhood were attributed by all nations to the people of this realm, whilst the kingdom's sovereign lord stood possessed of his lordship in the realm of France and duchy of Normandy; and what derogation, loss of merchandise, damaging of honour and villainy is reported generally of the English nation for the loss of the same; and this was especially so of the Duke of Somerset when he had the command and charge of these lands. This loss has caused and encouraged the king's enemies to conquer Gascony and Guienne. Now, daily, they make their advance intending to lay siege to Calais and to other places in the marches there. . . .

On the other hand, it is to be supposed that it is not unknown to you how, after my coming out of Ireland, as the king's true liegeman and servant (as I ever shall be to my life's end), I brought to his royal majesty's attention certain articles concerning the well-being and safeguard both of his most royal person and the tranquillity and conservation of all this his realm. These terms of advice, though they were thought fully necessary, were laid aside, to have no effect, through the envy, malice and untruth of the Duke of Somerset [who], because of the loyalty, faith and allegiance which I owe to the king, and the good will and favour that I have in all the realm, labours continually about the king's highness for my undoing, and to corrupt my blood, and to disinherit me and my heirs and such persons as are about me, without any desert or cause done or attempted on my part or theirs, as I make our Lord the judge.

[In order] that every man shall know my purpose, I signify to you that, [seeing that the Duke of Somerset] ever prevails and rules about the king's person, and that by this means the land is likely to be destroyed, I am fully determined to proceed in all haste against him, with the help of my kinsmen and friends, in such a way as to promote the ease, peace, tranquillity and safeguard of this land. . . . I pray and exhort you to strengthen, enforce and assist me, and to come to me with all diligence, wherever I may be or go, with as many goodly and likely men as you may to carry out this intention. . . .

9) *London Chronicle: Arundel 19*
(*Flemming*, pp. 122–3; *Lander*, pp. 67–8)
[On 16 February 1452] the king and his lords rode towards the Duke of York to take him, because he had raised men to come and take the Duke of Somerset; however, when the Duke of York heard of this, he took another route and so came towards London. As soon as the king heard of this he sent letters to the mayor, aldermen and commons of London [on 24 February, ordering] that they should secure the city and not let the Duke of York enter; as a result, great watch was made in the city. When the Duke of York learned of this, [he] went over Kingston Bridge. . . . [On Sunday 27 February] the king's vanguard came to London early in the morning and lodged in Southwark and, on the Monday after, in the morning, they moved from there into Kent. [In the] afternoon of the same day the king came to London with his host and went into Southwark, while the Duke of York pitched his field, with great ordnance, near Dartford. While the king remained in Southwark, bishops rode between the king and the Duke of York to set them at rest and peace; however, the Duke of York said he would have the Duke of Somerset or die in the attempt.

[On Friday 3 March] the king assembled his host on Blackheath before noon, awaiting the arrival of the Duke of York, [who] came with forty horse, [the] Earl of Devonshire and Lord Cobham, [and pledged] his allegiance. Then the king took them to grace. . . .

10) *Oath Sworn by Richard of York at St Paul's, 10 March 1452*
(*Paston Letters*, Vol. 1, pp. 101–2)
I, Richard Duke of York, confess and acknowledge that I am and ought to be humble subject and liegeman to you, my sovereign lord, King Henry VI, and ought therefore to bear you faith and truth as my sovereign lord and shall do so until my life's end. And I shall not at any time assent to anything that is attempted or done against your noble person. . . . I shall never hereafter make any assembly of your people without

your command or licence, or in my lawful defence. In the interpretation and declaration of my lawful defence, I shall report at all times to your highness and, if the case require, to my peers. . . . Whenever I find myself wronged or aggrieved, I shall sue humbly for remedy to your highness and proceed in accordance with your laws and in no other way. . . . All these things I promise truly to observe and keep, by the Holy Evangelists contained in this book that I lay my hands upon, and by the Holy Cross that I here touch, and by the blessed Sacrament of our Lord's body that I shall now with His mercy receive. . . . And this I have here promised and sworn proceeds of my own desire and free consent and by no constraining or coercion. . . .

11) London Chronicle: Rawlinson B355
(*Flenley*, p. 107; *Lander*, p. 69)
[In 1452/3] the king, complying with the counsel of the Duke of Somerset, rode to several of the Duke of York's townships where the tenants were compelled to come naked with choking cords around their necks, in the direst frost and snow, to submit to the king because, previously, they had supported their lord against the Duke of Somerset before his hour had come. Moreover, although the king himself pardoned them, the Duke [of Somerset] ordered them to be hanged.

12) Rolls of Parliament

a) Indictment of Richard of York, Coventry Parliament, 1459
(*Rotuli Parliamentorum*, Vol. 5, p. 346)
A short time after [Cade's rebellion, Richard of York] came out of Ireland, with great ostentation and a large number of followers, to your palace of Westminster. He came into your presence with a great multitude of people armoured and arrayed in manner of war. He there beat down the walls of your chamber, having no consideration for you. From this his disposition might be understood. At this time you answered his desires and demands in a way which made it seem to all your true subjects that the spirit of the wisdom of God was in you. Thus answered, he departed from you in confusion, and your true liege people, who heard of it, greatly rejoiced.

b) Commons' Petition for a Responsible and Wise Council, Reading Parliament, 1453
(*Rotuli Parliamentorum*, Vol. 5, p. 240)
[At] the beginning of this present Parliament at Reading [in March 1453], it was demonstrated and shown to the chancellor of England that there should be ordained and established a responsible and wise council, of right discreet lords and others of this land, to whom all people might have recourse for the administering of justice, equity and righteousness, of which they have no knowledge as yet. . . . [To] this it was answered, by Cardinal [Kemp] chancellor of England, that they should have good and comforting answer. . . .

c) Commons' Petition against Sir William Oldhall, Reading Parliament, 1453
(*Rotuli Parliamentorum*, Vol. 5, p. 265)

William Oldhall, knight, has long laboured, against the duty and fidelity of his allegiance, and by subtle, false and untrue means, against your most royal person and estate, your welfare and that of your realm, by all means in his power. He gave false and untrue counsel and aid, both to those men lately assembled on the field of Dartford, against your most royal person, and on several occasions to the great traitor John Cade [and others]. Let him be reputed and held a traitor, and a person attainted of high treason.

St Albans, 1455

Soon after John Talbot Earl of Shrewsbury was defeated and killed at the battle of Castillon on 17 July 1453, resulting in the rapid loss of Gascony and the reduction of the Lancastrian empire in France to Calais alone, Henry VI suffered a complete mental collapse. Initially, every effort was made to conceal the reality of the king's condition but, by the time Prince Edward of Lancaster was born in October 1453 and Queen Margaret of Anjou began to emerge as a political force, the need for more formal arrangements to ensure the smooth functioning of government in such unprecedented circumstances was becoming urgent (1, 2, 3). To this end, a great council was summoned to meet in November and, it soon became clear, Richard of York, so long in the political wilderness, had no intention of remaining there. Edmund Beaufort Duke of Somerset's efforts to prevent York attending the council failed; John Mowbray Duke of Norfolk presented a petition deploring the loss of Normandy and Gascony and demanding Somerset's impeachment; and, shortly afterwards, Somerset found himself a prisoner in the Tower: the pro-Yorkist *Benet's Chronicle* clearly approved of the arrest of 'this evil duke' but, perhaps significantly, the *Chronicon Angliae* stressed that Somerset was imprisoned despite the fact that 'no charge of treason against king or kingdom could be proved against him' (1, 2). Although, under the circumstances, the great council demonstrated considerable unity and solidarity, no permanent solution to the problem of Henry VI's incapacity was forthcoming and, over the next few weeks, the political crisis deepened: a newsletter penned in London on 19 January 1454, for instance, reported the king's entire lack of response to his newly born son, the ominous build-up of armed retinues by mutually antagonistic lords, and the fact that Margaret of Anjou had 'made a bill of five articles [the] first of which is that she desires the whole rule of this land' (4a). No less significantly, the winter of 1453/4 saw the forging of a political alliance between Richard of York and the Nevilles (Richard Neville Earl of Salisbury and his son Richard Neville Earl of Warwick, two of the most powerful nobles in England and, hitherto, attached to the court), an alliance which could both forward York's ambitions and be of assistance to the Nevilles in their now raging feud with the Percies in the north of England. The sudden death of Cardinal John Kemp, chancellor of England and a powerful opponent of York, on 22 March 1454, finally precipitated matters in favour of the York/Neville alliance: shortly after a Parliamentary delegation saw for itself just how incapacitated the King was, York became protector of the realm (but not regent) and Salisbury succeeded Kemp as chancellor (1, 2, 3, 5a, 6a, 6b).

Pro-Yorkist chroniclers tended to paint a glowing picture of Richard of York's months as protector: *Benet's Chronicle*, for instance, commented that in 1454 York 'governed the entire kingdom of England well and honourably [and] miraculously pacified all rebels and malefactors', while, according to *Bale's Chronicle*, too, he and Salisbury 'honourably ruled and governed' (1, 3). Perhaps effective measures were taken at last to curb lawlessness and aristocratic feuding, particularly in the north of England, but, although Somerset remained in prison, no formal charges were laid against him and many members of the council may well have been more concerned to prevent Margaret of Anjou securing power than provide York with unequivocal backing for full-scale reform of government and administration (1, 2, 4b, 7). At the end of 1454, moreover, Henry VI recovered at least most of his senses and, before long, Somerset was released from the Tower, York's protectorate terminated, and he and the Nevilles once more excluded from power (1, 2, 3, 4c, 6c, 6f). If we are to believe pro-Yorkist chronicles, York, Salisbury and Warwick had every justification for now retiring to their estates and even proceeding to arm since, as *Benet's Chronicle* put it, 'the evil Duke of Somerset' soon began 'conspiring to destroy the honourable Duke of York' (1); yet, according to the *Chronicon Angliae*, real culpability for the deteriorating political situation in the early months of 1455 lay with the Yorkist lords themselves: they 'left the royal household without either permission or formality', declared the chronicler, 'determined not to obey the king's commands' until they had sufficient forces to oust their opponents from the royal presence (2). When Somerset complained bitterly to the king in March 1455 that he had been imprisoned for over a year 'without any reasonable grounds or lawful process', Henry VI responded by openly declaring him a 'faithful and true liegeman' (8); however, when the Yorkist lords declared, in a letter to the new chancellor Thomas Bourchier Archbishop of Canterbury on 20 May 1455, that they, too, were the king's 'true and humble liegemen', resorting to arms only in order 'to clear ourselves' of unjust accusations, they received no such encouragement (5b). Prolonged negotiations certainly preceded the outbreak of hostilities but, whereas at Dartford in 1452 fighting had been averted, on 22 May battle was joined in the streets of St Albans (1, 9).

Although better documented than most battles of the Wars of the Roses, almost all surviving accounts of St Albans, whether contained in contemporary newsletters or later chronicles, present a firmly Yorkist perspective, designed to explain and justify the behaviour of the Yorkist lords. The *Chronicon Angliae*, which might well have been more sympathetic to the Lancastrians, ends shortly prior to the battle, while even Polydore Vergil says virtually nothing about the fighting: he is notably critical of the Yorkists, however, and also remarks that, since Henry VI 'had reposed all his hope' in Somerset, 'a noble captain who had fought valiantly so many years against the French', the king felt 'great and incredible sorrow' at his death (13). *Whethamsted's Register,* by contrast, very much sought to justify Richard of York's taking up arms, as well as expressing relief that, since fighting was confined to the streets of St Albans, the abbey itself remained unharmed. *Benet's Chronicle,* too, adopted a clearly pro-Yorkist stance on the battle and its outcome, as did *Bale's Chronicle,* the *English Chronicle* and *Gregory's Chronicle* (1, 3, 9, 10). Short reports of the battle and its immediate aftermath were penned, on 25 May, 31 May and 3 June, by Paston and Milanese correspondents (4d, 12a, 12b), while more substantial contemporary narratives, albeit again reflecting a Yorkist viewpoint, can be found in the so-called *Stow Relation* (emphasizing that the Yorkist lords, loyal throughout, had been forced to fight in order to preserve themselves) and the *Fastolfe Relation* (seeking to blame specific Lancastrians for the whole affair). The *Dijon Relation,* perhaps the best of the contemporary accounts, at least avoided lambasting the Lancastrians and sought to record objectively the sequence of events on 22 May 1455 (11).

The first battle of St Albans, essentially a skirmish in an English market town between rival lords and their retinues, had more political than military significance. Edmund Beaufort Duke of Somerset, Henry Percy Earl of Northumberland and Thomas Lord Clifford were all killed fighting for the king and it may well be they had been deliberately targeted by York and the Nevilles: if so, the events at St Albans in May 1455 may have set in motion a series of bloodfeuds that were to resurface with a vengeance at Wakefield in December 1460. More immediately, the balance of political advantage once more passed to York and the Nevilles. Henry VI, who had apparently been struck in the neck by a stray arrow during the fighting, fell into Yorkist hands, and the plums of government office rapidly followed: most notably, York himself became constable of England and Warwick captain of Calais (1, 4d, 9, 10). Even so, the Yorkist lords still lacked any substantial baronial support: hence, no doubt, their efforts to win over moderates like Thomas Bourchier Archbishop of Canterbury, who remained chancellor, and his brother Henry Viscount Bourchier, who became treasurer (1, 4d). Hence also, both at court and when Parliament met a few weeks after St Albans, their anxiety to present themselves as having behaved loyally to Henry VI throughout recent events and assign blame firmly elsewhere (4e, 5b, 5c). During the autumn of 1455, however, a new and violent flare-up of the Courtenay/ Bonville feud in the south-west and the prevalence of disorder elsewhere in the country resulted, on 19 November, in Richard of York once more becoming protector of the realm (1, 3, 5d, 6e). Perhaps, too, Henry VI had suffered another mental breakdown: certainly, at the end of October 1455, a Paston correspondent reported that 'some men are afraid that he [the king] is sick again' and, on 11 November, Richard of York was empowered 'to hold and dissolve Parliament' since 'the king cannot appear in person' (6d). Polydore Vergil, predictably, put an altogether more sinister gloss on it all, declaring that, following St Albans, the

Yorkist lords deliberately set out to get York made protector 'so Henry might be king in name but not in deed', as a preliminary to depriving him 'either of kingdom or of life at their pleasure' (13). As it turned out, however, York's second protectorate only lasted about three months: on 25 February 1456, perhaps at Margaret of Anjou's urging, Henry VI came to Parliament in person and formally dispensed with his services (1, 4f, 13).

1) Benet's Chronicle
(*Benet*, pp. 209–16; *Hallam*, pp. 210–16)
[Soon after Easter 1453] the king sent 1000 men to Gascony . . . [About 10 August] the Earl of Shrewsbury was killed [at Castillon], and his son Lord Lisle, [and] Lord Moleyns was captured by the French. . . . [About 29 September] the city of Bordeaux was again lost. . . .

[About 1 August 1453] the king became very ill at Clarendon and, although he eventually recovered, his sickness lasted a long time. [On 13 October 1453] Edward, son of King Henry VI, was born at Westminster and baptized in the abbey with great solemnity. When the royal council realized that the king's health was not improving and fearing the ruin of the realm under the Duke of Somerset's governance was imminent, the magnates of the kingdom sent for the Duke of York who, when he arrived in London with a small retinue [on 12 November], came to the council. The Duke of Norfolk, during a council meeting, charged the Duke of Somerset with treason on many counts: [as a result, on 23 November], this evil duke was arrested. . . .

[About 2 February 1454] the Dukes of York and Norfolk, the Earls of Salisbury, Warwick and Devon, and others, came to London, and on 11 February Parliament began at Reading [and] reopened at Westminster on 15 February. In this Parliament the Duke of York became lieutenant of the realm and the Duke of Buckingham steward of England. . . . [On 19 February] Cardinal John Kemp, Archbishop of Canterbury and chancellor of England, and a close friend of the Duke of Somerset (now in the Tower), died at Lambeth. At Canterbury he was succeeded by Thomas Bourchier Bishop of Ely. . . . On 10 April 1454 the Earl of Salisbury became chancellor of England and on 16 April Parliament appointed the Duke of York protector of England during the king's illness or until Prince Edward came of age.

[About 19 May 1454] the Duke of York, with a great number of men, rode to York to confront the Duke of Exeter and Lord Egremont, who had armed themselves in Yorkshire and rebelled against the king's peace. However, when they heard of the Duke of York's arrival, they fled. [On 23 July] the Duke of York seized the Duke of Exeter at Westminster, took him to his house and, later, imprisoned him in Pontefract castle. The Duke of York and the royal council also dismissed the Duke of Somerset from all his offices. . . . [On 31 October] Thomas Percy Lord Egremont, and his brother Richard, were captured near York by Sir Thomas Neville, [after] nearly 100 men had been killed [at Stamford Bridge] and many wounded. [On 31 December 1454] King Henry recovered his health at Greenwich, by God's grace.

On 6 February [1455], shortly after the Duke of Somerset was released on bail from the Tower of London, the Duke of York resigned his office. . . . Then the king, on the advice of the Archbishop of Canterbury and Duke of Buckingham, pardoned all those who had provided surety for the Duke of Somerset: thereafter the Duke of Somerset, who had previously almost ruined the whole of England by his evil rule, resumed his position as the crown's leading minister. On 7 March the Earl of Salisbury resigned as chancellor, Thomas Bourchier Archbishop of Canterbury replaced him, and the Earl of Wiltshire became treasurer.

Soon after Easter 1455 enmity once more broke out between the noble Duke of York and the evil Duke of Somerset and the Duke of Buckingham, since the Duke of Somerset was conspiring to destroy the honourable Duke of York by advising the king that [York] intended to remove him and rule in his place (a story falsely invented). On account of this, about the middle of May, the Duke of York, accompanied by the Earls of Salisbury and Warwick, Lords Clinton and [Grey of] Powis, set out for London with 7000 well armed men. When the Duke of Somerset learned of this, he advised the king that they were coming to destroy him. For this reason the king sided with the Duke of Somerset. [On 21 May] the king rode towards Watford, with the Dukes of Somerset and Buckingham, the Earls of Northumberland, Pembroke, Wiltshire, Stafford and Dorset, Lords Roos, Sudeley and Berners, and many other knights and men-at-arms. [On 22 May] he rode on to the well-fortified and guarded town of St Albans, where the Duke of York arrived with his supporters about 10 o'clock the same day, not to confront the king but to castigate the Duke of Somerset. The duke sent a message to the king [asking] him to send the Duke of Somerset under restraint to answer the Duke of Norfolk's charges, but he refused. Then the Earl of Warwick entered St Albans with 2000 men, all very well armed. Here the Duke of Somerset, the Earl of Northumberland, Lord Clifford, and many others, to the number of about 100, were killed fighting bravely. The king was wounded in the neck, the Duke of Buckingham (also wounded) was captured, Lord Stafford was wounded, the Earl of Dorset seriously wounded and captured, and the Earl of Wiltshire fled in panic. Thus all who supported the Duke of Somerset were killed, wounded or at least plundered. The king, who found himself deserted, fled to a tanner's house, where the Duke of York, and the Earls of Salisbury and Warwick, found him, and declared themselves humbly obedient. When the king saw this he was greatly relieved. . . .

[Following the king's return to London] Lord Bourchier was made treasurer and the Earl of Warwick captain of Calais. On 9 July [1455] the king opened Parliament at Westminster, and there the Duke of York once more became protector. . . .

[On 7 November 1455] Lord Egremont, who had been condemned at York for his disobedience and rebellion against the Earl of Salisbury, [was] committed to prison in London, along with his brother Richard. . . . [On 16 December] the Earl of Devon and Lord Bonville fought a battle [at Clyst] near Exeter, where Lord Bonville was defeated, twelve men killed on either side, and many wounded, after which William Bonville fled to London. The Duke of York sent for the Earl of Devon, who then accompanied him to London, where, with the consent of the council, he was imprisoned in the Tower of London, and Lord William Bonville in the Fleet.

[On 13 January 1456] Parliament met at Westminster, where the Duke of York and the house of Commons worked hard to obtain a resumption of royal grants, but most of the lords resisted. [Indeed] they went to the king and brought him to Westminster: there, in the king's presence, the Duke of York resigned his office. . . .

2) *Chronicon Angliae*
(*Giles*, pp. 44–7)

[In July 1453], at Clarendon, the king suffered a sudden and unexpected fright, becoming so ill that, for a year and a half, he lacked both natural sense and intelligence sufficient to govern the realm. No doctor or medicine could cure him. [On 13 October] his son Prince Edward was born. . . . Since the king had neither understanding nor strength to rule the kingdom, the leading magnates of the realm chose Richard Duke of York as regent. . . .

[The] Duke of Norfolk, backed by a number of fellow lords, accused the Duke of Somerset of betraying Normandy and other parts of France, [so vehemently that John Kemp chancellor of England] had to order his arrest and imprisonment in the Tower of London, even though no charge of treason against king or kingdom could be proved against him. . . .

[Following Kemp's death] Thomas Bourchier Bishop of Ely became Archbishop of Canterbury [and] Richard Earl of Salisbury chancellor of England. Also the Duke of Exeter and Thomas Lord Egremont began making war on the Earl of Salisbury and his sons in Yorkshire until, with the aid of the Duke of York, they were suppressed. Later Thomas Percy Lord Egremont took the field against Thomas Neville and his brother Sir John near Castleton Bridge in Yorkshire, where, after much slaughter, Egremont and his brother Richard were captured and imprisoned. At this time, too, the ancient feud between the Earl of Devon and Lord Bonville recommenced, [culminating in] the earl taking the field against Bonville, forcing him to flee, killing several of his men and plundering his tenants. Eventually, the Duke of York, as protector of the kingdom, and by the advice of the council, seized and imprisoned the Earl [of Devon, as he did also the Duke of Exeter soon after]. . . .

[Once the king] recovered his physical and mental health, and resumed the government of the kingdom, he immediately released the Dukes of Somerset and Exeter, and the Earl of Devon, from prison, [as a result of which] Richard Earl of Salisbury resigned the chancellorship. The king, on impulse, created Thomas Bourchier Archbishop of Canterbury chancellor of England. The Duke of York, and the Earls of Warwick and Salisbury, finding these changes unacceptable, left the royal household and council without either permission or formality, determined not to obey the king's commands until such time as they had enough forces and supporters to oust those lords so much higher in royal favour [than they].

3) Bale's Chronicle
(Flenley, pp. 140–3)

[At Clarendon in the summer of 1453] the king suddenly became indisposed [and] his wit and reason withdrawn. . . . [On 13 October] the queen, being at Westminster, had a prince, on account of which bells rang in every church and *Te Deum* was solemnly sung; and he was christened at Westminster, his godfathers being the chancellor Cardinal Kemp Archbishop of Canterbury and the Duke of Somerset, and his godmother the Duchess of Buckingham; of whose birth the people spoke strangely. . . . [Later] the Duke of Somerset was committed to the Tower as a prisoner.

[On] Friday 22 March [1454] Cardinal [Kemp] died suddenly at four in the morning, [and soon afterwards] the Duke of York was made protector of England and the Earl of Salisbury chancellor, and they honourably ruled and governed.

[On] 26 January [1455] the Duke of Somerset was taken out of the Tower by the Duke of Buckingham, the Earl of Wiltshire and Lord Roos; as a result, the Duke of York gave up the king's sword and ceased to be protector.

[On] Thursday 22 May [1455] the king assembled a great company of men at St Albans, including the Dukes of Buckingham and Somerset, the Earls of Northumberland and Wiltshire, Lords Clifford and Roos, and others, [where] the Duke of York was proclaimed a traitor. [Immediately] the Duke of York, and the Earls of Salisbury and Warwick, entered the town with their men arrayed for war, just as the king and his men were so arrayed. [There] the Duke of York, and the Earls of Salisbury and Warwick, slew the Duke of Somerset, the Earl of Northumberland and Lord Clifford, overthrew the king's banner [but] preserved his person, and took the Duke of Buckingham and Lord Roos, [although] the Earl of Wiltshire fled. [On] the second day after they brought the king to the city of London in great honour, the Duke of York riding on his right side and the Earl of Salisbury on his left, and the Earl of Warwick bearing his sword. . . .

[In November 1455] Lord Egremont and his brother were committed to Newgate and, in the same month, the Earl of Devonshire and Lord Bonville fought in the west country, and many people were slain on both sides. [In December] the Duke of York was made protector again, [but on 21 February 1456 the king] resumed his rule and discharged the Duke of York of the protectorship.

4) Paston Letters
(Paston Letters, Vol. 2, pp. 295–9, 329, Vol. 3. pp. 13–14, 31, 43–5, 75)

a) John Stodeley, in London, to the Duke of Norfolk, 19 January 1454
. . . at the prince's [Henry VI's infant son Edward] coming to Windsor, the Duke of Buckingham took him in his arms and presented him to the king in goodly

fashion, beseeching the king to bless him; but the king gave no answer. Nevertheless, the duke still stayed with the prince by the king, and, when he could obtain no answer, the queen came in, took the prince in her arms and presented him as the duke had done, desiring the king to bless him: however, all their labour was in vain, for they departed thence without any answer or expression from the king, saving only that he once looked on the prince and cast his eyes down again, without any more [sign of recognition].

Cardinal [Kemp] has charged and commanded all his servants to be ready with bows and arrows, swords and shields, crossbows, and all other weapons of war they can obtain, in order to safeguard his person. The Earl of Wiltshire and Lord Bonville have caused it to be proclaimed at Taunton in Somerset that every man who is able and willing to go with them, and serve them, shall have 6*d* every day as long as he abides with them. The Duke of Exeter, in person, has been at Tuxford near Doncaster in the north country, where Lord Egremont met him, and the two are sworn [to be allies]. The Earl of Wiltshire, Lords Beaumont, Poynings, Clifford, Egremont and Bonville gather all the men they can and may come here with them. . . . The Duke of Somerset's harbinger has taken up all the lodgings available near the Tower. . . .

The Duke of York will be in London next Friday night, as his own men tell for certain, and he will come with his household retinue, well attired and likely men. The Earl of March comes with him, but he will have another fellowship of good men who will be in London before him, with jackets, helmets and other armour. . . . The Earl of Salisbury will be in London on Monday or Tuesday next, with seven score knights and squires, besides other followers. The Earls of Warwick, Richmond and Pembroke come with the Duke of York, as it is said, each of them with a goodly fellowship, [and] the Earl of Warwick will have 1000 men awaiting on him besides the fellowship that comes with him, as far as I can tell. . . .

[Edmund and Jasper Tudor, Earls of Richmond and Pembroke, Henry VI's half-brothers] are likely to be arrested on their coming to London, if they come. . . .

Consequently, it is thought by my lord's servants and well-wishers here that my lord, at his coming, should bring a good and able company [to] have about him [and] have another goodly fellowship to wait on him and be here before him or soon after him, just as other lords of his blood will have. . . . [Here] every man who is of the opinion of the Duke of Somerset makes himself ready to be as strong as he can, [so] it is necessary my lord look well to himself and keep his followers about him, [for] it is to be feared that ambushes might be laid for him. . . . The Duke of Somerset has spies about in every lord's house of this land; some pose as friars, some as shipmen taken on the sea, and some as other kinds of men; they report to him all they see or hear concerning the duke. Therefore, keep good watch and beware of such spies.

[If the] chancellor [Kemp] or any others question my lord about his coming [in this manner, he should] answer that he was credibly informed that both the

Duke of Somerset, who is in prison, and others who are still at large and support his views against the welfare of the king and the land, have made great assemblies and gatherings of people to maintain the views of the Duke of Somerset and defeat my lord; and that the coming of my lord in such form as he shall come is only for the safeguard of his own person. . . .

b) William Paston to John Paston, July 1454
. . . my Lord of York has taken my Lord of Exeter into custody. The Duke of Somerset is still in prison, in worse case than he was.

c) Edmund Clere, in Greenwich, to John Paston, 9 January 1455
Blessed be God, the king is well amended and has been since Christmas Day, and on St John's Day commanded his almoner to ride to Canterbury with his offering, and commanded his secretary to offer at St Edward's [shrine]. On Monday afternoon the queen came to him and brought my lord prince with her. Then he asked what the prince's name was and the queen told him Edward; and then he held up his eyes and thanked God, [saying] he never knew [him] until that time, nor understood what was said to him, nor knew where he had been while sick until now. He asked who the godfathers were, the queen told him, and he was well pleased. She told him that the cardinal [Kemp] was dead and he said he never knew of it until then, [adding] that one of the wisest lords in this land was dead. [When] my Lord of Winchester and [the Prior] of St John's were with him, [he] spoke to them as well as ever he did, and, when they came out, they wept for joy. He says that he is in charity with all the world and wished that all the lords were so. Now he says matins of Our Lady, and evensong, and hears his mass devoutly. . . .

d) John Crane, in Lambeth, to John Paston, 25 May 1455
. . . as for such tidings as we have here, these three lords are dead: the Duke of Somerset, the Earl of Northumberland and Lord Clifford. . . . As for other lords, many of them are hurt, [and] as for any great multitude of people who were there, at most six score were slain. As for the lords who were with the king, they and their men were pillaged and robbed of all their armour and horses.

As for what rule we shall now have, I do not yet know, save only there are made certain new officers: my Lord of York, constable of England; my Lord of Warwick, captain of Calais; and my Lord Bourchier, treasurer of England. . . .

As for our sovereign lord, thank God he has no great harm.

e) Henry Windsor, in London, to John Bocking and William Worcester, 19 July 1455
. . . the king our sovereign lord, and all his true lords, are healthy in their bodies but not at ease in their hearts. Two days before the writing of this letter there was a quarrel between Lords Warwick and Cromwell before the king. When Lord Cromwell sought to excuse himself of all responsibility for the battle of St Albans,

Warwick swore he was not telling the truth since it was he who originated all the fighting there. So great is the ill-will between Lords Cromwell and Warwick at present that, at Cromwell's request, the Earl of Shrewsbury has lodged at the hospital of St James, for his security. Also, men of Lords Warwick, York and Salisbury proceed in armour daily to Westminster, having filled their lords' barges with weapons. . . .

The day before the writing of this letter, a bill passed [in Parliament] putting all the blame [for St Albans] on [Thomas] Thorp, [William] Joseph and my Lord of Somerset: by this bill all actions pending against any person or persons for any offences committed at that battle [are declared] extinct and void, [and it is affirmed that] all things done there were well done. . . . Many men complained bitterly now this bill is passed.

[After this letter] is read and understood, I pray you burn or break it, for I am loath to write anything of any lord but needs must.

f) John Bocking to Sir John Fastolfe, 9 February 1456
. . . this day my Lords of York and Warwick came to Parliament in good array, all in armoured jackets and coats of mail, and no other lord, on account of which men wondered. It was said on Saturday [7 February] that my Lord [of York] would have been discharged [from the protectorship] that same day, [and] if he had not come with strong support he would have been attacked. No man can say that any proof is available [to show by whom he might have been attacked].

The king, so it was told me by a great man, would have him [York] as his chief and principal councillor. . . . The resumption, men trust, shall proceed, and my Lord of York's first power of protectorship stand, or else not. The queen is a great and strong laboured [very active] woman, for she spares no pains to pursue her objectives towards an end and conclusion favourable to her power.

5) Rolls of Parliament

a) Henry VI's Incapacity and Richard of York's Appointment as Protector, March 1454
(*Rotuli Parliamentorum*, Vol. 5, pp. 241–2)
[On 25 March 1454] lords spiritual and temporal were in the king's high presence in the place where he dined. [Articles were put to the king expressing] great concern for his health and the great diligence of the lords in his Parliament, [but from him] they could get no answer or sign. [After dinner] they came to the king again [and] urged him for an answer, by all ways and means they could think of, but they received none. From that place [the king] was led, between two men, into the chamber where he slept and the lords pressed him once more, [but] they received no answer, word or sign. . . .

[On 27 March the lords spiritual and temporal in Parliament decreed that Richard Duke of York] be chief of the king's council and devised [for him the] name of protector and defender. . . .

b) Richard Duke of York, Richard Earl of Salisbury and Richard Earl of Warwick to Thomas Bourchier, Archbishop of Canterbury and Chancellor, 20 May 1455
(*Rotuli Parliamentorum*, Vol. 5, pp. 280–1)

. . . we hear that there is a great rumour and wonder at our coming, and of the manner thereof, towards the most noble presence of the king, [and] many doubts and ambiguities are created in the mind of his royal majesty and amongst the people concerning our faith and duty to his highness. [Yet] neither by our coming, nor by the manner thereof, do we intend to proceed to any matter except what, with God's mercy, shall be to His pleasure, and to the honour, prosperity and welfare of our sovereign lord, his land and people. . . .

We leave aside our own particular quarrels, which we shall never prefer above the duty, faith, love and affection which we owe to our sovereign lord and to his realm and people. Furthermore, [we] understand the calling and establishment of the king's council at his town of Leicester was based on the reason, by those whom we believe to have caused the arrangements of the meeting there, of the safety of his most noble person. This, by common assumption, implies a mistrust of some persons. We, therefore, his true and humble liegemen, have joined together better to act, in accordance with our duty, for the safety of his most noble person. . . . We believe there is a mistrust of us and we propose, with God's grace, to clear ourselves of this. . . .

c) Pardon for the Yorkists and Their Renewal of Allegiance, 24 July 1455
(*Rotuli Parliamentorum*, Vol. 5, p. 282)

We [Henry VI] declare that none of our cousins, the Duke of York, and the Earls of Warwick and Salisbury, nor any of the persons who came with them in their fellowship [to St Albans on 22 May] be impeached, sued, vexed, grieved, hurt or molested [for] anything supposed or claimed to have been done against our person, crown or dignity.

[On 24 July 1455], in the great council chamber, in the time of Parliament, in the presence of our sovereign lord, [every] lord spiritual [and] temporal freely swore and promised: 'I promise unto your highness [that] I shall truly and faithfully keep the allegiance that I owe unto you [and] do all that may be to the welfare, honour and safeguard of your most noble person, [and] at no time consent to anything [to] the hurt and prejudice of your most noble person, dignity, crown or estate. . . .'

d) Courtenay/Bonville Feud, November 1455
(*Rotuli Parliamentorum*, Vol. 5, pp. 284–5)

. . . there have been great and grievous riots in the west country betwen the Earl of Devon and Lord Bonville, as a result of which some men have been murdered, some robbed, and children and women taken. [The Commons in Parliament] have knowledge and understanding [that] great and grievous riots were committed in the city of Exeter by the Earl of Devonshire, accompanied by many riotous persons, as it is said by 800 horsemen and 4000 footmen, [who] have robbed the church of Exeter, and also taken gentlemen in that country: [consequently] a protector and defender must be [appointed to] abridge such riots and offences. . . .

6) Chancery Patent Rolls
(*Calendar of Patent Rolls*, 1452–61, pp. 153, 159, 226, 273, 278)

a) 13 February 1454
Power to Richard Duke of York, by assent of the council, to hold in the king's name Parliament [on] 14 February at the palace of Westminster, as the king cannot be present in person, and to do all things for the good governance of the realm, [and] to dissolve that Parliament by assent of the council.

b) 3 April 1454
Appointment, during pleasure, by the advice and assent of the lords spiritual and temporal and of the commonalty of England in the present Parliament, in consideration of the king's infirmity whereby his attendance [would be] prejudicial to his swift recovery, of Richard Duke of York, as protector and defender of the realm and church and principal councillor of the king, [the] authority of the duke ceasing when Edward, the king's first-born, arrives at years of discretion, if he should then wish to take upon himself the charge of protector and defender.

c) 31 March 1455
Edmund Duke of Somerset who, during the king's illness, was imprisoned in the Tower of London for more than a year and ten weeks until 7 February 1455, has been set free.

d) 11 November 1455
Power to Richard Duke of York, by assent of the council, to hold and dissolve Parliament (adjoined to 12 November) at the palace of Westminster, as the king cannot appear in person.

e) 19 November 1455
Appointment, on petition of the Commons in the present Parliament, of Richard Duke of York as protector and defender of the realm and church, and the king's principal councillor, until he be discharged by the king in Parliament by the advice and assent of the lords spiritual and temporal, [the duke's] authority ceasing when Edward, the king's first-born son, comes to years of discretion and wishes to assume the charge of protector and defender.

f) 9 March 1456
By letters patent dated 3 April 1454 the king appointed Richard Duke of York as

protector and defender of the realm and church, and the king's principal councillor, taking for his wages 2000 marks a year, of which sum £1139 9s remain unpaid from 3 April 1454 to 9 February 1455, and 1000 marks assigned to him by the lords spiritual and temporal in the present Parliament, as reward for personal labour in journeying and riding on the business of the realm, are still unpaid.

7) Henry VI to Sir Thomas Stanley and Sir Thomas Harrington, 16 May 1454
(*Proceedings and Ordinances of the Privy Council of England,* ed. N. H. Nicolas, Vol. 6, pp. 130–1)
[We] understand that our trusty and right well beloved cousin the Duke of Exeter, our right trusty and well beloved Lord Egremont, and others, make great assemblies and gatherings of our people to no good intent as it is rumoured. For which cause our right trusty and right entirely well beloved cousin the Duke of York, protector and defender of our realm, by the advice of our council, draws himself towards them to redress such inordinate demeaning and resist their malice if need be. Forsomuch we write to you willing and desiring that, if in the country where you are any persons resort to such gatherings, by all the means you can [prevent it]; and over that, wait upon our cousin the protector and assist him, if he command you to do so, with all the diligence, might and power you can muster for the redressing of such assemblies and evil disposed people.

8) Edmund Duke of Somerset's Grievances, and Henry VI's Response, March 1455
(*Flemming*, pp. 127–8)
[On 4 March 1455] at Greenwich, in the presence of the king and the lords of his council, Edmund Duke of Somerset declared that he, during the time of the disease of our sovereign lord, was committed to the Tower of London, and kept there for a whole year, ten weeks and more, and, as he believed, without any reasonable grounds or lawful process [until 7 February 1455], when he was, by the lords of the council, released on bail, under which he is now. [Then he requested] that his bail be discharged and he have full freedom as the king's faithful, true subject, which he has always been. . . .

[The king responded] that he well knew the duke had been, and is, his true and faithful liegeman and cousin, [and], in the presence of all the lords, openly declared the Duke of Somerset his faithful and true liegeman and subject. . . .

9) English Chronicle
(*Davies*, pp. 71–2)
[In May 1455] there was a mortal debate and variance between Richard Duke of York, Richard Earl of Salisbury and Richard Earl of Warwick [on the one hand] and Edmund Duke of Somerset [on the other], by whom at that time the king was principally guided and governed, as he had been before by the Duke of Suffolk. This Duke [of Somerset] always kept near the king, and dared not depart from his

presence, fearing always the power of the Duke of York and the [Neville] earls, and constantly exciting and stirring the king against them; notwithstanding that the commons of this land hated Duke Edmund and loved the Duke of York, because he loved the commons and preserved the common profit of this land. [Duke Richard and the Neville earls], realizing they might not prevail against or withstand the malice of Duke Edmund, who daily provoked the king to their final destruction, gathered secretly a power of people and kept them covertly in villages near the town of St Albans. When the king was there they encircled the town, and sent to the king, beseeching him to send out to them their mortal enemy, and enemy to all the realm, Edmund Duke of Somerset: if he would not do so, they would seize him by strength and violence. The king, by the advice of his council, answered that he would not deliver him. When the Duke of York and the earls heard this answer, although the town was strongly barred and arrayed for defence, they and their men violently broke down houses and fences on the east side of the town and entered St Peter's Street, slaying all that resisted them. Then the king came out of the abbey, with his banner displayed, into the same street, and Duke Edmund with him, and the Duke of Buckingham, the Earl of Northumberland and Lord Clifford, and Lord Sudeley bearing the king's banner; there was a sore fight; [and] there, at last, were slain Duke Edmund, the Earl of Northumberland and Lord Clifford. The king, who stood under his banner, was hurt in the neck by an arrow. Once Duke Edmund and the lords were slain, the battle ceased.

10) Gregory's Chronicle
(*Gregory*, p. 198)

[In 1455], the week before Whitsunday, there was a battle at St Albans between King Harry VI and the Duke of York, [where] King Harry was hurt with the shot of an arrow in his neck. . . . The Earl of Wiltshire bore the king's banner in the battle, [setting it] against a house end and fighting bravely with a helmet, fearful of losing his beauty, for he was named the fairest knight of this land. . . . The captains of this field under the Duke of York were the Earls of Warwick and Salisbury. In this battle were slain the Duke of Somerset, the Earl of Northumberland, Lord Clifford, and many others, both gentlemen and yeomen. [After it was over] the Duke of York brought [Henry VI] to London as king, not as a prisoner.

11) Dijon Relation: An Anonymous Contemporary Account of the First Battle of St Albans, 1455
(*Lander*, pp. 77–9; *EHD*, p. 277)

[The] Duke of York's men approached the town [of St Albans], placed good guards on all the roads nearby, and entered it so vigorously that they rapidly took and blockaded the market place, [where] the real fighting began. The battle started on the stroke of 10 o'clock but, because the place was small, few combatants could fight there and matters became so critical that four of the king's bodyguard were killed by arrows in his presence, and the king himself was wounded in the shoulder by an arrow, although it only grazed the skin. At last when they had fought for three hours the king's party, seeing they had the worst of it, broke away on one wing and began to flee. The Duke of Somerset retreated into a house to save himself by hiding but he was seen by the Duke of York's men who at once surrounded the house. The Duke of York ordered that the king should be taken out of the throng and put in the abbey for safety, and so it was done. The Duke of Buckingham, who was badly wounded by three arrows, also took refuge in the abbey. This done, York's men at once began to fight Somerset and his men, who were within the house and defended themselves valiantly. In the end, after the doors were broken down, Somerset saw he had no option but to come out with his men, as a result of which they were all surrounded by the Duke of York's men. After some were stricken down and the Duke of Somserset had killed four men with his own hand, so it is said, he was felled to the ground with an axe, and at once wounded in so many places that he died. And while Somerset thus made his defence, others of his party fought York's men, so that three of his lords there were slain: the Earl of Northumberland, Lord Clifford (a great pity for he was a brave man) and Sir Richard Harrington. [Altogether, on both sides] there died 200 men or thereabouts.

The battle lasted until 2.30 in the afternoon and, when it was over, the Duke of York's men went to the abbey to kill the Duke of Buckingham and the treasurer, namely the Earl of Wiltshire, who had retreated there with the king. The Duke of York would not allow it but sent his herald to the king to inform him that he must choose either to hand over the two lords as prisoners or see them killed in front of him and put himself in danger once more: so the king willingly agreed to let York arrest the two lords. Buckingham was taken but the treasurer could not be found, for he had already fled in a monk's habit, and even now, on 27 May, no one knows where he has gone.

When all these things were done the Duke of York entered the abbey and knelt before the king . . . protesting that he had not opposed him but had been against the traitors to his crown. Before York left the king pardoned him, and received him into grace, and on the same day the king, the Duke of York and all the other lords came to London, where they have been received with great joy and solemn procession. The Duke of York will now, without contradiction, be first after the king and have the government of all. God give him grace to carry out his tasks well. . . .

12) Milanese State Papers
(*CSPM*, pp. 16–17)

a) Newsletter from Bruges, 31 May 1455
. . . I learned here yesterday, by letters which came straight from Sandwich to Dunkirk, that fresh disturbances [have broken] out in England. . . . A great part of the nobles have been in conflict, and the Duke of Somerset, the Earl of

Northumberland and my Lord of Clifford are slain, with many other lords and knights on both sides. The Duke of Somerset's son [was] mortally wounded; my Lord of Buckingham and his son are hurt. The Duke of York has done this with his followers. On the 24th he entered London and made a solemn procession to St Paul's. They say he has demanded pardon from the king for himself and his men, and will have it. He will take up the government again, and some think that the affairs of that kingdom will now take a turn for the better. . . .

b) Newsletter from Bruges, 3 June 1455

I have further news of the battle in England brought by one who came here from Calais. They say that on the 21st of May the king left Westminster with many lords, including the Duke of Somerset, to hold a council at Leicester. . . . They went armed because they suspected that the Duke of York would also go there with men-at-arms. That day they travelled twenty miles to the abbey of St Albans. On the 22nd the king set out to continue his journey, but when they were outside the town they were immediately attacked by York's men, and many perished on both sides. The Duke of Somerset was taken and forthwith beheaded. With his death the battle ceased at once and, without loss of time, the Duke of York went to kneel before the king and ask pardon for himself and his followers, as they had not done this in order to inflict any hurt upon his majesty, but in order to have Somerset. Accordingly, the king pardoned them, and on the 23rd the king and York and all returned to London. On the 24th they made the solemn procession, and now peace reigns. The king has forbidden any one to speak about it upon pain of death. The Duke of York has the government, and the people are very pleased at this.

13) Polydore Vergil
(*Vergil*, pp. 97–8)

The Duke of York, after the victory [at St Albans], recalling how he had proclaimed at the beginning that his rising was for reform of the commonwealth, armed himself with mildness, mercy and liberality, and was so far from laying violent hands on King Henry that he brought him honourably to London, as conqueror of the field. Here, after consulting with the two Richard Nevilles and several other noblemen, [he] procured himself to be made protector of the realm, Richard Neville [Earl of Salisbury], the father, chancellor of England, and Richard Neville [Earl of Warwick], the son, captain of Calais. Thereby, the government of England might rest in him and the chancellor [Salisbury, Warwick] might have charge of the wars, and so Henry might be king in name and not in deed: [however], they thought it best to support [Henry VI] at that time, lest otherwise they might stir up the commonalty against themselves, [since the commonalty] loved, honoured and obeyed [the king] wonderfully for the holiness of his life. When matters were thus ordered, these three [York and the Nevilles] bore all the sway, as well concerning civil as foreign affairs; moreover, to the end that they might, following their own fantasies, without resistance, deprive King Henry either of kingdom or life at their pleasure, they removed from him, little by little, his old counsellors, put them from office and authority, and substituted in their places new men of their own. . . .

In the meantime, however, Henry Duke of Somerset and Humphrey Duke of Buckingham, with many other noblemen who held and stood with King Henry, lamenting his adversity, and not ignorant to what end all the Duke of York's crafty courtesy tended, [went] secretly to Queen Margaret, privately offered her their counsel, and declared that the Duke of York sought to deceive the king, yea, in very deed to kill him unawares. . . . The queen, much moved by this warning, and afraid both for herself and her husband, took occasion [to] persuade him [to] withdraw to Coventry. [The] king, seeing himself in danger, rode there and, calling an assembly of friends, discharged Richard Duke of York of the protectorship and the Earl of Salisbury of his office. . . .

Blore Heath and Ludford, 1459

Although, following the end of his second protectorate, Richard of York remained a prominent member of Henry VI's council, for several months he virtually disappeared from the political scene, spending much of the summer, in fact, at his Yorkshire castle of Sandal near Wakefield. Margaret of Anjou, at any rate if we are to believe Yorkist commentators, soon took advantage of this situation, as her hostility to the York/Neville connection became ever more implacable: indeed, not only did she engineer the court's withdrawal to the midlands in August 1456 (where she was joined, ominously, by the sons of the nobility killed at St Albans) but, over the next few years, deliberately sought to build up political support for the Lancastrian dynasty there and in the north-west, perhaps with the central aim of eliminating the Yorkist lords (not compromising with them). At a council held in Coventry in October 1456, a considerable and sustained verbal attack was launched on Richard of York, several moderates were dismissed from office and replaced by hardliners whose prime loyalty was to the queen and, arguably, what amounted to a political *coup* by the queen and her supporters ensured that York and his Neville allies became even more isolated than before; in November 1456 there was an attempted ambush of Warwick while he was journeying to London and, in December, York was assaulted in Coventry by the young Henry Beaufort Duke of Somerset; and, in November 1458, a determined effort to replace Warwick by Somerset as captain of Calais (despite, or perhaps even because of, a notable naval victory by the earl over a Spanish fleet in the English Channel earlier in the year) may well have been accompanied by another attempt on Neville's life (1, 2, 3a, 5, 7).

Why, then, did full-scale civil war not break out until the autumn of 1459? Perhaps Margaret of Anjou and her supporters were neither so powerful nor so malign as pro-Yorkist propagandists and chroniclers would have us believe. Perhaps the Yorkist lords, far from seeking to escalate political conflict, actually made every effort to prevent it. And, perhaps, Henry VI's own endeavours to promote peace and unity among the nobility, culminating in the so-called Loveday of 25 March 1458, should not be too easily discounted. Certainly, the extraordinary sequence of events in London early in 1458 very much caught the attention of contemporary and near-contemporary commentators (3b, 3c, 4, 5, 6, 7). At the king's summons, apparently, most of the great magnates of the realm (including Henry Beaufort Duke of Somerset, York and the Nevilles) arrived in

London, massively accompanied by their affinities (much to the alarm of the city authorities!), and mutually antagonistic to say the least; prolonged and complex negotiations eventually produced a reconciliation (when, most strikingly, the Yorkist lords agreed terms of restitution for the deaths of Edmund Beaufort Duke of Somerset, Henry Percy Earl of Northumberland and Thomas Lord Clifford at St Albans); and, on the Loveday itself, the king, the queen and all the lords solemnly processed through the streets to St Paul's: Henry VI, seemingly, wore his royal robes and crown; before him walked Richard Neville Earl of Salisbury and Henry Beaufort Duke of Somerset, as well as Henry Holland Duke of Exeter and Richard Neville Earl of Warwick; and, most remarkably of all, behind the king came Richard of York and Margaret of Anjou. And although, as the *English Chronicle* noted, 'peace and concord [did] not last long' (7), perhaps Henry VI's efforts did at least delay the resumption of hostilities. Even more important in preserving precarious peace, probably, was the reluctance of most of the nobility to take up arms at all: as in 1452 and 1455, the vast majority of lords remained loath to become involved in a civil war (particularly if an anointed king's possession of the throne might ultimately be challenged).

During 1459, however, the situation deteriorated markedly and, for this, responsibility probably lies primarily with Margaret of Anjou and her supporters rather than, as asserted at the Coventry Parliament later in the year, York, Salisbury and Warwick (2, 6). Indeed, if we are to believe the pro-Yorkist *English Chronicle*, the queen and her affinity now 'ruled the realm as she liked' and, in particular, 'sought the alliance of all the knights and squires of Cheshire', making her son Edward of Lancaster 'give a livery of swans to all the gentlemen of the countryside and to many others throughout the land, trusting through their strength to make her son king'. According to *Benet's Chronicle*, she firmly threw down the gauntlet in June 1459 at a great council held in Coventry where, in their absence and 'at the urging of the queen', the Yorkist lords were proclaimed traitors; when news of this reached the ears of York, Warwick and Salisbury, the chronicler continues, they 'resolved to journey to the king' (6). Certainly, the Yorkist leaders now began to arm with a vengeance and when, in September 1459, royal troops under the command of James Lord Audley intercepted a force led by Richard Neville Earl of Salisbury near Newcastle-under-Lyme in Staffordshire, bloodshed soon followed (6, 7). The battle of Blore Heath, fought on 23 September 1459, resulted, in fact, from Margaret of Anjou's determination to prevent Salisbury (journeying from his estates in north Yorkshire) joining his son Warwick (who had come over from Calais) and Richard of York at York's castle of Ludlow in the Welsh marches. There, according to the *English Chronicle*, both hosts fought 'a deadly battle' where, among the slain, were Audley himself and 'many of the notable knights and squires of Cheshire that had received the livery of the swans' (7). Following this confrontation, Salisbury marched to Worcester where he duly met York and Warwick; before long, however, the three lords did indeed proceed to Ludlow to await developments. Perhaps, as *Whethamsted's Register* tells us, their prime aim even now was to approach the king in person, 'with minds full of goodwill', and 'prostrate ourselves' at his feet 'to beg for grace' (1); alternatively, if we are to believe the version of events promulgated at the Coventry Parliament, 'intending the destruction of your most notable person', the Yorkist lords 'falsely and traitorously raised war against you' (2). In the end, no battle was fought at Ludlow: rather, on the night of 12/13 October 1459, the Yorkist lords simply fled (2, 6, 8, 9, 10). Chroniclers tend to emphasize, as critically important, the sudden desertion to Henry VI of Sir Andrew Trolloppe's Calais contingent but, in all probability, York, Salisbury and Warwick had already recognized the impossibility of defeating so powerful a royal force as that confronting them (8, 9, 10). Richard of York himself and his second son Edmund Earl of Rutland soon took ship for Ireland, while Salisbury, Warwick and York's eldest son Edward Earl of March (the future Edward IV) escaped to Calais (6, 8, 10). As for the Yorkist rank-and-file at Ludford, when confronted by the king in person and tempted by the promise of a free pardon, they simply melted away. When the Coventry Parliament met in November 1459 there was much deliberation as to whether (even now) the Yorkist lords should be pardoned or punished; however, in the end, the Parliament of Devils (as it was dubbed in Yorkist propaganda) settled for a detailed recital of Richard of York's alleged offences since 1450 and a vigorous character assassination of both York and his leading supporters, as a prelude to their attainder for treason (2).

1) Richard Neville Earl of Warwick's reasons for rejecting Henry VI's peace terms, October 1459
(*Whethamsted*, pp. 339–41; *Wilkinson*, pp. 131–2)
First, because we have had other and various pardons, and still have them. [Yet even] though we have had them confirmed [by] Parliament, they have not been of profit to us or done us good. . . . Nor were we summoned to councils or Parliaments, or admitted to any other business. It was as if [the king] had no faith at all in us; nor had he trust in his heart or mind.

Second, because, despite the pardons we obtained, the familiars of the king are so bold – almost all of them – and so stiff-necked that they do not fear to disobey royal commands. Nor do they fear, when they have transgressed, to be notorious on account of their misdeeds. They are a group of men without prudence or counsel. Would that they had wisdom and understanding, behaving more modestly in their manners and rule . . .

[Third], when the Earl of Warwick recently attended in person a certain council at Westminster [where] he gave counsel for the good of the kingdom, [he] would undoubtedly have been suffocated had God not sent aid from heaven . . .

For these three reasons, and especially because, in the opinion of many, general pardons are valueless these days [and] because we neither know how to, nor dare, approach the king's presence [or] enter his presence in person to beg for pardon, we must think therefore of [a] more infallible [stratagem]. We wish to approach in person, with minds full of good will, and to prostrate ourselves before [the king's] feet to beg for grace.

2) *Rolls of Parliament: Coventry Parliament, 1459*
(*Rotuli Parliamentorum*, Vol. 5, pp. 347–9)

. . . may it please your highness [Henry VI] to remember how, in the city of Coventry in your general council held there [in October 1456], the Duke of Buckingham, on behalf of the temporal lords, [sought] to make the Duke of York understand how badly he had conducted himself. [There] and then the Duke of Buckingham, and all the other lords, knelt on their knees and urged you, seeing the great danger to your noble person, and also considering that lords [such as York] had so often been charged [with disloyalty] and so often disturbed the great part of your realm, that you should no longer be pleased to show favour to the Duke of York, or any others, if they again attempted to act against your royal estate or to the disturbance of your realm. [Rather they should] receive what they deserved. . . . To which you were then pleased to say that you would do so, the Duke of York then being present, [and the] Duke of York then swore on the Holy Gospels, [promising] true and faithful obedience to you and your succession. . . .

[Following the Loveday of 1458] your highness trusted that tranquillity and due obedience would have followed on the part of the Duke of York and the Earls of Warwick and Salisbury. And you summoned them at different times to come to your councils. These summonses they disobeyed and they sent feigned and untrue excuses alleging frivolous business which, nevertheless, your highness accepted. Meanwhile, they enriched themselves by your gifts and grants, while continuing in their premeditated, malicious and damnable opinions and false and traitorous desires. . . .

[At Ludford in October 1459] Richard of York, Edward Earl of March, Richard Earl of Warwick, Richard Earl of Salisbury [and other lords], with other knights and people, whom they had blinded and assembled by wages, promises and other exquisite means, brought in certain persons to swear that you [Henry VI] were deceased, while mass was being said, [in order to] make the people less fearful of taking the field. . . . And intending the destruction of your most noble person, [they] falsely and traitorously raised war against you, shot their guns, and shot them as well at your most noble person as at the lords and people who were with you. . . .

Your highness offered pardon to all [the rebels, but the] leaders refused it. They tried to deceive their army by saying that Henry was dead. Henry, for his part, exhorted his troops. [But Almighty God] smote the hearts of the Duke of York and the Earls [of Salisbury and Warwick] suddenly from most presumptuous pride to the most shameful cowardice, so that about midnight [immediately after the events at Ludford], they fled out of the town [of Ludlow] unarmed, with a few followers, into Wales, [for they understood] that your people's hearts, blinded by them before, were now mostly converted by God's inspiration to repent, humbly submit themselves to you, and ask your grace, which the greater number of them did . . . Robert Radcliffe, one of the fellowship of the Duke of York, and the Earls of Warwick and Salisbury, confessed at his death that they would have seized, at their will and pleasure, both the crown of England and the duchy of Lancaster. . . .

Let it please your highness, by the advice and consent of your lords spiritual and temporal, and of your Commons assembled in this Parliament, [to] ordain, establish and enact [that] Richard Duke of York, Edward Earl of March, Richard Earl of Salisbury, Edmund Earl of Rutland, Richard Earl of Warwick [and others], for their treacherous levying of war against your most noble person at Ludford, [be] declared attainted of high treason, as false traitors and enemies against your most noble person, high majesty, crown and dignity. . . . And that they, and every one of them, forfeit from them and their heirs, all their estates, honours and dignities. . . .

3) Paston Letters
(*Paston Letters*, Vol. 3, pp. 108–9, 125, 127)

a) James Gresham to John Paston, 16 October 1456
. . . my lord chancellor is discharged. In his stead is my Lord of Winchester, my Lord of Shrewsbury is treasurer [and] Master Laurence Booth is [keeper of the] privy seal. And it is said that my Lord of York has been with the king, and has left again, in right good and favourable esteem with the king but not in favourable esteem with the queen. And some men say that if my Lord of Buckingham had not prevented it, my Lord of York would have been attacked as he left.

On Monday last there was a great affray at Coventry between the Duke of Somerset's men and the watchmen of the town; and two or three men of the town were killed, to the great jeopardy of all the lords there. For the alarm bell was rung, and the town arose, and would have attacked the Duke of Somerset had not the Duke of Buckingham prevented it.

Also it is said that the Duke of Buckingham has reacted most unfavourably to both his brothers being so suddenly discharged from their offices of chancellor and treasurer. This, among other things, causes his opinion to be opposed to the queen's intentions, and that of many others also, as it is said.

Also, some men say that the council [at Coventry] is dissolved, and that the king has left for Chester; also, some say many of the lords will return here, to London, by [1 November 1456].

b) William Botoner to Sir John Fastolfe, 1 February 1458
The king came to Westminster last week; the Duke of York came to London with his own household, [but] only to the number of 140 horse, as it is said; and the Earl of Salisbury with 400 horse in his company, four score knights and squires.

The Duke of Somerset came to London on the last day of January with 200 horse, and lodges outside the Temple Bar, and the Duke of Exeter shall be here this week, with a great and strong fellowship, as it is said.

The Earl of Warwick has not yet come, because the wind is not yet favourable for him: the Duke of Exeter is greatly displeased that my Lord of Warwick occupies his office, and takes upon him the keeping of the sea.

c) John Bocking, in London, to Sir John Fastolfe, 15 March 1458

. . . the council, in the morning, [is] at the Black Friars, for the convenience of the lords who are within the town, and, in the afternoon, at the White Friars in Fleet Street, for the lords outside the town. All matters shall come to a good conclusion with God's grace; for the king shall come here this week, and the queen also, as some men say, and my Lord of Buckingham with her, and many people. . . .

4) Contemporary Ballad: the Loveday of 1458
(*Robbins*, pp. 194–5)

. . . Love has put out malicious governance,
In every place both free and bond.
In York, in Somerset, as I understand,
In Warwick also is love and charity,
In Salisbury too, and in Northumberland,
That every man may rejoice in concord and unity.
Egremont and Clifford, with others foresaid,
Be set in the same opinion.
In every quarter love is thus laid,
Grace and wisdom have thus the domination. . . .
At [St] Paul's in London, with great renown,
On our Lady day in Lent this peace was wrought;
The king, the queen, with lords many a one,
To worship that Virgin as they ought,
Went in procession, and spared right nought,
In sight of all the commonalty,
In token that love was in heart and thought,
Rejoice, England, in concord and unity.

5) Short English Chronicle
(*Three Fifteenth Century Chronicles*, ed. J. Gairdner, pp. 70–1)

[In 1457] Sir Thomas Percy broke out of Newgate and, in the same year, there was a rising [in London] by mercers and other crafts against the Lombards. Afterwards, by command of the king, 28 mercers' men and others were sent to Windsor castle. . . . And in the same year the seneschal of Normandy Sir Pierre de

Brézé and [Robert de] Flocques came, with 3000 men, landed near Sandwich, and took the town and pillaged it, taking away much merchandise, slaying several people and taking many prisoners: [eventually they were] driven away and, while fleeing to their ships, more than 120 Frenchmen were drowned.

[In 1458], as the Duke of York and the Earl of Salisbury lay peaceably in London, there came to the city the Duke of Somerset, the Earl of Northumberland and Lord Egremont, and other lords of their affinity, [intending] to fight with the Duke of York. In the meantime the Earl of Warwick came from Calais with a goodly fellowship to help the Duke of York and his father [the Earl of Salisbury]. However, the mayor of London, with a goodly fellowship of armed men, kept the peace. . . . And the same year the Earl of Warwick defeated a Spanish fleet near Flanders. . . .

6) Benet's Chronicle
(*Benet*, pp. 221, 223–4; *Hallam*, pp. 218, 220)
[Early in 1458] a great council met at Westminster and, despite the king's absence, the council strove for peace between the lords: for there was a great quarrel between the Duke of Somerset and the Earl of Northumberland on one side, as a result of the deaths of their fathers at St Albans, and the Duke of York and the Earls of Warwick and Salisbury on the other. All these lords brought many men with them, the former [lodged] outside London and the latter inside . . . [On] 20 March the king and queen came to London [where on 25 March] the king, with great difficulty, engineered an agreement between the lords. Thereafter, as a sign of their amity, the king, queen and all the lords went in procession to St Paul's. . . .

[In late June 1459] the king held a great council at Coventry in the presence of the queen and prince but in the absence of the Archbishop of Canterbury, the Duke of York, the Earls of Salisbury, Warwick and Arundel, the Bishops of Ely and Exeter, Lord Bourchier, and others: there, at the urging of the queen, all the absent lords were indicted. . . . When they learned of this the Duke of York, and the Earls of Warwick and Salisbury, resolved to journey to the king. . . .

[On Friday 21 September 1459] the Earl of Warwick came to London, with 500 very well armed men, and then proceeded to Warwick. On the following Sunday the Earl of Salisbury, intent on approaching the king, was confronted, near Newcastle-under-Lyme, by 8000 men-at-arms of the queen's affinity. When they refused him passage the earl, accompanied by 3000 men, fought them [at Blore Heath], killed or captured 2000 of them and forced the rest to flee. [Soon afterwards] the Duke of York, and the Earls of Warwick and Salisbury, assembled an army of 25,000 near Worcester. The king and his lords, with 40,000 men arrayed for war and banner unfurled, advanced towards them. The Duke of York, however, not willing to give battle, retreated to Worcester as he saw the king approaching. When the king followed him he fell back to Tewkesbury and, since the king continued in pursuit, he crossed the Severn and made for Ludlow, [where] some of his men planned to betray him . . . [On 13 October] the Duke of York fled to Wales, while the Earls of Warwick and March made for Calais. The king, in response, created the Duke of Somerset captain of Calais and ravaged all the Duke of York's lands between Worcester and Ludlow. . . .

7) *English Chronicle*
(*Davies*, pp. 77–90)

[About Shrovetide 1458] a council was held at Westminster, to which came the young lords whose fathers had been slain at St Albans: the Duke of Somerset, the Earl of Northumberland and his brother Lord Egremont, and Lord Clifford, with a great power. They were lodged outside the walls of London, about Temple Bar and Westminster. The city could not receive them because they came against the peace. The Duke of York and the Earl of Salisbury came, but only with their household men, in peaceable manner, thinking no harm, and they were lodged within the city. [The former lords] came in order to destroy utterly the Duke of York and the Earls of Salisbury and Warwick, and the city was armed every day to withstand the malice of the young lords, if need had arisen. And soon after the Earl of Warwick came from Calais, of which he was captain, and lay within the city.

[Now] the bishops and other lords treated between them concerning peace and accord and, after long deliberation, both parties submitted to the judgement and arbitration of the king and his council, who, after thorough deliberation, gave this award and arbitration: a yearly rent of £45 should be funded in perpetuity by the Duke of York and the earls, in the abbey of St Albans where the slain [Lancastrian] lords were buried, to maintain prayer for their souls and for the souls of all who were slain there, and, in addition, the Duke of York and the earls should pay to the Duke of Somerset and his mother, to the Earl of Northumberland, and to the Lords Egremont and Clifford, a notable sum of money, to compensate for their fathers' deaths and for the wrongs done to them. Upon this, a document was written and security given and, so, trouble ceased, and peace and accord made between them: however, it did not last long. . . .

[On 9 November 1458], the king and queen being at Westminster, there occurred a great quarrel between Richard Earl of Warwick and men of the king's household, so much so that they would have slain the earl [had he not] escaped to his barge and went soon after to Calais, of which he had been made captain shortly before by authority of Parliament. Soon afterwards the young Duke of Somerset, by canvassing those who hated the Earl of Warwick, became captain of Calais, and a privy seal was directed to the earl to discharge him of the captainship: however the earl, forasmuch as he had been made captain by authority of Parliament, would not obey the privy seal but continued exercising the office for many years after. . . .

[On 23 September 1459] Richard Earl of Salisbury, having with him 7000 well arrayed men, fearing the malice of his enemies and especially of the queen and her company, which hated him mortally, and the Duke of York and Earl of Warwick also, took his way towards Ludlow where the Duke of York lay at that time, so that they both together would have ridden to the king at Coleshill in Staffordshire, to have cleared themselves of certain articles and false accusations touching their allegiance laid against them maliciously by their enemies. When the king heard of their coming, those who were about him counselled him to gather a power to withstand them, and informed him that they came to destroy him. The queen lay then at Eccleshall, and at once by her urging the king assembled a great power, whereof Lord Audley was chief and had the leading of them, and went forth to a field called Blore Heath, by which the Duke of York and the earl must needs pass. And there both hosts met and encountered together and fought a deadly battle. And there was Lord Audley slain, and many of the notable knights and squires of Cheshire that had received the livery of the swans [from Margaret of Anjou and her son earlier in the year]. And there were taken prisoner the Earl of Salisbury's two sons, Thomas and John. . . . After this discomfiture the earl went to Duke Richard at Ludlow, and thither to them, from Calais, the Earl of Warwick. . . .

8) Brut Chronicle
(*Brut*, pp. 526–7)
[Following the battle of Blore Heath] the Duke of York and the Earls of Warwick and Salisbury saw that the governance of the realm was exercised mostly by the queen and her council, while the great princes of the land were not called to the council but set apart. [Also] it was proclaimed throughout the realm that these lords should be destroyed utterly. [So they] assembled together with many people [in] the west country, to whom came the Earl of Warwick from Calais, with many old soldiers, such as Andrew Trollope and others. . . . When they were thus assembled, and made their field, the king sent out commissions and privy seals to all the lords of his realm to come and await upon him in their most defensible array. So every man came, in such numbers that the king was stronger and had far more people than the Duke of York and the Earls of Warwick and Salisbury: for it is here to be noted that no lord in England at this time dare disobey the queen, for she ruled all that was done about the king, who was a good, simple and innocent man.

When the king had come to the place where they all were, the Duke of York and his fellowship had made their field in the strongest manner and had prepared to fight, [during] the night Andrew Trollope and all the old soldiers of Calais, with a great fellowship, suddenly left the duke's host and went straight to the king's, where they were received joyously. . . . Then the Duke of York and the other lords, seeing themselves so deceived, took counsel briefly the same night and departed from the field, leaving behind most of their people. . . . Then the

Duke of York, with his second son, departed through Wales towards Ireland, leaving his eldest son the Earl of March with the Earls of Warwick and Salisbury, who, together with three or four men, rode straight to Devonshire. There, by the help and aid of one Dinham, a squire, who secured a ship for them, [they] sailed to Guernsey, where they refreshed themselves, and thereafter to Calais. . . .

9) Jean de Waurin
(*Lander*, p. 95)
[In October 1459] the Duke of York, like a valiant prince, ordered that, the following day in the morning, each should take himself to the field, which they did, and took themselves towards Ludlow hoping to find the king's company in disorder. However, they did not do so, for the king's people still held together, so much so that they came to battle the one against the other, and my Lord of Warwick drew up his forces putting Andrew Trollope to lead the vanguard because he trusted him more than he trusted anybody else. This Andrew had received news by a secret and extremely well written message from the Duke of Somerset which rebuked him because he was coming to wage war against the king his sovereign lord, saying as well that the king had proclaimed among his host that all those who were adherents to the opposing party but wished to return to serve the king would receive both great rewards and a pardon for everything. Then Andrew Trollope secretly went to the members of the Calais garrison and so exhorted them that they all came together to the Earl of Warwick and told him that they did not wish to fight against their sovereign lord and immediately turned tail without anyone being able to stop them.

10) Crowland Chronicle: Second (1459–1486) Continuation
(*Crowland*, pp. 108–11; *Ingulph*, pp. 453–4)
[In October 1459] preparations for a battle were well advanced, near the town of Ludlow in the Welsh marches, between King Henry and those faithful to him on the one side, and Richard Duke of York, his sons, kinsmen, connections and affinity, especially the Earls of Salisbury and Warwick, father and son, on the other. The king's party, however, got stronger every day, with the gathering of great numbers both of nobles and common people, particularly after Andrew Trollope and his mercenaries from Calais, who had been summoned by their captain the Earl of Warwick from overseas, as though for the service of the king, had deserted the duke. For, finding that, contrary to their expectations, they had been committed against the king, they chose instead to support the king who had provided their keep and their wages. As a result, the duke's army was disbanded and, while he himself retreated to Ireland, his eldest son Edward Earl of March, together with the two earls, father and son, sailed to Calais. In the mean time, a Parliament having been summoned to Coventry, the duke and the earls were attainted, and their goods and inheritances transferred to new owners.

Northampton and Wakefield, 1460

Richard Neville Earl of Warwick had been a notably high-profile captain of Calais in the later 1450s and, although Henry Beaufort Duke of Somerset now held the office in theory, Warwick, his father Richard Neville Earl of Salisbury and York's eldest son Edward Earl of March found a safe refuge there following the rout at Ludford in October 1459: indeed, for several months Calais became the main centre of Yorkist operations (1, 2a, 2b). Superior Yorkist intelligence, moreover, foiled all efforts to dislodge the Yorkist earls: early attempts by Somerset to take Calais failed, not least since, so the *Brut* tells us, 'the shipmen owed more favour to the Earl of Warwick than the Duke of Somerset' (1); when Richard Lord Rivers and his son Sir Anthony Woodville gathered a fleet at Sandwich to help him, the Yorkist John Dinham raided the town during the night of 15 January 1460, seized both the Woodvilles and many of their ships, and brought them to Calais, where they were thoroughly humiliated (1, 2a, 2b); and, in June 1460, a similar fate befell a second Lancastrian fleet assembled at Sandwich (1). Meanwhile, the Yorkist earls launched a vigorous propaganda campaign from Calais, even enlisting the services of a Papal legate Francesco Coppini (5a), and particularly targeting south-eastern England. In March 1460 Warwick sailed to Ireland to consult with Richard of York and perhaps, as Ralph Griffiths has speculated, the possibility of deposing Henry VI was first seriously discussed at this time (1). Three months later the Yorkist earls embarked from Calais, landing at Sandwich on 26 June 1460, and, although the Lancastrian government had put defence measures in place in anticipation of an invasion, they proved ineffective (1, 2b, 5a). The anti-government sentiment in south-eastern England that had produced Cade's rebellion a decade earlier remained as powerful as ever and, as the Yorkist lords made their way towards London, they attracted a great deal of support; the city authorities, if only after considerable soul-searching (for London had hitherto been more or less loyal to Lancaster), opened the capital's gates to Warwick, Salisbury and March on 2 July (and, henceforth, London proved a great asset to the Yorkists); and shortly afterwards, Warwick and March set off in search of Henry VI (1, 3, 5a, 5b). At Northampton they ran him to ground and, after prolonged but abortive negotiations, battle was joined outside the town on 10 July (1, 3, 4, 5b). Most battles of the Wars of the Roses tend to be poorly reported, and this is certainly true of Northampton, although the *English Chronicle* does remark, intriguingly, that the 'ordnance of the king's guns availed not, for that day was so great rain that the guns lay deep in the water and were so quenched that they might not be shot'. Victory went to the Yorkists and, most importantly, Henry VI now fell into their hands. At this stage, despite rumours to the contrary (5b), there was no question of removing the king from the throne: rather, as the second Crowland continuator learned, 'the victorious earls paid all honours of royalty to King Henry', conducting him to London 'in solemn procession', the Earl of Warwick, 'bare-headed, carrying a sword before the king, in all humility and respect' (4). Soon, a Yorkist-controlled regime was established in Henry VI's name, albeit a partisan and narrowly-based administration very much dominated by the Nevilles (2c), exercising little authority beyond London and south-eastern England.

Strangely absent, for several weeks, was Richard of York until, perhaps out of the blue, he returned from Ireland early in September 1460. From the moment of his arrival in Cheshire, moreover, he probably made it clear that he had come to claim the throne for himself and, when he entered London early in October, it was like a king: surrounded by a substantial body of retainers, trumpets blaring, banners (charged with the arms of England) held aloft, and with his sword borne upright before him in truly regal fashion (1, 3, 4, 6). Several chronicles relate the dramatic sequence of events that now took place in Westminster Hall where Parliament was meeting (1, 3, 4, 6). The most graphic description, probably an eye-witness account, is provided by *Whethamsted's Register*: Richard of York, declared the chronicler, entered the Parliament chamber 'with great pomp and splendour and in no small exaltation of mood', made directly for the royal throne, and 'laid his hand on the drape or cushion as if about to take possession of what was his by right' (6). If he expected acclamation, he certainly did not get it. Indeed, if we are to believe Jean de Waurin, even York's friends were dismayed by his actions, particularly Richard Neville Earl of Warwick (7). Nevertheless, York now submitted a formal claim to the throne and, after prolonged and probably heated debate in Parliament, a compromise was cobbled together in the so-called Act of Accord on 24 October 1460: under the terms of this, Henry VI was to retain the crown as long as he lived but, after his death, Richard of York and his heirs were to succeed (1, 3, 4, 8b). Less surprisingly, the Coventry Parliament and all its proceedings were declared null and void (8a). As for Henry VI, he became, even more than before, a virtual prisoner of the Yorkists (3, 4, 6, 7).

Clearly, none of this was acceptable to stalwart Lancastrians, most particularly Margaret of Anjou, since the Act of Accord (if ever fully implemented) would have disinherited her beloved son Prince Edward of Lancaster. The queen, in fact, had every intention of fighting back with every weapon in her considerable armoury; she enjoyed a great deal of northern support; and, as the *Annales Rerum Anglicarum* record, the Yorkshire estates of both the Nevilles and Richard of York were targeted for vandalism and devastation (9). The Lancastrian leadership, meanwhile, demonstrated real military panache in establishing a powerful force in the vicinity of Hull (3, 4, 5c, 6, 9, 10). Richard of York, in response, marched north in December

1460, accompanied by Richard Neville Earl of Salisbury and Edmund Earl of Rutland, and, shortly before Christmas, arrived at York's castle of Sandal near Wakefield (3, 4, 5c, 6, 9, 10). A few days later, on 30 December, he made the foolish decision to engage a much larger army than his own at the battle of Wakefield and, perhaps partly as a result of treachery in his own ranks, sustained a major defeat in the field (3, 4, 5c, 6, 9, 10, 11). Among the slain was Salisbury's son Sir Thomas Neville and worse was to follow when, next day, Salisbury himself was executed at nearby Pontefract (3, 5c, 6, 9, 10): thus, arguably, the deaths of Henry Percy second Earl of Northumberland at St Albans in 1455 and his son Thomas Lord Egremont at Northampton earlier in 1460 were revenged. Despite the colourful story in *Whethamsted's Register*, Richard of York almost certainly lost his life during the fighting at Wakefield (3, 4, 5c, 6, 9, 10, 11). Soon after the battle, probably, York's second son Edmund of Rutland fell into the hands of John Lord Clifford: 'Butcher' Clifford apparently wasted no time, given such a splendid opportunity, of avenging *his* father's death at St Albans too (3, 5c, 9, 10). Thereafter, according to the *Annales*, the heads of all the leading Yorkists who had lost their lives were despatched to the city of York and placed on 'various gateways' there: the head of Richard of York himself, the annalist adds, was 'in contempt crowned with a paper crown' (9).

1) Brut Chronicle
(*Brut*, pp. 528–30)

[Following the rout of Ludford] the king ordained the Duke of Somerset to be captain of Calais, [who] made himself ready in all haste to go to Calais and take possession of his office. [However] when he came he found the Earl of Warwick resident there as captain, and the Earls of March and Salisbury also, [so he] went to Guisnes. [Thereafter] some of the ships which had come over with him entered the harbour of Calais of their own free will, for the shipmen owed more favour to the Earl of Warwick than the Duke of Somerset. . . . After this, men came over the sea daily to these lords in Calais, who began to become stronger. [The] Duke of Somerset in Guisnes also got people to him, who came out and skirmished with those of Calais, and they with them, for many days. . . .

[In January 1460] the lords of Calais sent over Master [John] Dinham, with a great company, to Sandwich, where he took the town, captured Lord Rivers and his son Lord Scales, seized many ships in the harbour and brought them all to Calais; [yet] many mariners of their own free will came to Calais with the ships in order to serve the Earl of Warwick.

After this the Earl of Warwick, by the advice of the lords, took all his ships, manned them well and sailed to Ireland to speak with the Duke of York and take his advice about how they should enter into England again. When he had been there, and done his errands, he returned to Calais, bringing with him his mother the Countess of Salisbury. While he was sailing near the west country the Duke of Exeter, admiral of England, aboard the *Grace Dieu* and accompanied by many ships of war, met with the Earl of Warwick's fleet: however, they did not fight, since many of the men with the Duke of Exeter owed better will and more favour to the earl than to him; so they departed, and came to Calais in safety, blessed by God!

The king's council, seeing that these lords had seized ships from Sandwich and taken Lord Rivers and his son, ordered the setting up of a garrison at Sandwich, made [Osbert] Mundford captain of the town, and warned men and merchants visiting Flanders not to go to Calais. They of Calais, seeing this, sent Master Dinham and many others to Sandwich, [where] they assaulted the town by water and land, and struck off the head of its captain Mundford; and, daily, men came over to Calais from all parts of England.

After this the Earls of March, Warwick and Salisbury came over to Dover [in June 1460] with many people and landed there, drew all the country to them, and came armed to London, [where] they informed the lords of the king's council that, although they intended no harm to the king's person, they would put from him such people as were about him. And so they departed from London, with a great company, towards Northampton, where the king was [and who], with many lords, had made a strong field outside the town. There both forces met and a great battle was fought, in which were slain the Duke of Buckingham, the Earl of Shrewsbury, Viscount Beaumont, many knights and squires, and others. The king himself was taken in the field and afterwards brought to London. . . .

[While] Parliament was meeting at Westminster the Duke of York came out of Ireland [in September 1460], with the Earl of Rutland. Riding with a great company into the palace of Westminster, he took the king's palace, came into the Parliament chamber, took the king's place and claimed the crown as his proper inheritance and right, putting in writing his title and claim to be rightful heir. After much debate, it was decreed and concluded that King Henry should reign and be king during his natural life, forasmuch as he had so long been king and was in possession [of the crown]. After his death the Duke of York should be king and his heirs after him and, immediately, he should be proclaimed heir apparent and also protector of England during the king's life. [Moreover] if King Henry during his life broke the agreement, or any article concluded in this Parliament, he should be deposed, and the duke should take the crown and be king. All these things were enacted by the authority of Parliament. [While] the Commons of the realm were assembled in the common house, debating the title of the Duke of York, the crown hanging in the midst of their house suddenly fell down: this was taken as an omen that the reign of King Henry was ended. The crown which stood on the highest tower of the steeple in Dover castle also fell down this year.

2) Paston Letters
(*Paston Letters*, Vol. 3, pp. 203, 204–5, 226)
a) William Botoner, in London, to John Berney, January 1460
. . . . Lord Rivers, Sir Anthony his son, and others, have been taken to Calais,

following a slight assault on Sandwich by [John] Dinham, with 800 men, on Tuesday between 4 and 5 o'clock in the morning. . . . The Duke of York is in Dublin, strengthened by his earls and homagers. . . . God send the king victory over his enemies, and rest and peace among his lords!

b) William Paston, in London, to John Paston, 28 January 1460

. . . my Lord Rivers was brought to Calais and, before the lords with eight score torches, my Lord of Salisbury berated him, calling him knave's son, that he should be so rude as to call him and [his fellow] lords traitors, for they shall be found the king's true liegemen when he should be found a traitor. And my Lord of Warwick berated him, and said that his father was but a squire, and brought up with King Henry V, and since made himself by marriage, and also made lord, and that it was not his place to use such language about lords of the king's blood. And my Lord of March berated him likewise. And Sir Anthony was berated for his language about all three lords. . . .

[The] king comes towards London and, as it is said, raises people as he comes: it is certain commissions have been directed to several shires, every man to be ready, in his best array, to come when the king sends for him. . . .

c) Friar Brackley to John Paston, October 1460

. . . God save our good lords, Warwick and all his brothers, and Salisbury, [and] preserve them from treason and poison, [for] if anything but good come to my Lord of Warwick, farewell ye, farewell I, and all our friends, [since] this land would be utterly undone . . . God defend them, and grant them grace to know their friends from their enemies, and to cherish and prefer their friends and lessen the might of all their enemies throughout the shires of the land.

3) Gregory's Chronicle
(*Gregory*, pp. 207–10)

[Following the arrival of the Yorkist lords at Sandwich in June 1460] the commons of Kent and their well-wishers brought them to London, and so on to Northampton. There they met with the king and fought courageously with the king's lords and company, but there was much favour in that field towards the Earl of Warwick. They took the king there, and created new officers of the land as chancellor, treasurer and others, but did not occupy them immediately [since they were awaiting] the coming of the Duke of York out of Ireland. In that field were slain the Duke of Buckingham, standing still at his tent, the Earl of Shrewsbury, Lords Beaumont and Egremont, and many other men. And many men were drowned in the river near the field. . . .

[In September 1460] the Duke of York came out of Ireland, [journeyed] towards London, [gave] banners charged with the arms of England to trumpeters and, commanding his sword be borne upright before him, rode to King Harry's palace at Westminster, and there claimed the crown of England. He kept King Harry there by force and strength until, at last, the king, for fear of death, granted him the crown: for a man that has little wit will soon be afraid of death, [although] I trust and believe there was no man that would have done him bodily harm. However, the lords asked earnestly that King Harry should retain the crown during his life, the crown returning to the duke's heirs after his death, and thereupon swore to be faithful and true to King Harry; also that it should be treason to speak any evil of the Duke of York, his wife or any of his children. All the lords agreed to this, and so it was proclaimed in London and many places in England. [Also it was decreed that] the duke should receive from the crown yearly, for his expenses and those of his heirs during King Harry's life, 10,000 marks in money. This accord was made on the last day of October [1460].

That same night the king was moved [from Westminster] to London, against his will, to the Bishop of London's palace, and the Duke of York came to him that same night by torchlight, behaving as if he were king, and said in many places that 'this is ours by very right'. The queen, hearing this, went away into Wales [but] one of her own servants, whom she had [created] an officer of her son the prince, plundered and robbed her, and put her in doubt of her life and her son's life also. Then she came to the castle of Harlech in Wales, where she received many great gifts and was greatly comforted, of which she had need. . . . Thereafter she moved very secretly to Jasper Earl of Pembroke, for she dare not stay in any place that was open, but only secretly. The reason was that counterfeit tokens were sent to her as though they had come from her most revered lord Henry VI; however, they were not of his sending [but] forged things, for they that brought the tokens were of the king's house, and some of the prince's house, and some of her own house, and warned her beware of the tokens, so she gave no credence to them. For, at the king's departure from Coventry towards the field of Northampton, he kissed her and blessed the prince and commanded her not to come to him till he should send her a special token that no man knew but the king and she. For the lords would have liked to have got her to London, for they knew well that all the arts that were done were encouraged by her, for she was more intelligent than the king. . . .

The queen, having knowledge of these matters, sent to the Duke of Somerset, at that time in Dorset at the castle of Corfe, and for the Earl of Devon and Alexander Hody, and prayed them to come to her as hastily as they could, with their tenants as strong in armour as men of war, for Lords Roos, Clifford, Greystoke, Neville and Latimer were waiting upon the Duke of Exeter to meet with her at Hull. This matter was not delayed but very secretly done, and she sent letters to all her chief officers that they would do the same, and that they should warn all those servants that loved her or meant to preserve and encourage her royal office, to wait upon her at Hull by the day she appointed. All these people were gathered and conveyed so secretly that they were assembled to the number of 15,000 before any man would believe it; so that if any man said, or told, or talked of such a gathering, he would be disgraced; and some were in great danger, for the common people said to those that told the truth, 'You talk just as if you wished it were so', and gave no credence to their saying.

Eventually the lords [in London] learned the truth and, on 9 December [1460] the Duke of York, the Earl of Salisbury, the Earl of Rutland (who was the Duke of York's second son, one of the best disposed lords in this land) and Sir Thomas Harrington, and many more knights, squires and numerous people with them, set off from London towards York. [On 30 December] the Dukes of Exeter and Somerset, the Lords Roos, Neville and Clifford, many more knights, squires and gentlemen, and the commons of the queen's party, met with the Duke of York at Wakefield. There they made a great assault on the Duke of York, and took him and the Earl of Salisbury, the Earl of Rutland, and Lord Harrington, and Sir Thomas Neville and Sir Thomas Harrington, and many more knights were taken and slain beside all the commons. This good Duke of York, with his lords aforesaid, lost their heads: God have mercy on their souls, for they lost in that encounter 2500 men, [while] in the queen's party were slain but 200.

4) Crowland Chronicle: Second (1459–1486) Continuation
(*Crowland*, pp. 111–13; *Ingulph*, pp. 454–6)

[In June 1460 the Earls of March, Salisbury and Warwick] crossed from Calais and landed in Kent and a great battle was fought near Northampton [on 10 July] between King Henry and the earls with their respective supporters. There fell on the king's side the Duke of Buckingham, the Earl of Shrewsbury, Viscount Beaumont, Lord Egremont and other nobles, as well as innumerable common men. The victorious earls paid all honours of royalty to King Henry and conducted him to London in solemn procession, Richard Neville Earl of Warwick, bare-headed, carrying a sword before the king, in all humility and respect.

[In October 1460] the Duke of York came over from Ireland to Westminster, at the time of the beginning of Parliament, and, as soon as he had entered the upper chamber of the royal palace where the lords spiritual and temporal were sitting, he approached the royal throne and claimed the sole right of sitting upon it; he then put forward a genealogy tracing his lineal descent from Lionel Duke of Clarence, to whose successors, he asserted, the kingdom of England rightly belonged, since he was the elder [son of Edward III], rather than to the descendants of John Duke of Lancaster, the younger brother [of Lionel] from whom King Henry was descended; he also protested that he would no longer endure the injustices which the three Henrys, who were usurpers, had for so long inflicted upon his line. Thereafter, he immediately entered the inner rooms of the palace, compelled King Henry to remove to the queen's apartments, and took over the king's apartments himself. This disturbance continued, albeit without killing or bloodshed, for about three weeks [until 31 October], during which time the whole Parliament was occupied with discussion of the duke's lineage and rights. [On 31 October] a settlement of the differences was concluded in the following manner: the duke and his sons, Edward Earl of March and Edmund Earl of Rutland, who had both reached the age of discretion, were to swear fealty to the king and to recognize him as their king for as long as he might live – this much having already been decreed in Parliament – but it was added, with the king's own consent, that immediately upon the king's death the duke and his heirs be sanctioned to claim and take possession of the crown of England. Matters being so arranged, the duke withdrew from the palace of Westminster to his London house, leaving the king and his men in peace.

At this time Queen Margaret, with Prince Edward, the only son of the king and herself, was staying in the north. Since the queen's northern supporters found Parliament's decree both odious and execrable, the people and nobles of those parts rose up with the aim of altering it; thereupon the Duke of York, accompanied by his son the Earl of Rutland and Richard Earl of Salisbury, set out for Wakefield to put down the rising and, in the ensuing battle, he was defeated and slain.

5) Milanese State Papers
(*CSPM*, pp. 24, 27, 42)
a) Francesco Coppini, Bishop of Terni and Papal Legate, to Henry VI: open letter displayed at St Paul's Cross, 4 July 1460
. . . on coming to Calais, owing to recent events I found almost everything in turmoil, and [the Yorkist] lords all ready to cross to England, declaring they could not wait any longer in the existing state of affairs. Nevertheless, after I had conferred with them and exhorted them to peace and obedience, they gave me a written pledge that they were disposed to devotion and obedience to your majesty, and to do all in their power for the conservation and augmentation of your honour and the good of your realm. However, they desired to come to your majesty and be received into their former state and favour, from which, they declare, they had been ousted by the craft of their opponents. They begged me to cross the sea with them to interpose my efforts and prevent bloodshed, assuring me that they would do anything honourable and just that I should approve for the honour and estate of your highness and the welfare of your realm, especially certain things contained in documents under their own seals and oaths, which they handed over, and which I am confident your serenity would approve after viewing them with a tranquil and open mind, as they tend to the honour and glory of your lordship, the public exaltation of the realm and the honour and advantage of princes and lords . . . [Seeing] danger in delay, I crossed with them, there being no other way. Their business, passage and progress were more speedy than they themselves had at first anticipated or hoped for, on account of people flocking to them out of a remarkable eagerness for their arrival and the reunion

of the whole realm . . . [They] crossed the sea on Thursday and went straight on till they reached London. . . .

b) Newsletters from Bruges, 7/15 July 1460, and London, 7/10 July 1460: A Digest
. . . the Earls of Warwick, Salisbury and March, and other lords and knights passed from Calais, took Sandwich and then went on to London, where they were received by the people of the place. With them was Francesco Coppini, the papal legate, with about 20,000 people. This happened on Wednesday, and they remained until Saturday, when all left and went towards the king, except the Earl of Salisbury who remained here [in London]. The Archbishop of Canterbury went with them, and the Bishop of Exeter and his followers and all their power. . . . They also say that the Duke of York will descend upon the country with a large number of troops. . . .

When the king heard of Warwick's arrival, he took himself to a valley between two mountains, a strong place. But Fortune, who throughout showed herself favourable to Warwick, ordained that it should rain so heavily that they were forced to come out of that place and encounter Warwick. Without a serious fight, or much slaughter, Warwick very soon had the king in his power. He forthwith put to death the Duke of Buckingham, one of the great lords of that country, and the Lords Beaumont, Egremont and Shrewsbury, all great lords. That happened last Friday, and today he should be in London, the king having come from Warwick. In that place are several other lords, and there also the Duke of York and all their friends will soon go, where they will gather for mutual support, appoint new officers and arrange the government of the country. This will remain in the hands of Warwick. It is not thought that he will stay his hand, but will put to death all those who have acted against him. It is also thought that they will make a son of the Duke of York king, and that they will pass over the king's son, as they are beginning already to say that he is not the king's son. Similarly, the queen also runs great danger. . . . Thus one may say that today everything is in Warwick's power and the war at an end, and that he has done marvellous things. God grant him grace to keep the country in peace and union. . . .

c) Newsletter from London, 9 January 1461
Some of the lords of the queen's party, rendered desperate by the victory of the lords here, and especially by the Earl of Warwick, assembled a force in the northern parts, [to] come and attack their opponents here who are with the king, and get the king back into their power. Accordingly, the Duke of York, with two of his sons and Warwick's father the Earl of Salisbury, went out to meet them [at Wakefield]. And it came to pass that, although they were three times stronger, yet from lack of discipline, because they allowed a large part of the force to go pillaging and searching for victuals, their adversaries, who are desperate, attacked the duke and his followers. Ultimately they routed them, slaying the duke and his younger son the Earl of Rutland, Warwick's father, and many others.

6) *Whethamsted's Register*

(*Whethamsted*, pp. 376–8, 381–2; *Wilkinson*, p. 170; *Lander*, p. 108; *EHD*, pp. 283–4)

[When Richard of York returned from Ireland] there were varied and contrary rumours amongst the people about his return. Some said that his arrival was peaceful and that he intended nothing else but the restoration of harmony among the quarrelling lords of the realm, bringing peace to the kingdom, and reforming it, by his authority. Yet others, including those who were older and wiser, suspected that he meant to act litigiously against the king for the royal crown and claim it for himself by title of hereditary right. . . .

[Almost] at the beginning of a Parliament assembled at Westminster for the good government of the realm, the Duke of York suddenly arrived, with great pomp and splendour and in no small exaltation of mood, for he came with trumpets and horns, men-at-arms and a very large retinue. Entering the palace there, he marched straight through the great hall until he came to the solemn chamber where the king, with the Commons, was accustomed to hold Parliament. When he arrived he made directly for the king's throne, where he laid his hand on the drape or cushion, as if about to take possession of what was his by right, and held his hand there for a brief time. At last, withdrawing it, he turned towards the people and, standing quietly under the cloth of state, looked eagerly at the assembly awaiting their acclamation. Whilst he stood there, turning his face to the people and awaiting their applause, Thomas Bourchier Archbishop of Canterbury arose and, after a suitable greeting, enquired whether he wished to come and see the king. The duke, who seemed irritated by this request, replied curtly: 'I do not recall that I know anyone in the kingdom whom it would not befit to come to me and see my person, rather than I should go and visit him.' When the archbishop heard this reply, he quickly withdrew and told the king of the duke's response. After the archbishop had left, the duke also withdrew, went to the principal chamber of the palace (the king being in the queen's apartments), smashed the locks and threw open the doors, in a regal rather than a ducal manner, and remained there for some time. When news of the duke's high-handedness became known to the people, and they heard how, of his own ill-considered judgement and without any weighty discussion, he had so entered, everyone, of whatever estate, rank, age, sex, order or condition, immediately began to grumble fervently against him and assert he had acted rashly. . . .

[Soon afterwards Richard of York] by authority of the king journeyed northwards to subdue the people of that region who, at the instigation of Queen Margaret and many lords who had taken her side, had rebelled against him . . . [There] set out with him the distinguished and eminent lord Richard Neville Earl of Salisbury. [Following their arrival at the Duke of York's town of Wakefield] they heard that the northern men were coming in large numbers: [nevertheless, they] relaxed in their castles and went foraging for victuals. [The northerners], before the appointed day of battle, attacked them and, overcoming them by the weight of their numbers, killed many and put many to flight. They took the two lords [York and Salisbury] alive in the battle and treated them with great mockery, especially the Duke of York. They stood him on a little anthill and placed on his head, as if a crown, a vile garland made of reeds, just as the Jews did to the Lord, and bent the knee to him, saying in jest: 'Hail King, without rule. Hail King, without ancestry. Hail leader and prince, with almost no subjects or possessions'. And, having said this and various other shameful and dishonourable things to him, at last they cut off his head. . . . The Lord Salisbury they took to the castle of Pontefract and there, at the impious, shameless and savage instigation of certain perverse men, they beheaded him.

7) Jean de Waurin
(*Lander*, pp. 109–10)
[On arrival in London in October 1460] the Duke of York rode straight to the palace [of Westminster], at which the people were greatly taken aback. When he had dismounted he went to lodge in the royal chamber and the king was placed in the custody of six of the duke's men. The Earl of Salisbury, observing the manner of these proceedings, without saying anything, left and went to London to his son the Earl of Warwick [where] he recounted to him all the ordering and government of the Duke of York, and how the king had been put out of his chamber. When the Earl of Warwick heard his father speak he became very angry [and] said he would go [to Richard of York] himself: so he called on Thomas Neville and other supporters, entered his barge on the Thames and went to the palace (which he found full of armed men). When he saw this disposition, he doubted whether the duke intended to come to an understanding with him. Nevertheless, the earl did not abandon his enterprise but entered the duke's chamber and found him leaning on a cupboard. When the duke saw him he walked forward and so they greeted each other: there were angry words between the two of them, for the earl disclosed to the duke how the lords and people were unhappy at his desire to strip the king of the crown. During these exchanges the Earl of Rutland, brother to the Earl of March, arrived and said to the Earl of Warwick: 'Fair cousin, you must not be angry, for you know that it is our right to have the crown, which belongs to my lord my father, and he will keep it as anyone may see.'

8) Rolls of Parliament

a) Reversal of the Coventry Attainders, October 1460
(*Rotuli Parliamentorum*, Vol. 5, p. 374)
[Several] seditious and evil disposed persons, having no regard [for] your most noble person and realm, sinisterly and importunately begged your highness [Henry VI] to call a Parliament to be held at Coventry [on 30 November 1459], for the sole intention of destroying certain of the great, noble, faithful and true

lords of your blood, and other true liege people of this your realm. [This] Parliament was duly summoned, and a great part of the knights for several shires, and many citizens and burgesses for several cities and towns, [were] returned and accepted, some of them without due and free election, and some of them without any election, against your laws and the liberties of the commons, by the means and labour of these seditious persons. . . .

Please it your highness [to] ordain, enact and establish, by the advice and assent of the lords spiritual and temporal in this Parliament, that the Parliament held at Coventry be void and declared no Parliament, and all acts, statutes and ordinances made by its authority be reversed, annulled, repealed, revoked, and of no force or effect. . . .

b) Act of Accord, 24 October 1460
(*Rotuli Parliamentorum*, Vol. 5, pp. 378–9)
. . . Richard Duke of York, tenderly desiring the weal, peace and prosperity of this land, and to set apart all that might be trouble to the same, [considering that] King Henry the Sixth [has] been named, taken and reputed King of England and of France [during] his natural life, [agrees], without hurt or prejudice to his own right and title, [to] take, worship and honour him [Henry VI] for his sovereign lord.

. . . it is accorded, appointed and agreed that Richard Duke of York be entitled, called and reputed from henceforth, very and rightful heir to the crowns [of England and France] and, after the death of Henry [VI], the duke and his heirs shall immediately succeed to these crowns. . . .

. . . Richard Duke of York shall have, by authority of Parliament, castles, manors, lands etc [to] the yearly value of 10,000 marks, of which 5000 marks shall be to his own estate, 3500 marks to Edward Earl of March, his first son, for his estate, and £1000 to Edmund Earl of Rutland, his second son. . . .

9) Annales Rerum Anglicarum
(*Annales*, pp. 774–5; *Thornley*, pp. 8–9; *EHD*, pp. 285–6)
The Earl of Northumberland, the Lords Clifford, Dacre and Neville, held a council at York [in November 1460] and plundered the tenants of the Duke of York and the Earl of Salisbury. And the Duke of Somerset and the Earl of Devon, with many knights and gentlemen of the west parts, fully armed, came through Bath, Cirencester, Evesham and Coventry to York. . . .

The Duke of York, with the Earl of Salisbury and many thousands of soldiers, started from London towards York. . . . On 21 December [1460] the Duke of York and the Earl of Salisbury, with 6000 fighting men, came to Sandal castle, where they spent Christmas, while the Duke of Somerset and the Earl of Northumberland with the opposite party lay at Pontefract. King Henry with the Earl of Warwick and others spent Christmas in the Bishop of London's palace at St Paul's. Edward Earl of March spent Christmas in the town of Shrewsbury at the friary.

On 29 December [1460] at Wakefield, while the Duke of York's men were roaming about the countryside in search of victuals, a fierce battle was fought between the Duke of Somerset, the Earl of Northumberland and Lord Neville with a great army, and the other party: there fell in the field the Duke of York, Thomas Neville, son of the Earl of Salisbury, Thomas Harrington, [many] other knights and squires, and 2000 of the common people. And in the flight after the battle Lord Clifford killed Edmund Earl of Rutland, son of the Duke of York, on the bridge at Wakefield. And the same night the Earl of Salisbury was taken by a servant of Andrew Trollope. And next day the Bastard of Exeter slew the Earl of Salisbury at Pontefract, where by the counsel of the lords they beheaded the dead bodies of the Duke of York, the Earls of Salisbury and Rutland, Thomas Neville, Thomas Harrington [and four others], and placed their heads on various gateways at York. And also, in contempt, they crowned the head of the Duke of York with a paper crown.

When the battle was over, Queen Margaret came from Scotland to York, where, by the counsel of the lords, it was decided to march with all possible strength to London and rescue King Henry from the hands of his enemies. . . .

10) English Chronicle
(*Davies*, pp. 106–7)

[In December 1460] the Duke of Somerset and the Earl of Devon went to the north country with 800 men; and, immediately after, the Duke of York, the Earl of Rutland his son, and the Earl of Salisbury, a little before Christmas, with a few people, also went to the north, intending to repress the malice of the northern men who loved not the Duke of York nor the Earl of Salisbury, and they were lodged at the castle of Sandal and at Wakefield. Then Lord Neville, brother of the Earl of Westmorland, under a false colour went to the Duke of York, desiring a commission from him to raise men in order to chastise the rebels of the country: the duke granted this request, believing him to be true and of his party. When he had this commission he raised to the number of 8000 men, and brought them to the lords of the country: that is to say, to the Earl of Northumberland, Lord Clifford and the Duke of Somerset, who were adversaries and enemies of Duke Richard. When they saw a convenient time to fulfil their cruel intentions, on the last day of December, they fell upon Duke Richard, and killed him, his son the Earl of Rutland, and many other knights and squires; that is to say, Lord Harrington, a young man, Sir Thomas Harrington, Sir Thomas Neville, son to the Earl of Salisbury, and Sir Harry Radford; and other people to the number of 2200. The Earl of Salisbury was taken alive and led by the Duke of Somerset to the castle of Pontefract, and granted his life in return for a great sum of money. But the common people of the country, who loved him not, took him out of the castle by violence and struck off his head. When the death of these lords was known, there was great sorrow for them.

11) Crowland Chronicle: First (Prior's) Continuation
(*Ingulph*, p. 421)

[During] the week of our Lord's Nativity [1460], Richard Duke of York incautiously engaged the northern army fighting for the king [Henry VI] at Wakefield, without waiting to bring up the whole of his own forces; upon which a charge was made by the enemy on his men and he was, without mercy or respect, relentlessly slain. There fell with him at the same place many noble and distinguished men; and countless numbers of the common people, who had followed him, met their deaths there; and all to no purpose.

Mortimer's Cross, St Albans and Towton, 1461

Soon after Margaret of Anjou returned from Scotland to York early in January 1461, she and her advisers took the decision to march south; moreover, with Richard of York and Richard Neville Earl of Salisbury dead, and a large northern force (flushed with victory at Wakefield) at her disposal, the prospect of successfully reaching London, removing Henry VI from Warwick's clutches, nullifying the Act of Accord and finally defeating the Yorkists must have seemed promising indeed. Faced with this possible scenario, the Yorkist propaganda machine in Westminster no doubt went into overdrive, as Warwick deliberately stoked up hysteria at the probability of a huge and unruly northern army creating havoc in southern England. Clement Paston certainly took on board such tales when he reported, on 23 January, that 'the people in the north rob and steal' and now were primed to threaten 'men's goods and livelihoods in all the south country' (11a). Pro-Yorkist chroniclers, too, paint a picture of appalling mayhem: the *English Chronicle*, for instance, put on record that, as they marched south, the northern men robbed 'all the country and people as they came [as] if they had been pagans or Saracens and not Christian men' (3); the first Crowland continuator deplored this pillaging and plundering 'whirlwind from the north' which, 'in the impulse of [its] fury, attempted to overrun the whole of England' (1); and, according to *Whethamsted's Register*, in 'every place through which they came' the northerners 'robbed, plundered and devastated' (2). Obviously, such sources need to be treated with considerable caution but they cannot be dismissed out of hand as mere retailers of anti-northern prejudice and propaganda. Margaret of Anjou's army clearly was a notably undisciplined force but, nonetheless, scored a considerable victory over Warwick the Kingmaker in the field at the second battle of St Albans on 17 February 1461. Several sources, including the probably well-informed *Whethamsted's Regester*, provide information about the confrontation and its significance (2, 3, 4, 6, 12a), but *Gregory's Chronicle* is exceptional in its detailed coverage of the fighting (5). Warwick had brought Henry VI with him to St Albans and, as a result of her success there, Queen Margaret once more took control of her hapless husband (3, 4, 6, 12a): *Gregory's Chronicle* tells us, indeed, that 'in the midst of the battle' the king 'went to the queen and forsook all his lords, trusting better to her party' than the Yorkists (5). When news reached London of the events of 17 February, panic seems to have broken out at the prospect of hosting so notorious a force of northerners and urgent negotiations soon began between representatives of the city authorities and the queen (3, 6, 12a, 12b). Fortunately for the capital, Margaret of Anjou decided against either entering London by agreement or taking the city by force: instead, and probably foolishly, she retreated back to the north, taking both her husband and her victorious army with her (3, 4, 6). As a result, the initiative now passed once more to the Yorkists.

When Richard of York's eldest son Edward Earl of March heard of his father's death at Wakefield he was probably in the Welsh marches. Soon afterwards he defeated a largely Welsh Lancastrian force at the battle of Mortimer's Cross near Hereford (3, 4, 5, 6). So ill-documented is this affair, however, that even its date has been disputed: was it 2 February, as suggested by *Gregory's Chronicle* and the *Annales Rerum Anglicarum* (5, 6), or 3 February, as the *English Chronicle* (probably rightly) has it (3)? Despite his own defeat at St Albans a fortnight later, Warwick was able to rendezvous with Edward in the Cotswolds about 22 February and, together, the two earls now journeyed to London where, on 26 February, they were enthusiastically admitted and, on 4 March, the young Edward was proclaimed king as Edward IV (3, 4, 7, 12c). Since contemporaries put so much emphasis on popular support among Londoners in enabling Edward Earl of March to seize the throne (7, 12c), it would be foolish to discount this as no more than politically engineered enthusiasm. Nevertheless, it was the Yorkist lords themselves (few though they were at this stage) who were primarily responsible for Edward becoming king: indeed, they had little choice in the matter, arguably, now Henry VI was no longer available to provide a figurehead (4, 7, 12c). No time was wasted, however, in confronting the threat posed to the fragile new regime by Margaret of Anjou's as yet undefeated Lancastrian army in the north of England (8, 9, 12c). The result was the biggest and bloodiest confrontation of the entire Wars of the Roses. In a preliminary skirmish at Ferrybridge near Pontefract, on 28 March, the Lancastrian John Lord Clifford was killed and, according to *Gregory's Chronicle*, the 'Earl of Warwick was hurt in his leg by an arrow'. Next day, at Towton near Tadcaster, the main battle was fought, despite, if we are to believe Polydore Vergil, Henry VI being 'rather minded to have prayed than fought' on what was, in fact, Palm Sunday (9)! The total number of men involved may well have exceeded 50,000 and, undoubtedly, it was a long and hard-fought struggle, hampered by atrocious weather and producing massive casualties: in the end, however, victory went to Edward IV and the Lancastrians sustained a devastating defeat (8, 9, 10, 11b, 12d). Chronicle accounts of the battle are certainly rich in hyperbole: the first Crowland continuator, for instance, recorded that '38,000 warriors fell on that day', bodies were 'piled in pits and trenches', and the blood of the slain 'mingling with the snow' eventually 'ran down in the furrows and ditches along with the melted snow, in a most shocking manner, for a distance of two or three miles'; the author of the *Great Chronicle of London* learned that, at Towton, 'there was the son against the father, the brother against brother, the nephew against nephew' (8); and, according to Polydore Vergil, there was 'so great slaughter that the dead carcasses hindered them as they fought' (9). As for Warwick the Kingmaker's brother George Neville, writing on 7 April 1461, he particularly emphasized both the length of the battle and the great numbers who lost their lives: indeed, he declared, by the end 'so many dead bodies were seen as to cover an area six miles long' and more than three broad (12d). Many northern Lancastrian lords, most notably Henry Percy third Earl of Northumberland, were certainly killed, while Margaret of Anjou herself (accompanied by Henry VI, Prince Edward of Lancaster and Henry Beaufort Duke of Somerset, among others) was lucky to escape capture in York and, eventually, find refuge in Scotland (8, 10, 11b, 12d).

1) *Crowland Chronicle: First (Prior's) Continuation*
(*Ingulph*, pp. 421–3)
[Richard Duke of York] being removed from this world [at Wakefield], the northern men, [aware] that there was no one now who would care to resist their inroads, swept onwards like a whirlwind from the north, and in the impulse of their fury attempted to overrun the whole of England. At this time too, fancying that everything tended to ensure them freedom from molestation, paupers and beggars flocked from those quarters in infinite numbers, just like so many mice rushing from their holes and everywhere devoted themselves to pillage and plunder, regardless of place or person. For, besides the vast amounts of property they collected outside, they also irreverently rushed, in their unbridled and frantic rage, into churches and other sanctuaries of God, and most wickedly plundered them of their chalices, books and vestments and, unutterable crime!, broke open the pixes in which were kept the body of Christ and shook out the sacred elements from them. When priests and others of Christ's faithful in any way sought to resist, like so many abandoned wretches as they were, they cruelly slaughtered them in the very churches or churchyards. Thus did they proceed with impunity, spreading in vast crowds over a region of thirty miles in breadth and, covering the whole surface of the earth just like so many locusts, made their way almost to the very walls of London, all the movables they could possibly collect in every quarter being placed on beasts of burden and carried off. With such avidity for plunder did they press on that they dug up the precious vessels which, out of fear of them, had been buried in the earth, and with threats of death forced people to produce those treasures they had hidden in remote and obscure spots. [Then] word came to us [at Crowland] that this army, so execrable and so abominable, had approached to within six miles of our boundaries. [Fortunately], after the adjoining counties had been given up to dreadful pillage and plunder, [our abbey], by Divine grace and clemency, was preserved.

2) Whethamsted's Register
(*Whethamsted*, pp. 388–92; *Thornley*, pp. 10–11)

[The northern men], with the queen and the prince, made their way towards the southern parts [after Wakefield] and advanced without interruption until they came to the town and monastery of the English protomartyr Alban. In every place through which they came on both sides of the Trent, but especially on this side, they robbed, plundered and devastated, and carried off with them whatever they could find or discover, whether clothing or money, herds of cattle or single animals, or any other thing whatsoever, sparing neither churches nor clergy, monasteries nor monks, chapels nor chaplains. . . .

The northern men, coming to the town [of St Albans] and hearing that the king, with a great army and some of his lords, was lying near, immediately entered the town, desiring to pass through the middle of it and direct their army against the king's [the Earl of Warwick's] army. However, they were forced to turn back by a few archers who met them near the Great Cross, and to flee to the west end of the town, where, entering by a lane which leads from that end northwards as far as St Peter's Street, they had a great fight with a certain small band of men of the king's army. Then, after not a few had been killed on both sides, going out to the heath called Barnet heath, lying near the north end of the town, they fought a great battle with certain large forces, perhaps 4–5000, of the vanguard of the king's army. . . . The southern men, who were fiercer at the beginning, [were] broken very quickly afterwards, and the more quickly because, looking back, they saw no one coming up from the main body of the king's army, or preparing to bring them help, whereupon they turned their backs on the northern men and fled. . . . The northern men, seeing this, [pursued] them very swiftly on horseback and, catching a good many, ran them through with their lances. . . .

3) English Chronicle
(*Davies*, pp. 107–10)

[Following the battle of Wakefield], by the king's command, writs and commissions were directed to sheriffs and other officers to raise men to chastise the people and rebels of the north. They of the north, hearing this, secretly gathered a great people and came down suddenly to the town of Dunstable, robbing all the country and people as they came, spoiling abbeys, houses of religion and churches, and bearing away chalices, books and other ornaments, as if they had been pagans or Saracens and not Christian men.

[On 12 February 1461] King Harry and his lords, that is to say, the Dukes of Norfolk and Suffolk, the Earls of Warwick and Arundel, Lord Neville and others, left London and came with their people to the town of St Albans, not knowing that the people of the north were so near. When the king heard that they were so near him, he went out and took his field [not far] from St Albans [where] he stood and saw his people slain on both sides. At the last, as a result of the withdrawal of the

Kentishmen [and] also the indisposition of the people of the king's side, King Harry's party lost the field. The lords who were with the king, seeing this, withdrew and went away.

When the king saw his people dispersed and the field lost, he went to his queen, Margaret, who came with the northern men, and her son Edward; for they of the north said that they had come to restore the king to the queen his wife, and deliver him out of prison, forasmuch as, since the battle of Northampton, he had been under the rule and governance of the Earls of Warwick and Salisbury, and others. . . .

When this battle was over, London, dreading the manners and malice of the queen, the Duke of Somerset and others, lest they would have plundered the city, [sent] the Duchess of Buckingham, and knowledgeable men with her, to negotiate with them to show benevolence and goodwill to the city, which was divided within itself. Some worthy men and aldermen, dreading and weighing the inconvenience and mischief that might follow, contrary to the commonweal of the city, [promised] a certain sum of money to the queen and the Duke of Somerset, suggesting he come to the city with only limited numbers. [Consequently], certain spearmen and men-at-arms were sent by the duke to enter the city before he came: of these, some were slain, some sore hurt, and the rest put to flight. Immediately after, the commons, for the salvation of the city, took the keys of the gates where they should have entered, and courageously kept and defended it from their enemies, until the coming of Edward the noble Earl of March.

Thereafter King Harry, with Margaret his queen and the northern men, returned homeward towards the north again: which northern men, as they went homeward, did harms innumerable, taking men's carts, horses and beasts, and robbing the people, [so that] men in the shires through which they passed had almost no beasts left to till their land. . . .

[On 3 February 1461] Edward, the noble Earl of March, fought with the Welshmen near Wigmore in Wales, whose captains were the Earl of Pembroke and the Earl of Wiltshire, [and] he won a victory over his enemies, put the two earls to flight, and slew 4000 Welshmen. [On 28 February] he came to London and innumerable people flocked to him at once, ready to go with him to the north in order to avenge the death of his father the noble Duke Richard. [Soon afterwards] Edward the noble Earl of March was chosen king in the city of London and began to reign.

4) Crowland Chronicle: Second (1459–1486) Continuation
(*Crowland*, pp. 112–13; *Ingulph*, p. 456)
[Following the battle of Wakefield] the northerners invaded the southern parts [of England] until they reached St Albans, where they put to flight the Earl of Warwick, who had brought along King Henry as if to make him fight against the queen, his wife, and his son. [Yet] the northerners failed to follow up their victory,

[instead] leading the king and queen back with them to the north. Meanwhile the duke's eldest son, Edward Earl of March, campaigning against the queen's supporters in Wales, won a glorious victory over them at Mortimer's Cross. When he heard of his father's death and how eagerly the people of the south were awaiting him as their future king, he assembled his forces together and proceeded to London. Here, after proper deliberation with his council, it was decided, irrevocably, that since King Henry, by associating with the murderers of his father and endeavouring to annul the decree of Parliament, had broken the accord, the earl no longer need observe his fealty to him. [On 4 March 1461 Edward IV] commenced his reign, amidst the acclamation of the whole populace, [and so] he gained a thoroughly deserved victory and the crown. . . .

5) *Gregory's Chronicle*
(*Gregory*, pp. 211–14)

[On 2 February 1461] Edward Earl of March, the Duke of York's son and heir, won a great victory at Mortimer's Cross in Wales, where he put to flight the Earls of Pembroke and Wiltshire, and took and slew knights, squires and others to the number of 3000. [In] that conflict Owen Tudor was taken and brought to Haverfordwest [sic: Hereford], where he was beheaded in the market place: his head was set on the highest pinnacle of the market cross, and a mad woman combed his hair, washed away the blood off his face, got candles, and set about him, burning, more than a hundred. . . .

[On 17 February] next following King Harry rode to St Albans, accompanied by the Duke of Norfolk, the Earls of Warwick and Arundel, Lords Bourchier and Bonville, many great lords, knights and squires, and commons numbering 100,000 men. There they had a great battle with the queen, who had come from Wakefield to St Albans with all her lords, and every lord's man bore his lord's livery, so that every man might know his own fellowship by his livery. Besides all that, every man and lord bore the prince's livery, a band of crimson and black with ostrich feathers. The core who won that field were householdmen and feedmen. I believe less than 5000 men fought in the queen's party, for most of the northern men fled away, some being taken and plundered of their armour on the way as they fled. And some of them ever robbed as they fled, a pitiful thing to hear. . . .

In the midst of the battle King Harry went to his queen and forsook all his lords, trusting better to her party than his own lords. Then, through great labour, the Duke of Norfolk and the Earl of Warwick escaped away; the Bishop of Exeter, brother to the Earl of Warwick and at that time chancellor of England, Lord Bourchier, and many other knighs, squires and commons fled, and many men were slain on both sides. Lord Bonville was beheaded. . . . The number of men slain was 3500 or more.

[At this second battle of St Albans] the lords in King Harry's party pitched a field and fortified it very strongly, and like unwise men broke their array and field and took another, and before they were prepared for the battle the queen's party was at hand with them in the town of St Albans, and then everything was out of order, for their scouts did not come back to them to bring news of how near the queen was, save one who came and said she was nine miles away. Before the gunners and Burgundians could level their guns they were busily fighting, and many a gun of war was provided that was of little or no avail; for the Burgundians had such instruments as would shoot both pellets of lead and arrows of an ell in length with six feathers, three in the middle and three at one end, and a very big head of iron at the other end, and would fire, all together. All these three things they might shoot well and easily at once but, in time of need, they could not shoot one of them, for the fire turned back upon those who would shoot these three things. Also they had nets of great cords four fathoms in length and four feet wide, like a hedge, and at every second knot there was a nail standing upright, so that no man could pass over it without a strong chance of getting hurt. Also they had body shields borne like a door, made with a prop folding up and down to set the shield where they liked, and loop holes with shooting windows to shoot out of. . . . And, when their shot was spent and finished, they cast the shield before them, so that no man could get over the shield because of the nails that stood upright, unless he wished to do himself a mischief. Also they had a thing made like a lattice full of nails as the net was, but it could be moved as a man would: a man might squeeze it together so that the length would be more than two yards long and, if he wished, he might pull it wide, so that it would be four square. And that served to lie at gaps where horsemen would enter. . . . And since worthy men will not dissemble or curry favour for any bias, they could not understand how these devices did either good or harm, except on our side with King Harry. Therefore they are much neglected, and men take to themselves mallets of lead, bows, swords, glaives and axes. As for spearmen, they are only good to ride before the footmen and eat and drink up their victuals, and many more such fine things they do. Hold me excused [for these opinions] but I speak for the best, for in foot soldiers is all the trust.

6) *Annales Rerum Anglicarum*
(*Annales*, pp. 775–6; *Thornley*, pp. 9–10; *EHD*, pp. 286–7)

[On 2 February 1461] a battle was fought near Wigmore at Mortimer's Cross, where the Earl of March with 51,000 men attacked the Earl of Pembroke with 8000, and there fled from the field there the Earl of Pembroke, the Earl of Wiltshire and many others. . . .

[Not long after] Queen Margaret, with the prince, the Dukes of Exeter and Somerset, the Earls of Northumberland, Devon and Shrewsbury, [several barons], and many others, to the number of 80,000 fighting men, came towards St Albans. [On 17 February 1461] the battle of St Albans was fought, where the Duke of Norfolk and the Earls of Warwick and Arundel and many others fled from the field. And King Henry was captured on the field. . . . And the prince came to the king in the field, where the king, his father, dubbed him knight. And in the battle were killed 20,000 men. . . .

When the battle was over, the aldermen of London sent the Duchesses of Bedford and Buckingham to sue to the queen for grace and the peace of the city. [Soon afterwards] the king and queen turned back from St Albans to Dunstable with their army, fearing that, if their men had entered London, they would have sacked the city. And this was the downfall of King Henry and his queen for, if they had entered London, they would have had all at their mercy.

7) *London Chronicle: Gough 10*
(*Flenley*, pp. 161–2)

[On Thursday 26 February 1461] the Earl of March and the Earl of Warwick came to London with a great power and, on the Sunday afterwards, all the host mustered in St John's field and there were read among them certain articles and points in which King Harry VI had offended against the realm. Then it was demanded of the people whether Harry were worthy to reign still and the people cried 'Nay!'. Then they were asked if they would have the Earl of March as king and they cried 'Yea!'. Certain captains then went to the Earl of March's place at Baynard's Castle, and many people with them, and told him that the people had chosen him as king: he thanked them and, by the advice of the Archbishop of Canterbury, the Bishop of Exeter and the Earl of Warwick, and others, consented to take it upon him. [On Tuesday 3 March] he caused it to be proclaimed that all manner of people should meet him on the morrow [Wednesday 4 March] at St Paul's at 9 o'clock and so they did. Thither came the Earl of March with the lords in goodly array and there went on procession through the town singing the litany. After the procession was over the Bishop of Exeter, the chancellor, delivered a sermon and, at the end of the sermon, declared the Earl of March's right and title to the crown and demanded of the people whether they would have him as their king as their right demanded. They cried 'Yea!'. Then all the people were asked to go with him to Westminster to see him take his possession and so the people did. The Earl of March, with the lords spiritual and temporal, then rode thither and, when he came to the hall, he alighted and went in, and so up to the Chancery, where he was sworn before the Archbishop of Canterbury, the chancellor of England, and the lords, that he should truly and justly keep the realm and maintain its laws as a true and just king. Then they put royal robes on him, and the cap of estate, and he went and sat in the chair as king: the people were then asked if they would have him as king, and maintain, support and obey him, as true king, and they cried 'Yea!'. Thereafter he went through the palace to Westminster church, where the abbot and a procession awaited him in the church porch with St Edward's sceptre, which he grasped, and so he went into the church, offered with great solemnity at the high altar and at St Edward's shrine, before coming down into the chair where he sat in the seat while *Te Deum* was solemnly sung. Then he went into the palace again, changed his array, came down by water, went to St Paul's to the bishop's palace, and there lodged and dined. . . . So King Edward IV began his reign. . . .

8) Great Chronicle of London
(*Great Chronicle*, pp. 196–7)

[In March 1461 Edward IV] journeyed northwards [until] he came upon a village named Sherborn near York where, on Palm Sunday [29 March] he encountered with King Henry's host, which was of great multitude and in it many lords of name, with knights and other men of honour. But that notwithstanding, after a sore and long and unkindly fight – for there was the son against the father, the brother against brother, the nephew against nephew – the victory fell to King Edward, to the great loss of people on both sides. [Of supporters of Henry VI there] were slain above 20,000, besides lords and men of name [who included] the Earls of Northumberland, Westmorland and Wiltshire, Lords Welles, Clifford, Fitzwalter and Dacre, and the Earl of Westmorland's brother Sir John Neville. . . . When the field was won by King Edward, and word thereof soon after brought to King Henry and Queen Margaret in York, at once they fled towards Scotland with such small company as they had, among which were the Duke of Somerset and Lord Roos. . . .

9) Polydore Vergil
(*Vergil*, pp. 110–II)

[In March 1461 Edward IV] marched towards York and, when he came about eleven miles from the city, he camped at a village called Towton. When King Henry knew that his enemies were at hand, he did not at once issue out of his tents, since the solemn feast of Palm Sunday was at hand, on which he was rather minded to have prayed than fought, so next day he might have better success in the field. But it came to pass by means of the soldiers who, as their manner is, dislike lingering, that very same day, by daybreak, [he] was forced to sound the alarm. His adversaries were as ready as he. The archers began the battle but, when their arrows were spent, the matter was dealt with by hand strokes with so great slaughter that the dead carcasses hindered them as they fought. Thus did the fight continue more than ten hours in equal balance when, at the last, King Henry saw the forces of his foes increase, and his own somewhat yield, [and the battle was lost].

10) Jean de Waurin
(*Hallam*, pp. 224, 227)

There was a great slaughter that day [at] Towton and for a long time no one could see which side would gain the victory, so furious was the fighting. But at last the supporters of the king, queen and Duke of Somerset were utterly defeated. . . . When Edward Duke of York had won the day at Towton, he gave thanks to God for his glorious victory. Then many knights, earls and barons came into his presence, bowed to him and asked what they ought now to do for the best: he replied that he would never rest until he had killed or captured King Henry and his wife, or driven them from the country, as he had promised and sworn to do. The princes and barons of his company said: 'My lord, then we must make for York, for we are told that Queen Margaret and some of her supporters have gone there for safety.' But as soon as the queen heard this news, she and her people packed up everything they could carry and left York in great haste for Scotland.

11) Paston Letters
(*Paston Letters*, Vol. 3, pp. 250, 267)

a) Clement Paston to John Paston, 23 January 1461
. . . I have heard it said that the [northern] lords will be here sooner than men expected, I have heard within three weeks. . . . In this [southern] country every man is very willing to go with the lords here, and I hope God will help them, for the people in the north rob and steal, and be agreed to pillage all this country, and give away men's goods and livelihoods in all the south country. . . . The lords here have as much as they can do to keep down all this country, more than four or five shires; for they would be upon the men in the north [since] it is for the weal of all the south. . . .

b) William Paston and Thomas Playters to John Paston, 4 April 1461
. . . our sovereign lord [Edward IV] has won the field [at Towton] and, on the Monday after Palm Sunday, he was received into York with great solemnity and procession . . . King Harry, the queen, the prince, the Dukes of Somerset and Exeter are fled into Scotland, and they be chased and followed.

12) Milanese State Papers
(*CSPM*, pp. 48–50, 54, 61–2)

a) Newsletter from London, 19 February 1461
[On 17 February] not far from St Albans the king took the field with the party from here; those of the queen encountered them in order to have him. About an hour after midday a skirmish was begun with the king's foreguard. They say that it lasted until six, and in the end the party from here was routed and the queen's side recovered the king, and he is with the queen and prince. They say that many were slain. . . . When the news was known here, the mayor sent to the king and queen, it is supposed to offer obedience, provided they were assured that they would not be plundered or suffer violence. In the mean time they keep a good guard at the gates, which they keep practically closed, and so through all the

district they maintain a good guard, and those who are here, thank God, feel no harm or lack of governance. Yet the shops keep closed, and nothing is done either by the tradespeople or by the merchants, and men do not stand in the streets or go far away from home. We are all hoping that, as the queen and prince have not descended in fury with their troops, the gates may be opened to them upon a good composition, and they may be allowed to enter peacefully. . . .

b) Newsletter from London, 22 February 1461

[The envoys from London to St Albans] returned on the 20th, and reported that the king and queen had no mind to pillage the chief city and chamber of this realm, and so they promised; but at the same time they did not mean that they would not punish the evil doers. On the receipt of this reply by the magistrates, a proclamation was issued that every one should keep fast to his house and should live at peace, in order that the king and his forces might enter and behave peacefully. But less than an hour later all the people run to arms and reports circulated that York [*sic*] with 60,000 Irish and March with 40,000 Welsh had hastened to the neighbourhood and would guard their place for them; and they said that the mayor must give them the keys of the gates. They called for a brewer as their leader, and that day this place was in an uproar, so that I was never more afraid than then that everything would be at hazard. But, by the grace of God and the excellent arrangements of the mayor and aldermen and of the notables who were at the counsel, they decided last Saturday to send to the king and queen four aldermen [and others to] fetch four cavaliers in whom the king and queen had perfect confidence, and treat here with the magistrates in the presence of the people, and come to an arrangement that they might enter, that is the king, queen, prince and all the nobles with their leaders without the body of the army. . . .

c) Newsletter from London, 4 March 1461

[In my last letter I sent news of] how, at St Albans on carnival day, the forces of the queen and prince routed those of the king and Warwick, with a great slaughter, and that everyone believed that Warwick had gone to Calais. But it was not so, as he went to meet the Earl of March, and last Friday after dinner they came here with about 5000 persons, including foot and horse. A great crowd flocked together and, with the lords who were there, they chose the Earl of March as their king and sovereign lord, and that day they celebrated the solemnity, going in procession through the place amid great festivities. It remains to be seen how King Henry, his son, the queen and the other lords will bear this, as it is said that the new king will shortly leave here to go after them.

d) George Neville, Bishop of Exeter and Chancellor of England, to Francesco Coppini, London, 7 April 1461

[At Towton] there was a great conflict, which began with the rising of the sun, and lasted until the tenth hour of the night, so great was the pertinacity and boldness of the men, who never heeded the possibility of a miserable death. Of the enemy who fled, great numbers were drowned in the river near the town of Tadcaster, eight miles from York, because they themselves had broken the bridge to cut our passage that way, so that none could pass, and a great part of the rest who got away [were] slain and so many dead bodies were seen as to cover an area six miles long by three broad and about four furlongs. In this battle eleven lords of the enemy fell, including the Earl of Devon, the Earl of Northumberland, Lords Clifford and Neville, with some cavaliers; and from what we hear from persons worthy of confidence, some 28,000 persons perished on one side or the other. . . .

Let us now return to our puppet [Henry VI] who, with [Queen] Margaret, his son, the Duke of Somerset, and some others, took refuge in a new castle [Newcastle] about sixty miles north of York. . . .

Hexham, 1464

Even after Edward IV had won his great victory at Towton on 29 March 1461, Lancastrianism was by no means a spent force: indeed, the new king's position on the throne often seemed far from secure, at any rate until the summer of 1464, and he contrived actually to lose his crown (if only for a few months) as late as 1470/1. During Edward IV's early months, in particular, there is considerable evidence of disturbances in various parts of England and Wales; of fears that internal disorder and resistance in southern and south-western shires might be linked with an imminent French invasion; and of the serious threat to northern counties posed by dissident Lancastrians in a politically well-disposed Scotland (2, 4, 5a, 6b). Yorkist fears of Lancastrian sedition are graphically demonstrated by the speed and vigour of the government's reaction to the Earl of Oxford's conspiracy in February 1462 (1, 5b). Late 1463, moreover, saw Henry Beaufort Duke of Somerset and several fellow Lancastrians trying to coordinate rebellion in both Wales and England culminating, early in 1464, in an apparent effort to secure Edward IV's overthrow when anti-government disturbances and risings broke out in several English and Welsh counties: the stark reality of their failure is perhaps less significant than the fact that they occurred at all.

The main Lancastrian threat to Yorkist rule in the early 1460s clearly centred on Scotland and north-eastern England. In the aftermath of Towton Scotland not only gave refuge to Henry VI, Margaret of Anjou and several leading Lancastrian lords but also provided positive backing for their cause; while, time and time again during Edward IV's first years, Northumberland's great fortresses – notably Alnwick, Bamburgh and Dunstanburgh castles – provided highly visible rallying points for Lancastrian resistance (1, 2, 3, 4, 5a, 6a). The potential Scottish menace became immediately apparent when, on 25 April 1461, Margaret of Anjou surrendered the border town and castle of Berwick to Scotland; soon afterwards a Paston correspondent reported that 'Berwick is full of Scots' and speculated on the imminence of 'another battle now between the Scots and us'; and news reached Bruges at the beginning of June 1461 that the Lancastrian leadership was 'negotiating for a marriage alliance between the sister of the late King of Scots and [Edward of Lancaster] Prince of Wales' (1, 5a). Yet Scotland never provided the substantial and sustained backing Margaret of Anjou so clearly needed, while Edward IV, too, struggled to find sufficient resources to mount an all-out campaign in the far north of England. As a result, a classic cat-and-mouse game was played out in

Northumberland for several years, neither Lancaster nor York ever managing to convert temporary advantage into permanent gain. During the autumn of 1461 the Yorkists seemed to have secured firm control of the Northumberland castles yet, by November 1462, they had reverted back to Lancaster: indeed, after securing a modest degree of support from Louis XI of France, Margaret of Anjou even attempted a sea-borne invasion of north-eastern England at this time, only to withdraw in disarray when news reached her of an imminent Yorkist offensive spearheaded by Edward IV himself (1, 6c, 7). The king, in fact, never got beyond Durham (where he was apparently laid low by measles) but Warwick the Kingmaker did mount serious sieges of the great Northumberland fortresses and, by the end of January 1463, not only were Alnwick, Bamburgh and Dunstanburgh once more in Yorkist hands but even Henry Beaufort Duke of Somerset appeared to have abandoned Lancaster for York (1, 7). Within months, however, the Yorkists lost control of the castles again and, at the end of the year, Somerset returned to the Lancastrian fold. Yet, by then too, so disillusioned had Margaret of Anjou become following a short-lived Yorkist resurgence in the summer of 1463 that she and Edward of Lancaster had sailed for Burgundy, never again to set foot on Scottish soil (6c, 7).

Not until the spring of 1464 did the Yorkists, at last, mount a major and sustained campaign to secure north-eastern England once and for all (7). Crucial to its success was the ending of Scottish support for Lancaster and it was while John Lord Montagu, Warwick the Kingmaker's brother, was on a mission to escort Scottish ambassadors to York that the so-called battle of Hedgeley Moor was fought, probably on 25 April 1464: the Lancastrians were routed in what was, in fact, little more than a skirmish in Northumberland, the Scottish envoys duly reached York and a fifteen year Anglo-Scottish truce resulted (8). Soon afterwards, in another Northumberland battle fought at Hexham on 15 May, the industrious Montagu inflicted a decisive defeat on the Lancastrians (1, 2, 4, 5c, 7, 8, 9). Moreover, almost all Henry VI's leading supporters were captured either on the field or soon after and the Yorkists' determination to put an end for good to Lancastrian resistance is amply demonstrated by the ensuing round of executions (1, 2, 4, 5c, 7, 8, 9). All that remained was to secure the speedy surrender of the Northumberland castles and, equipped with a substantial force and siege artillery, Montagu now marched on them: Alnwick and Dunstanburgh capitulated without resistance on 23 June, while Bamburgh, after a short siege, surrendered two days later (7, 8). Finally, in July 1465, Henry VI himself was captured in Lancashire, escorted to London, and imprisoned in the Tower (1, 2, 3, 8, 9, 10).

1) Short English Chronicle
(*Three Fifteenth Century Chronicles*, ed. J. Gairdner, pp. 77–80)
[Following Towton] King Harry fled, with his queen and several lords, to Berwick, where they delivered that town, and many other castles in the north, to the Scots and the French. . . .

[In February 1462 there was] a great treason against the king by the followers of the Earl of Oxford and his son Aubrey, with other knights, and the king's rebels, traitors and adversaries outside the land. God sent the king himself knowledge of these treasons and, at once, they were taken and condemned to death. First, Lord Aubrey was drawn through London to Tower Hill on 20 February, and there beheaded; on 23 February Sir Thomas Tuddenham, Sir William Tyrel and John Montgomery, squire, were drawn through London to Tower Hill, and there beheaded on a scaffold; and on the 26th day of the same month John de Vere Earl of Oxford was led through London to Tower Hill, and beheaded on the same scaffold. [Also] this year several castles in the north were again yielded to King Edward.

[Later in 1462] Queen Margaret took Bamburgh, Alnwick and Dunstanburgh with 6000 Frenchmen and, in the same year, the king obtained great guns and other great ordnance in London, and carried them up to the north country. There the king, with his lords, laid siege to these castles, which were yielded up. . . . Also this year the Duke of Somerset became the king's sworn liegeman, but he did not keep his oath, for he went over to the other side again [in 1463]. . . .

[In May 1464] several lords and gentlemen of the queen's affinity came to Hexham. Lord Montagu, with other knights and squires, gained knowledge of them and there took most of them, [including] Harry Duke of Somerset, who was beheaded on 15 May at Hexham. . . .

[In 1465] King Harry was taken in the north country, and two doctors with him, Doctors Manning and Bedon, all three of whom were brought to London. The Earl of Warwick met with them at Islington by the king's command, arrested King Henry on certain charges, and so brought him in at Newgate, [leading him] through Cheapside and all London to the Tower [on 24 July].

2) *Warkworth's Chronicle*
(*Warkworth*, pp. 1–2, 4, 5)

[In] the first year of his reign, [Edward IV] ordained a Parliament, at which were attainted King Harry and all others that fled with him into Scotland out of England. . . .

[Queen] Margaret, Harry Duke of Exeter, the Duke of Somerset and other lords that fled from England kept certain castles in Northumberland, as Alnwick, Bamburgh, Dunstanburgh, and also Warkworth; which they had victualled and stuffed both with Englishmen, Frenchmen and Scotsmen; by which castles they had the most part of Northumberland. . . .

[In May 1464] the Duke of Somerset, Lord Roos, Lord Moleyns [and others] gathered a great people of the north country. And Sir John Neville, that time being Earl of Northumberland, with 10,000 men, came upon them, and there [at Hexham] the foresaid lords were taken and afterwards beheaded. . . .

[In 1465] King Harry was taken beside a house of religion in Lancashire, by means of a black monk of Abingdon, in a wood called Clitherwood, near Bungerly stepping-stones, by Thomas Talbot, son and heir to Sir Edmund Talbot of Bashall, and John Talbot his cousin of Colebury, being at his dinner at Waddington Hall, and was carried to London on horseback, with his legs bound to the stirrups, and so brought through London to the Tower, where he was kept a long time by two squires and two yeomen of the crown, and their men; and every man was suffered to come and speak with him, by licence of the keepers.

3) *Crowland Chronicle: First (Prior's) Continuation*
(*Ingulph*, pp. 426, 439)
[Following Edward IV's victory at Towton] King Henry fled, together with a few of his followers, into Scotland, in which country and in the castles bordering it, he lay concealed, in great tribulation, during the four following years. Queen Margaret, however, with her son Edward, whom she had borne to King Henry, took flight to parts beyond the sea, not to return very speedily. . . .

[In 1465], having taken refuge in Scotland or lurked in secret hiding places in the bordering castles of England, [Henry VI] was taken prisoner. Being captured in the northern parts, he was led by a strong body of men to the Tower of London, where King Edward ordered all possible humanity to be shown towards him, consistent with his safe custody, and, at the same time, gave directions that he should be supplied with all suitable necessaries and treated with becoming respect.

4) *Crowland Chronicle: Second (1459–1486) Continuation*
(*Crowland*, pp. 112–15; *Ingulph*, pp. 456–7)
[Following Edward IV's victory at Towton there occurred] sieges of castles in Northumberland and various clashes on the Scottish borders between the remnants of Henry's forces, who made frequent raids from Scotland, and John Neville Lord Montagu, lately created Earl of Northumberland [in 1464] and other faithful partisans of King Edward. Fortunes varied but, most frequently, [such engagements] ended to the greater glory of King Edward. In all this raiding and conflict many nobles on Henry's side, such as Henry Duke of Somerset, and other lords, namely Hungerford and Roos, and the distinguished knights Ralph Grey and Ralph Percy, and others, were routed and slain by the prowess of the Earl of Northumberland.

5) *Milanese State Papers*
(*CSPM*, pp. 93, 106–7, 110–11)

a) *Newsletter from Bruges, 2 June 1461*
King Henry, the queen, their son, the Duke of Somerset and Lord Roos, his brother, have taken refuge in Scotland. It is said that they are negotiating for a marriage alliance between the sister of the late King of Scotland and the Prince of Wales. . . . They also say that King Henry has given away a castle called Berwick, which is one of the keys of the frontier between England and Scotland.

b) Newsletter from Bruges, 25 March 1462

. . . a great conspiracy [has been discovered], at the head of which was the Earl of
Oxford, and he, his eldest son and many other knights and esquires lost their
heads. . . . This earl and his accomplices sent letters to King Henry and the queen
in Scotland, by a servant of his who, after having been to York, returned to King
Edward and presented the letters, which were read as well as copied, and then
sealed up again and sent by the same messenger to King Henry with a promise
that he would return with the reply. He did so and it was done very secretly. After
the reply had been read, the Earl of Worcester, who has been made constable of
England, was sent to take the earl and the others. . . . Their plan was as follows: to
follow the king [Edward IV], as his servants, towards the north [and] once among
the enemy they were to attack the king and murder him and all his followers. In
the mean time the Duke of Somerset, who was at Bruges and is still there, was to
descend upon England, and King Henry was also to come with the Scots, and the
Earl of Pembroke from Brittany. . . .

c) Newsletter from Antwerp, 1 June 1464

I have heard recently that fresh disturbances have taken place in England
between the two kings [Edward IV and Henry VI] and subsequently that King
Edward has pursued his adversaries and has taken the Duke of Somerset and Lord
Moleyns, with others since, and had them all beheaded. King Henry has retreated
to some castle, where they say he is besieged. . . . One may say that that party is
utterly dispersed. . . .

6) Paston Letters
(*Paston Letters*, Vol. 3, pp. 306–7, 312, Vol. 4, p. 51)

*a) Robert Lord Hungerford and Robert Whittingham, in Dieppe, to Margaret of Anjou, 'the
Queen of England in Scotland', 30 August 1461*

Madam, fear you not, but be of good comfort, and beware not to risk your
person, nor my lord the prince, by sea, until you have other word from us [or
unless] your person cannot be secure where you are and extreme necessity drive
you from there. And, for God's sake, give the same advice to the king . . . [We
trust death will not take us] until we see the king and you peaceable again in your
realm. . . .

b) Henry Windsor to John Paston, 4 October 1461

. . . all the castles and strongholds in south Wales and north Wales are given and
yielded up into the king's hand. And the Duke of Exeter and the Earl of
Pembroke are flown and taken to the mountains, and several lords with great
power are after them; and the most part of gentlemen and men of worship are
come into the king, and have grace, of all Wales.

c) Thomas Playters to John Paston, July 1462

. . . King Harry and his adherents in Scotland shall be delivered. . . . The queen and the prince have been in France [and persuaded] many people to come to Scotland, where they trust to have succour, and then to come into England. What will happen I cannot say but I heard that these agreements were accepted by the young lords of Scotland but not by the old.

7) Great Chronicle of London
(*Great Chronicle*, pp. 199–202)

[In November 1462] Queen Margaret, with a small army, came out of France into Scotland and, enjoying the aid of the King of Scots, crossed the border into England and made sharp war. When the king [Edward IV] learned this, he assembled his people in all haste and sped northwards. However, when the queen knew of his coming with so great a strength, she fled back into Scottish territory: whence she was so sharply pursued that she was forced to take a carvel and, with a small number of supporters, sail to some coast for her safeguard. Not long after, such a tempest arose that she had to abandon her carvel and take a fishing boat: by this means, she was preserved and able to land at Berwick, for shortly after the carvel was sunk and, with it, much of the queen's riches. Shortly after about 400 Frenchmen of her retinue were, by the force of this tempest, driven ashore near the castle of Bamburgh: seeing they might not now recover their ships, they set them on fire and, afterwards, rode to an island off Northumberland, where they met a squire named Manners and the Bastard of Ogle who, with such small retinue as they then had, skirmished with the Frenchmen, and took and slew most of them.

[Edward IV] had intended to employ his ordnance at the town of Berwick but he was suddenly taken with the sickness of the measles and so vexed by that infirmity that he was forced to abandon his plans. And once he was somewhat recovered, he learned that the queen had left [the town], so he soon afterwards returned southwards. When the Scots knew of the king's departure, they at once assembled a power of knights and came into the land intending to have rescued such people as had held the castle of Alnwick; but, as soon as they knew of its surrender and of the power of the English under the command of Lord Hastings, they retreated. . . . Between Christmas and Candlemas [1462/3] the castles of Bamburgh and Dunstanburgh were yielded up to Lord Hastings, and the Duke of Somerset, Sir Ralph Percy and others of their retinue submitted to the king's grace [and the king] granted them pardons: however, shortly afterwards, the duke, fearing those who were about the king, went secretly into Scotland again to King Henry, and there tarried with him and the queen.

[During 1463] the Scots came again to the castle of Bamburgh and, finding it but weakly defended by soldiers, won it from them, stuffed it with soldiers, and appointed as one of their captains an English captain Sir Ralph Grey. This season thus passing, King Henry, being still in Scotland, at the urging of the queen and the Scots, gathered a new power, intending to have again crossed the border. Soon after the king [Edward IV], being warned, assembled his knights and made ready to ride northwards, sending ahead of him Lord Montagu, the Earl of Warwick's brother, to array the men of Northumberland. Additionally, he victualled many ships and manned them with good soldiers in various ports, some at London, some in the west country, some at Sandwich, [intending] to sail to the coasts of Scotland. . . . When he had thus provided for his army, both by sea and by land, he then journeyed northwards, [holding] his course until he came to York, where he rested and sent a part of his host to Lord Montagu . . . [When Montagu] encountered the vanguard of King Henry, [a] sharp fight took place [in May 1464]. Victory fell to Lord Montagu and, in this skirmish and ensuing chase, the Duke of Somerset, Lord Hungerford, Lord Roos [and others] were taken. So closely pursued was King Henry that Lord Montagu took several of his followers, clad in blue velvet, one of whom wore a cap on his head richly garnished with two crowns of gold, which Lord Montagu gave to King [Edward] shortly afterwards. . . . [The] Duke of Somerset was beheaded at Hexham, [while] Lord Hungerford, Lord Roos and others were put to death at Newcastle . . . [Edward IV also] sent Lord Montagu with a competent company of soldiers to Bamburgh castle, which he assaulted so fiercely that, in a short time, they won, notwithstanding the Scots, and took Sir Ralph Grey [who], for that treason and others, was drawn, hanged and quartered at York.

8) Gregory's Chronicle
(*Gregory*, pp. 223–4, 227, 232–3)

[About Easter 1464] the Scots sued unto our sovereign lord the king [Edward IV] for peace. . . . And then was Lord Montagu assigned to fetch the Scots [and] took his journey towards Newcastle. [In response] it was plotted by the false Duke of Somerset, [Sir Ralph] Percy and their followers that, a little way from Newcastle, in a wood, the false traitor Sir Humphrey Neville, with four score spearmen and bowmen too, should suddenly attack and slay Lord Montagu. However, God be thanked, their false treason became known. Then Lord Montagu took another way, gathered a great fellowship, went to Newcastle, and then journeyed towards Norham. On the way there met with him that false Duke of Somerset, Sir Ralph Percy, Lord Hungerford and Lord Roos, with all their company, to the number of 5000 men-at-arms [at Hedgeley Moor on 25 April 1464], and that same day was Sir Ralph Percy slain: when he was dead, all fled with full sorry hearts. Then Lord Montagu took his horse and rode to Norham, fetched the Scots, [and] there was concluded a peace for fifteen years. . . .

[On 14 May 1464] Lord Montagu took his journey towards Hexham from Newcastle, [where] he took the false Duke Harry of Somerset, Lord Roos, Lord Hungerford [and others]: lo, so courageous a man is this good Earl Montagu, for he spared not their malice, nor falseness, nor guile, nor treason, for he took and slew many a man during that encounter. [A round of executions followed, including the Duke of Somerset, Lord Hungerford and Lord Roos]. Beside Newcastle, in the same month, [Sir William] Tailboys was taken in a coal pit, who had much money with him, both gold and silver, which should have gone to King Harry: if it had reached him, it would have caused much sorrow for, although he had sufficient armour and ordnance, men would not go one foot with him until they had money. . . .

Also, the same summer, [the Earl of] Warwick and his brother Lord Montagu, who was made Earl of Northumberland by the king, laid siege to the castle of Dunstanburgh by the same means. Then they laid siege to the castle of Bamburgh, with great ordnance and guns, and courageously got it by force, taking therein that false traitor Sir Ralph Grey. They brought him to the king at Pontefract castle, from where he was led to Doncaster, and there his head was struck off, sent to London, and set upon London Bridge. . . .

[In 1465] King Harry came out of Scotland into Lancashire and, until he reached Furness Fells, he was never known; but there he was recognized and taken [and on 25 July] he was brought to the Tower of London. . . .

9) Polydore Vergil
(*Vergil*, pp. 114–15)
[Early in 1464 in Scotland] an exceedingly great number of men, in hope of plunder, assembled quickly from every hand, so that for force King Henry was thought not much inferior to his enemy. This rumour was augmented when, everywhere he went, [they] wasted, burnt and plundered town and field. Thus robbing and destroying he came to a village called Hexham, where he met and encountered John Marquis Montagu [on 15 May] and, after a sharp fight, as often happened before, was discomfited, losing the most part of his army. [Henry VI], with continual flight, retreated to Scotland, and others by similar means saved themselves. There were taken Henry Duke of Somerset, Robert Earl of Hungerford and Thomas Roos. The Duke of Somerset, for altering his mind, was beheaded out of hand; the others were brought to Newcastle and executed not long after . . . [King] Edward, although he thought his affairs now at last, by reason of this victory, to be sufficiently assured, yet he was very careful that Margaret, wife to King Henry, should by no means return to England to move the people there to future sedition. . . . [Henry VI], whether he was past all fear or driven deeply to some kind of madness, [when] enterprising to enter England in disguise had scarce set foot there when he was taken, brought to King Edward in London and committed to prison.

10) John Blacman
(*Blacman*, p. 43)
. . . after the horrid and ungrateful rebellion of his subjects had continued a long time, and after these rebels had fought many hard battles against him, [Henry VI]

fled at last with a few followers to a secret place prepared for him by those that were faithful to him. And, as he lay hid there for some time, an audible voice sounded in his ears for some seventeen days before he was taken, telling him how he should be delivered up by treachery, and brought to London without all honour like a thief or an outlaw, and led through the midst of it, and should endure many evils devised by the thoughts of wicked men, and should be imprisoned there in the Tower: of all which he was informed by revelation from the Blessed Virgin Mary and Saints John Baptist, Dunstan and Anselm, [and] was thereby strengthened to bear with patience these and like trials.

Barnet, Tewkesbury and the End of the Lancastrian Dynasty, 1471

As early as February 1465 Margaret of Anjou, a politically disgruntled and financially embarrassed exile on the continent since the summer of 1463, was lobbying the aid of Louis XI of France to recover the crown of England for her husband Henry VI and, ultimately, her son Edward of Lancaster who, by February 1467, was already showing signs of being far more like his grandfather Henry V than his own father; in May 1467 it was reported that the French king had sent for Margaret; and, by October 1468, Louis had apparently hinted that he would indeed 'help the old Queen of England' (1a, 1b, 1c, 1e). Already, too, the notion of 'treating with the Earl of Warwick to restore King Henry in England' had been canvassed (1d) and, certainly, by the later months of 1468 Warwick the Kingmaker was becoming increasingly resentful at Edward IV's policies, the growing prominence at court of Queen Elizabeth Woodville and her family, and his own apparently waning influence on events. Lancastrianism, moreover, had shown recent signs of revival, particularly in Wales (2), and several known Lancastrian sympathizers, most notably John de Vere Earl of Oxford, had been imprisoned. In the summer of 1469 Warwick's hand can surely be detected behind the rebellion of Robin of Redesdale in Yorkshire, a rising that culminated in a victory for Edward IV's opponents at the battle of Edgecote near Banbury on 26 July and the Yorkist king's imprisonment (3): yet Edward's release (or possibly escape) only a few weeks later may partly have resulted from a pro-Lancastrian rebellion in the far north of England, as Warwick struggled in vain to make his *de facto* control of government a reality. During the Lincolnshire rising of March 1470 there are indications of both Warwick's key role and the existence of Lancastrian sentiments among the rebels (4): this time, however, Edward IV came out on top and Warwick became an unwilling exile in France. Louis XI now set himself the task of reconciling Warwick and Margaret of Anjou as an essential prerequisite to replacing the Yorkist king by his predecessor. Clearly, it took all the wily French king's very considerable negotiating skills to pull this one off, not least since Margaret of Anjou's hostility to Warwick (whom she regarded as mainly responsible for her husband losing his throne in the first place) bordered on the fanatical (1f). Eventually, however, it was agreed that a marriage between Prince Edward of Lancaster and Warwick's daughter Anne be contracted, as a prelude to the earl's crossing to England, driving out Edward IV and restoring Henry VI: once he had accomplished this task, but only then, Margaret and her son would themselves cross to England (1g, 1h, 1i, 1j, 4).

Warwick the Kingmaker, accompanied by a number of diehard Lancastrians such as John de Vere Earl of Oxford and Jasper Tudor Earl of Pembroke (as well as Edward IV's own brother George Duke of Clarence), and supplied with ships by the French king, finally set sail for England early in September 1470 (1j, 1k, 4). After landing in the west country (an area traditionally Lancastrian in sympathy), Warwick, Clarence, Pembroke and Oxford issued a proclamation declaring their commitment to Henry VI, condemning Edward IV as a usurper and calling on all men of fighting age to join them; moreover, not only did they attract considerable popular support there and elsewhere (4) but, within three weeks of their coming, Edward IV had fled the country and sailed for Burgundy. Early in October 1470, following the arrival of Warwick and Clarence in London, Henry VI was restored to the throne (4, 5, 6). Several years of imprisonment in the Tower had all too obviously left their mark on him: indeed, if we are to believe John Blacman, 'like a true follower of Christ', he had 'patiently endured hunger, thirst, mockings, derisions, abuse and many other hardships' (10). More mundanely, *Warkworth's Chronicle* remarks that, when freed from incarceration, the king was neither 'honourably arrayed' nor 'so cleanly kept as should be such a prince' (4). Clearly, Henry VI was even less capable of ruling in 1470/1 than he had been a decade earlier and the government now established in his name was very much dominated by Richard Neville Earl of Warwick. Over the next six months Warwick did seek to reconcile as many Yorkist supporters as he could, as well as trying to ensure continued Lancastrian backing (4), but, in practice, he found it almost impossible to satisfy one faction without alienating another. The situation was certainly not helped either by the failure of Margaret of Anjou and Edward of Lancaster, whether as a result of caution or adverse weather, to fulfil their promise to cross the Channel (1l, 1m, 4, 6). Perhaps the second Crowland continuator was at his most perceptive when judging Henry VI's 'Second Reign': although in October 1470 'innumerable folk' regarded Henry VI's restoration as 'a miracle and the transformation the work of the All Highest', he commented, by the spring of 1471 'no one dared admit to having been his partisan' (5).

Edward IV returned to England in March 1471 and, after a none-too-enthusiastic reception in Yorkshire, began to attract increasing support as he marched south. Once news of his imminent arrival in London became known, a desperate attempt was made in the city to rally support for Henry VI: if we are to believe *Warkworth's Chronicle*, when the people were urged to be true to the king, 'every man said they would', only to be betrayed by the city authorities (4); however, according to the *Great Chronicle of London* (whose author may well have been an eyewitness), Henry's pathetic progress through the city was 'more like a play than the showing of a prince to win men's hearts', not least since he was ever displayed 'in a long blue gown of velvet as though he had no more to change with' (6). Certainly, on 11 April 1471,

Edward IV entered the capital unopposed and, apparently, had an audience with his Lancastrian rival before once more imprisoning him (4, 6). Indeed, so we are informed in a letter written soon afterwards by Edward's sister Margaret of Burgundy, the two kings shook hands and Henry even naively declared, 'My cousin of York, you are very welcome: I know that in your hands my life will not be in danger.' Edward IV remained in London just two days before marching out to confront Warwick's army as it, too, approached London: Henry VI, so the *Great Chronicle* tells us, was 'conveyed secretly after him' (6). The extraordinary battle of Barnet was fought, in a thick mist, early on Easter Sunday morning (14 April). The *Arrival of Edward IV* provides a detailed, probably eyewitness, account of the fighting and, despite its all too obvious pro-Yorkist stance, remains indispensable (7). Clearly, confusion reigned for much of the time but, in the end, it was a notable Yorkist victory: the turning point almost certainly came when, as *Warkworth's Chronicle* relates, the 'star with streams' livery of John de Vere Earl of Oxford's men was mistaken, in the mist, for the Yorkist 'sun with streams' device, and Oxford's force came under attack by their fellow Lancastrians; moreover, by the time it was all over, both Warwick the Kingmaker and his brother John Neville had lost their lives (1n, 4, 6, 7, 8a, 8b).

On the very same day that Barnet was fought, ironically enough, Queen Margaret of Anjou, accompanied by her son Prince Edward of Lancaster, at last set foot on English soil again when she landed at Weymouth in Dorset (1l, 1m, 1n, 4, 5, 6, 8a). Although initially shattered by news of Barnet, Margaret of Anjou, urged on by stalwart Lancastrians such as Edmund Beaufort Duke of Somerset and John Courtenay Earl of Devon, soon rallied: interestingly, a Milanese correspondent writing in Bruges on 7 May 1471 (before news of Tewkesbury reached Burgundy) reported considerable optimism about her prospects (1n) and, clearly, Margaret attracted considerable support as she journeyed towards south Wales (4, 5). Edward IV, determined to confront the queen and her supporters before her force had grown too large, lost no time in responding to her arrival and, on 4 May, the battle of Tewkesbury was fought (1o, 4, 5, 6). The only substantial account of the fighting is that provided by the partisan author of the *Arrival* (7) but several sources comment on the outcome and significance of the battle (1o, 4, 5, 6). The death of Prince Edward of Lancaster was clearly a devastating blow for the Lancastrians and, although there is considerable disagreement in the sources, the balance of likelihood is that he was killed during the action (1o, 4, 5, 6, 7). John Courtenay Earl of Devon and Somerset's brother John Beaufort also lost their lives on the field, while Edmund Beaufort Duke of Somerset himself and a number of other Lancastrian diehards, probably forcibly removed by Edward IV from Tewkesbury abbey where they had taken refuge after the battle, were executed (4, 5, 7). The victory at Tewkesbury, following so quickly on the heels of Barnet, finally put paid to Lancastrian hopes, despite a spirited attempt by Thomas Neville Bastard of Fauconberg to raise the south east and seize London (9). On 21 May 1471 Edward IV entered the capital once more amid considerable spectacle, apparently displaying the recently captured Margaret of Anjou as a veritable trophy of his success, and now (at last!) he was fully secure on the throne (4, 5, 6, 7): indeed, a Milanese correspondent, writing on 2 June, now judged King Edward 'the peaceful lord and dominator' of England (1o). A few years later Margaret of Anjou was ransomed by Louis XI, destined to spend the rest of her life as a politically toothless exile from her adopted country (1q). An even worse fate befell her husband when, probably on the very night of Edward IV's triumphant entry into London following Tewkesbury, his miserable life finally came to an end in the Tower. The official Yorkist version of this event in the *Arrival* – that he died 'of pure displeasure and melancholy' – can surely be discounted, while any role Edward's younger brother Richard of Gloucester (the future Richard III) may have had in the hapless Henry's demise is far from clear: Edward IV himself, in all probability, was responsible for ordering both his rival's death and the disposal of his corpse once the deed was done (1p, 4, 5, 6, 10, 11, 12). So ended the Lancastrian dynasty.

1) Milanese State Papers
(*CSPM*, pp. 117, 120, 126, 139–42, 150–1, 154, 156–7, 223)

a) Axieto, 6 February 1465
[Queen Margaret of Anjou] begs the king here [Louis XI of France] to be pleased to give her help so that she may be able to recover her kingdom. . . . The king remarked: 'Look how proudly she writes'. . . .

b) Bourges, 14 February 1467
This boy [Edward, son of Henry VI and Margaret of Anjou], though only thirteen years of age, already talks of nothing but cutting off heads or making war, as if he had everything in his hands or was the god of battle or the peaceful occupant of [the English] throne.

c) Chartres, 5 May 1467
[The] son of Duke John [of Calabria, Margaret of Anjou's brother] has left Nancy in Lorraine and gone to visit the late Queen of England, who has also withdrawn to Lorraine with her son aged thirteen, because she had no other asylum. She is to come and stay at the court here, and the king has sent [to] fetch her, and she should soon be here.

d) Chartres, 9 May 1467
[There has been talk] of treating with the Earl of Warwick to restore King Henry in England, and the ambassador of the old Queen of England is already here.

e) Paris, 1 October 1468
[King Louis XI] now gives out that he means to help the old Queen of England

[and] favour her in that enterprise as much as possible. However, so far I hear of nothing actual being done. . . .

f) Amboise, 29 June 1470
The Queen of England, wife of King Henry, and the prince, her son, arrived in this place on the 25th inst., and were received in a very friendly and honourable manner by his majesty the king and the queen. His majesty has spent and still spends every day in long discussions with that queen to induce her to make the alliance with Warwick and to let the prince, her son, go with the earl to the enterprise of England. Up to the present the queen has shown herself very hard and difficult, and although his majesty offers her many assurances, it seems that on no account whatever will she agree to send her son with Warwick, as she mistrusts him. Nevertheless it is thought that in the end she will let herself be persuaded to do what his majesty wishes.

g) Angers, 20 July 1470
The Queen of England, wife of King Henry, has been induced to consent to do all that his majesty desires, both as regards a reconciliation with Warwick and the marriage alliance. The queen and Warwick are expected here in a day or two, to arrange everything finally, and then Warwick will return to England without losing time. The Prince of Wales will not go with him this first time, but one of his uncles will go, a brother of King Henry, who is here. If matters go prosperously, then the prince will go back immediately, otherwise he will not set foot there.

h) Angers, 24 July 1470
The Queen of England and the Prince of Wales, her son, arrived here the day before yesterday, and on the same day the Earl of Warwick also arrived. With great reverence Warwick went on his knees and asked her pardon for the injuries and wrongs done to her in the past. She graciously forgave him and he afterwards did homage and fealty there, swearing to be a faithful and loyal subject of the king, queen and prince as his liege lord unto death. They have not yet spoken of the marriage alliance, though it is considered as good as accomplished.

i) Angers, 28 July 1470
The marriage of Warwick's daughter to the Prince of Wales is settled and announced. . . . In two days Warwick will leave for his fleet, to direct it [to] the enterprise of England. King Henry's brother, the Earl of Pembroke, is going with him, and if their affairs prosper the king himself [?Prince Edward of Lancaster] will immediately follow them.

j) Angers, 31 July 1470
The Queen of England and the Earl of Warwick left this morning together for Normandy to celebrate the nuptials of their children, as Warwick wishes to see

them united before he proceeds to England. Immediately afterwards he will proceed with his enterprise.

k) Omans, 14 September 1470

The Earl of Warwick, in the name of St George, left port with all his fleet, and with the fleet of Queen Margaret, on the 9th inst., and sailed towards England.

l) Beauvais, 28 March 1471

[The Queen of England] has delayed crossing [to England] up to the present, but now she is going in God's name, and it is reckoned that at this moment she has either crossed, or is on the sea in the act of doing so. She would have gone earlier still if the escort to take her had come sooner, for she took leave of the king at Amboise more than three months ago.

m) Beauvais, 9 April 1471

The Queen of England embarked these last days, but a contrary wind drove her back again. She is only waiting for a wind to start.

n) Bruges, 7 May 1471

[You] will have heard of the fighting which has taken place in England and how the Earl of Warwick and his brother have been slain by King Edward. A Spaniard, who left London on the 24th of April, relates that King Edward has set out with his power to look for the queen and the prince, who had landed and had gone to the parts of Wales. We have heard nothing since, although we are greedy for news. There are many who consider the queen's prospects favourable, chiefly because of the death of the Earl of Warwick, because it is reckoned she ought to have many lords in her favour, who intended to resist her because they were enemies of Warwick. . . .

o) Ham, 2 June 1471

Yesterday his majesty heard with extreme sorrow, by clear and manifest news from England, so it appears, that King Edward has recently fought a battle with the Prince of Wales, towards Wales, where he had gone to meet him. He has not only routed the prince but taken and slain him, together with all the leading men with him. He has also taken the queen and sent her to London to keep King Henry company, he also being a prisoner there; and so at length King Edward remains the peaceful lord and dominator of that kingdom of England without having any further obstacle whatever.

p) La Fere, 17 June 1471

King Edward has not chosen to have the custody of King Henry any longer, although he was in some sense innocent, and there was no great fear about his proceedings, the prince his son and the Earl of Warwick being dead as well as all those who were for him and had any vigour, as he has caused King Henry to be secretly assassinated in the Tower, where he was a prisoner. They say he has done the same to the queen [*sic*], King Henry's wife. He has, in short, chosen to crush the seed.

q) Lausanne, 21 April 1476
We hear that the King of France has bought, for 24 or 30,000 crowns, Queen Margaret of England, daughter of King Réné, widow of King Henry and prisoner of King Edward in England, and has fetched her to France, it is supposed in order to get her to give up her claims to Provence as the daughter of King Réné.

2) Gregory's Chronicle
(*Gregory*, p. 237)
[In 1468] Lord Herbert of Wales got the castle of Harlech in Wales, a castle so strong that men said it was impossible for any man to get it, but it was secured by surrender; and some of the petty captains were beheaded at Tower Hill in London, for that castle was fortified and victualled by such as loved King Harry. . . . Also that year, a little before the siege of [Harlech] castle, old Lord Jasper [Tudor], sometime Earl of Pembroke, was in Wales, who rode over the country and held many assizes in King Harry's name. . . .

3) Crowland Chronicle: First (Prior's) Continuation
(*Ingulph*, pp. 445–6)
[In] 1469 there arose a great disagreement between the king [Edward IV] and his kinsman Richard, the most illustrious Earl of Warwick. . . . [In] the summer season a whirlwind again came down from the north, in the form of a mighty insurrection of the commons of that part of the country. They complained that they were grievously oppressed with taxes and annual tributes by the favourites of the king and queen [Edward IV and Queen Elizabeth Woodville] and, having appointed one Robin of Redesdale to act as captain over them, proceeded to march, about 60,000 in number, to join the Earl of Warwick, who was then in London. . . .

[The] army of the northern men unexpectedly met [William Herbert Earl of Pembroke] on the plain of Edgecote, near Banbury, in the county of Northampton [on 26 July 1469], when, the two armies engaging, a great battle was fought and a most dreadful slaughter, especially of the Welsh, ensued; so much so that 4000 men of the two armies are said to have been slain. The Earl of Pembroke, and several other nobles and gentlemen of Wales, were made prisoners and, by order of the Earl of Warwick without any opportunity of ransom, beheaded at Northampton. . . .

4) Warkworth's Chronicle
(*Warkworth*, pp. 8–13, 15–19, 21)
[In March 1470 there] gathered all the commons [of Lincolnshire] to the number of 30,000, and cried 'King Harry' and refused King Edward. And the Duke of Clarence and the Earl of Warwick caused all this, like as they did Robin of Redesdale to rise before that at Banbury field [in July 1469]. . . .

[When] the Duke of Clarence and the Earl of Warwick were in France [in July 1470, they] could find no remedy but to send to Queen Margaret and make a marriage between Prince Edward, King Harry's son, and [one] of the Earl of Warwick's daughters, which was concluded. . . . And there it was appointed and accorded that King Harry should [be restored to the throne] and reign as well as he did before, and after him Prince Edward and his heirs of his body lawfully begotten. . . . Also it was appointed and agreed that Harry Duke of Exeter, Edmund Duke of Somerset, brother to Harry that was slain at Hexham field, the Earl of Devonshire called Courtenay, and all other knights, squires and all others that were put out and attainted for King Harry's quarrel, should come into England again. [All this was] written, indented and sealed between Queen Margaret and the prince her son on the one part and the Duke of Clarence and the Earl of Warwick on the other. . . .

[A] little before Michaelmas [1470] the Duke of Clarence and the Earl of Warwick landed in the west country and gathered there a great people. . . . [In October 1470] the Bishop of Winchester, by the assent of the Duke of Clarence and the Earl of Warwick, went to the Tower of London, where King Harry was in prison by King Edward's commandment, and there took him from his keepers, who was not honourably arrayed as a prince and not so cleanly kept as should be such a prince; they had him out, newly arrayed him and did to him great reverence, and brought him to the palace of Westminster, and so he was restored to the crown again, [of which] all his good lovers were full glad, and the more part of the people. . . .

[In February 1471] Harry Duke of Exeter, Edmund Duke of Somerset, Lord John of Somerset, his brother the Earl of Ormond, Jasper Earl of Pembroke, brother to King Harry, and the Earl of Richmond, with many other knights, squires, gentlemen and yeomen, came into England, and entered into their lordships and lands, [since] all attainders made in King Edward's time were annulled by Parliament, King Harry admitted to his crown and dignity again, and all his men to their inheritance. . . .

[On 10 April 1471] King Harry and, with him, the Archbishop of York, rode about London and desired the people to be true to him; and every man said they would. Nevertheless, [Christopher] Urswick, recorder of London, and several aldermen, who had the rule of the city, commanded all the people who were in arms, protecting the city and King Harry, to go home to dinner; and during dinner time King Edward was let in, and so went to the Bishop of London's palace, and there took King Harry and the Archbishop of York and put them in prison. . . .

[On] Easter eve [Edward IV] and all his host went towards Barnet, and carried King Harry with him, [and on 14 April] King Edward won the field [of Barnet]. And there was slain of the Earl of Warwick's party the earl himself, Marquis Montagu, Sir William Tyrel and many others. The Duke of Exeter fought courageously there that day, and was greatly plundered, and wounded, and left naked for dead in the field, and so lay there from seven of the clock till four in the afternoon, [when he was] brought to a house by a man of his own, and a leech brought to him, and so afterwards brought into sanctuary at Westminster. . . . And King Harry, being in the van during the battle, was not hurt; but he was brought again to the Tower of London, there to be kept.

[Meanwhile] Queen Margaret and Prince Edward her son, with other knights, squires and other men of the King of France, had ships to bring them to England [but], when they were embarked in France, the wind was so contrary to them for seventeen days and nights they could not come from Normandy, [whereas] with a wind they might have sailed it in twelve hours. [Eventually, on the same day that Barnet was fought], they landed at Weymouth, and so, by land, from Weymouth they rode to Exeter. There met with [the queen] at Weymouth Edmund Duke of Somerset, Lord John his brother, brother to Harry Duke of Somerset slain at Hexham, and Courtenay Earl of Devonshire, and many others. And on Easter Monday tidings were brought to them that King Edward had won the field of Barnet and King Harry put into the Tower again. And at once they made out commandments, in the queen's name and the prince's, to all the west country, and gathered great people, and made their way towards the town of Bristol.

When [Edward IV] heard that they were landed, and had gathered many people, he took all his host and went out of London the Wednesday of Easter week, and courageously took his way towards them. [When] Prince Edward heard thereof, he hastened himself and all his host towards the town of Gloucester; however, he did not enter the town but made his way to Tewkesbury and there he made a field not far from the River Severn, [where] King Edward and his host came upon him on Saturday the fourth day of May 1471. And Edmund Duke of Somerset and Sir Hugh Courtenay left the field, as a result of which the field was broken; and most people fled away from the prince, so the field was lost to their party. And there was slain in the field Prince Edward, who cried for succour to his brother-in-law the Duke of Clarence; also there was slain Courtenay Earl of Devonshire, Lord John of Somerset, Lord Wenlock [and others]; and these were taken and beheaded afterwards, where the king had pardoned them in the abbey church of Tewkesbury, by a priest that turned out at his mass and the sacrament in his hands, when King Edward came with his sword into the church, who required him by virtue of the sacrament that he should pardon all those whose names here follow: the Duke of Somerset [and fourteen others]; which, upon trust of the king's pardon, given in the same church on the Saturday, abode there still, when they might have gone and saved their lives; however, on Monday after, they were beheaded notwithstanding the king's pardon. And afterwards these ladies were taken: Queen Margaret; Prince Edward's wife, the second daughter of the Earl of Warwick; the Countess of Devonshire. . . .

[The] same night that King Edward came to London, King Harry, being inward in prison in the Tower of London, was put to death, the 21st day of May, on a

Tuesday night, between 11 and 12 o'clock, being then at the Tower the Duke of Gloucester, brother to King Edward, and many others. And on the morrow he was put in a coffin and brought to St Paul's, and his face was open so that every man might see him. And in his lying, he bled on the pavement there, and afterwards he was brough to the Blackfriars and there he bled anew and afresh; and from thence he was carried to Chertsey abbey in a boat, and buried there in the chapel of Our Lady.

5) *Crowland Chronicle: Second (1459–1486) Continuation*
(*Crowland*, pp. 122–3, 126–31; *Ingulph*, pp. 463, 465–6, 468)

[In October 1470] King Henry VI was taken out of the Tower, where he had so long been held in captivity, and restored to the throne and [on 13 October], ceremonially and in public, the crown was placed on his head. All laws were now re-enacted in Henry's name. . . . You might then have come across innumerable folk to whom the restoration of the pious King Henry was a miracle and the transformation the work of the All Highest; but how incomprehensible are the judgements of God, how unfathomable his ways: for it is well known that less than six months later no one dared admit to having been his partisan. . . .

[In April 1471 Queen Margaret of Anjou] and her followers sailed a straight course from Normandy and landed in the region of Cornwall and Devon. The queen's army grew daily, for there were many in those western parts who preferred King Henry's cause to the claims of all others. Edmund Duke of Somerset, first in rank in the whole company after Prince Edward and an exile from his boyhood, together with his brother, John Beaufort by name, Thomas Earl of Devon, John Lord Wenlock and Brother John Langstrother, Prior of the Order of St John in England, considered in council how they might pass swiftly along the western coast – perhaps through Bristol, Gloucester and Chester – to reach Lancashire, where considerable numbers of archers were to be found. They were confident that the nobility and common people in those parts, beyond all others in the kingdom, were well affected to the Lancastrian line. Nor perhaps might that belief have failed them had not King Edward marched against them from London so speedily, in spite of having so few troops with him, in order that, while still in the county of Gloucester, their further progress might be intercepted. And that in fact happened.

When both armies were too fatigued and thirsty to march any further, they joined battle near Tewkesbury. After the result had long remained doubtful, in the end King Edward gained a glorious victory. Of the queen's forces, either on the battlefield or afterwards by the avenging hands of certain persons, there were killed Prince Edward himself, King Henry's only son, the Duke of Somerset, the Earl of Devon [and others]. Queen Margaret was captured and kept in security so that she might be borne in a carriage before the king at his triumph in London, and so it was done. . . .

I shall pass over in silence the fact that, at this time, King Henry's lifeless body was discovered in the Tower of London: may God have mercy upon and give time for repentance to the person, whoever it might be, who dared to lay sacrilegious hands on the Lord's Anointed! And so, let the perpetrator merit the title of tyrant and the victim that of glorious martyr. The body was put on view for a few days in St Paul's church in London and then carried along the Thames, in an illuminated barge solemnly equipped with torches for the purpose, to the monastic church of Chertsey in the diocese of Winchester, fifteen miles from the city, for burial. The miracles which God has performed in answer to the prayers of those who devoutly implored his intercession bear witness to his life of innocence, love of God and of the church, patience in adversity and other remarkable qualities.

6) Great Chronicle of London
(*Great Chronicle*, pp. 212, 214–16, 218, 220)
[On 12 October 1470] the Tower was given up by appointment, and King Henry fetched out of the place where he was long before imprisoned, and then lodged in the king's lodging where the queen before lay. [On 15 October the Duke of Clarence], accompanied by the Earls of Warwick, Derby and Shrewsbury, Lord Stanley, and many other noble men, rode to the Tower and fetched thence King Henry, and conveyed him through the high streets of the city, riding in a long gown of blue velvet to St Paul's, and when he had there offered at the rood of the north door he was then conveyed through the church to the bishop's palace and there lodged. . . . [Thus] was this ghostly [spiritual] and virtuous prince King Henry VI, after long imprisonment and many injuries, derisions and scorns sustained by him patiently of many of his subjects, restored unto his right and regality; in which he took no great pride but meekly thanked God and gave all his mind to serve and please him, and partook little or nothing of the pomp or vanities of this world. . . .

[On 27 February 1471 there] came to London the Earl of Warwick, who had tarried for a long while at the seaside to receive Queen Margaret and her son, of whom he was brought certain and true knowledge that they had lain at a haven in France, abiding there for a convenient wind, from the beginning of November last past. . . .

[On 11 April 1471, in order to] cause the citizens [of London] to bear more favour to King Henry, [the king] was conveyed from the palace of St Paul's through Cheap and Cornhill, and so on about to his lodging again by Candlewick Street and Watling Street, accompanied by the Archbishop of York, who held him by the hand all the way, and Lord Zouch, an old and impotent man, [who] bore the king's sword; and so, with a small company of gentlemen going on foot before, one on horseback carrying a pole or long shaft with two fox tails fastened on the end, and a small company of serving men following, this progress was held, more like a play than the showing of a prince to win men's hearts; for by this means he lost many and won none or right few, and ever he was shown in a long blue gown of velvet, as though he had no more to change with. But before this progress was fully finished, King Edward's foreriders had come to Shoreditch and Newington, wherefore the archbishop, having small confidence that the citizens would resist King Edward or his people shifted for himself and left King Henry alone in the palace, and the rest of any reputation did as the bishop had done. . . . [Edward IV, on arrival in London], commanded King Henry to his presence, communed the fill of his pleasure, and commanded him again to such a place within the palace where he might safely be kept. . . .

[When Edward IV left London on 13 April] King Henry was conveyed secretly after him, and so held his way to Barnet [where] King Edward won the field [on 14 April], and upon the same afternoon was King Henry brought through the city riding in the same blue gown [as] before, and so conveyed to Westminster, and thence to the Tower, where he remained a prisoner while he lived. . . .

[Queen] Margaret, with Prince Edward her son, landed in the west country with a strength of Frenchmen. . . . The king assembled his people and drew towards his enemies, and finally met with them at a place or village called Tewkesbury, where after a short fight he subdued his enemies and took Queen Margaret and her son alive, the which [Prince Edward] being brought into his presence, after the king had questioned a few words of the cause of his so landing within his realm, and he gave unto the king an answer contrary to his pleasure, the king struck him on the face with the back of his gauntlet, after which stroke so received by him, the king's servants rid him out of life forthwith. And then was Queen Margaret sent towards London. . . .

Upon Ascension Eve the corpse of King Henry VI was brought through Cornhill from the Tower with a great company of men of that place bearing weapons as if they would have led him to some place of execution, and so they conveyed him to St Paul's, where that night he was set in the body of the church beside the image of Our Lady of Grace, open visaged that he might be known. And upon the morrow with a few torches, as he was brought thither, so was he thence conveyed to the waterside, and from thence to Chertsey and there buried, for whom shortly afterwards God showed sundry miracles. Of whose death the common rumour then went that the Duke of Gloucester was not all guiltless.

7) Arrival of Edward IV
(*Historie of the Arrivall of Edward IV*, ed. J. Bruce, pp. 19–20, 28–31, 38)
On the morning [of 14 April 1471], despite a great mist preventing the opposing armies seeing each other, the king [Edward IV] committed his cause and quarrel to Almighty God [on the battlefield of Barnet]. Displaying banners and sounding trumpets, he set upon his opponents, first with shots and then with hand-strokes, all courageously received by them when battle was joined. The joining of the two battle lines was not directly front to front, however, as it would have been had not

the mist prevented each seeing the other clearly: this probably caused the battle to be more cruel and mortal. For, as it was, one end of their line over-reached the end of the king's line: so, at that west end where their force was much stronger, they defeated the king's men and, when many of them fled towards Barnet (and then London), they chased them and did much harm. Because of the great mist, however, neither the defeat, flight nor chase were observed by the rest of the king's force, so they were in no way discouraged; nor, for the same reason, were their enemies greatly encouraged. Likewise, at the east end, the king's force over-reached their line, and so defeated their opponents there, before drawing near to the king who was in the midst of the battle, sustaining all its might and weight [in the centre]. Nevertheless, as a result of the setback at the west end, news spread to Westminster, London and beyond that the king had been defeated and the field lost: it was not so. Rather, the king courageously determined to take revenge on all those who had falsely and traitorously conspired against him and, with the faithful and mighty assistance of his fellowship, vigorously and valiantly attacked his opponents in the midst and at the strongest point of their battle line: there, with great violence, he beat and bore down before him all who stood in his way [and as a result] won the field. . . .

[On 4 May 1471] the king armoured himself, and set all his host in good array, displayed his banners, blew trumpets, committed his cause and quarrel to God, and advanced directly upon his enemies [at Tewkesbury, despite the fact that they] were pitched in a very strong ground, very difficult to assail. Nevertheless, the king's ordnance was so conveniently positioned, and his vanguard so sore oppressed them with shots of arrows, that they gave them a right sharp shower, [for his opponents] had not so great a supply [of arrows and guns] as the king. In front of their field were such narrow lanes and deep dikes, so many hedges, trees and bushes, that it was right hard to approach near them and come to hand fighting. Moreover, Edmund, called Duke of Somerset, having that day the vanguard, [advanced] with his fellowship somewhat on one side of the king's vanguard, and by certain paths and ways, previously surveyed and unknown to the king's party, departed out of the field, passed a lane and came [to a] close just in front of the king [and], from the hill that was in one of the closes, set right fiercely on the end of the king's force. The king, most courageously, at once set upon them, entered and won the dike and hedge and, with great violence, pushed them back up the hill; so also the king's vanguard, being in the rule of the Duke of Gloucester. Here it is to be remembered that when the king had come to the field, before he set upon them, he noticed that, on the right of the field, there was a park, and therein much wood, and he, thinking to provide a remedy in case his enemies had laid an ambush of horsemen in that wood, chose out of his fellowship 200 spears and set them in a plomp [compact group] about a quarter of a mile from the field, charging them to keep a close watch on that corner of the wood, and do what was necessary if the need should arise, and if they saw no such need

[to] employ themselves in the best way they could. This provision proved as valuable at this time of the battle as could well have been devised, for these spears of the king's party, seeing no likelihood of any ambush in that corner of the wood, and seeing also a good opportunity to employ themselves well, all at once and unexpectedly burst out upon the Duke of Somerset and his vanguard. [Upon this Somerset's men] fled into the park and nearby meadow, and into lanes and dikes, where they best hoped to escape the danger. Nevertheless, many were defeated, taken and slain. And, even at the time of their flight, the king courageously set upon the other part of the field, where was Edward called prince, and in a short time put them to discomfiture and flight: so it befell, in the chase, that many of them were slain; at a mill, in the meadow, many of them were drowned; and many ran towards the town, many to the church, to the abbey, and elsewhere, as best they might.

In the winning of the field [at Tewkesbury] those who endured hand-strokes were slain at once. Edward, called prince, was taken, fleeing towards the town, and slain in the field. There were also slain Thomas, called Earl of Devonshire, John of Somerset, called Marquis Dorset, Lord Wenlock, and many others in great numbers. When this was done and achieved with God's might, the king took the direct way to the abbey to give unto Almighty God praise and thanks for the victory; [moreover, since] there had fled into the church many of his rebels [hoping] there to be relieved and saved from bodily harm, he gave them all his free pardon. [Nevertheless, since there] were found, in the abbey and other places in the town, Edmund called Duke of Somerset [and others, they] were brought before the king's brother [Richard] Duke of Gloucester and constable of England, and [John] Duke of Norfolk, marshal of England, [and] so were judged to death. . . . [On 7 May 1471] the king departed from Tewkesbury, towards his city of Worcester, and, on the way, he obtained certain knowledge that Queen Margaret was to be found not far from there in a poor religious house, where she had hidden herself, for the security of her person, early in the morning [of 4 May], after her son Edward called prince had gone to the field. . . .

Here it is to be remembered that, from the time of Tewkesbury field where Edward called prince was slain, then, and soon after, were taken and slain at the king's will all the noblemen that came from beyond the sea with Edward [of Lancaster] . . . Queen Margaret herself was taken and brought to the king and, in every part of England where any commotion was begun for King Henry's party, they were rebuked, so that it appeared to every man, at once, that the [queen's] party was extinct and repressed for ever, without any kind of hope of revival. . . . The certainty of all this came to the knowledge of Henry, lately called king, being in the Tower of London: not having, before that, knowledge of these matters, he took it to such great hatred, anger and indignation that, of pure displeasure and melancholy, he died the 23rd day of the month of May [1471]. The king caused his body to be brought to the Friars Preachers of London, and there his funeral service was sung.

Then the body was carried by water to an abbey called Chertsey by the Thames, sixteen miles from London, and there it was honourably interred.

8) Paston Letters
(*Paston Letters*, Vol. 5, pp. 99–100)

a) Sir John Paston, in London, to Margaret Paston, 18 April 1471
. . . my brother John is alive and fares well, and is in no peril of death. Nevertheless, he is hurt with an arrow on his right arm beneath the elbow: I have sent him a surgeon, who has dressed it, and he tells me that he trusts he shall be all whole in a right short time. . . .

There were killed upon the field, half a mile from Barnet, on Easter day, the Earl of Warwick, Marquis Montagu [and others]. . . . As for other tidings, it is understood here that Queen Margaret is verily landed, and her son, in the west country, and I believe that tomorrow or the next day King Edward will depart from here towards her to drive her out again. . . .

b) John de Vere Earl of Oxford to Margaret Countess of Oxford, April 1471
. . . I am in great heaviness at the making of this letter but, thanked be God, I have escaped and suddenly departed from my men, for I understand my chaplain would have betrayed me. . . .

[Do] give credence to the bearer of this letter, [reward] him for his costs, since I was not able to do so, [speedily] send me all the ready money you can raise and as many men as can come well horsed. . . .

[Be] of good cheer and [do not worry], for I shall bring my purpose about by the grace of God. . . .

9) London Journal
(*EHD*, p. 316)
[On Sunday 12 May 1471] Kentish men and others [led by Thomas Neville Bastard of Fauconberg], rebels of the king, mounted an attack on London Bridge. . . . [On 14 May] Kentish seamen and other rebels made an attack with great force and set fire to thirteen buildings on London Bridge. The Kentish seamen and others to the number of 3000 also launched an attack from the Thames on the gates at Aldgate and Bishopsgate and set fire to several buildings. The citizens [of London], however, sallied out of the gates, offered stout resistance, and put them to flight. . . .

10) John Blacman
(*Blacman*, p. 41)
. . . after a long time spent in hiding in secret places wherein for safety's sake he was forced to keep close, [Henry VI] was found and taken, brought as a traitor and criminal to London, and imprisoned in the Tower there; where, like a true

follower of Christ, he patiently endured hunger, thirst, mockings, derisions, abuse, and many other hardships, and finally suffered a violent death of the body that others might, as was then the expectation, peaceably possess the kingdom. But his soul, as we piously believe upon the evidence of the long series of miracles done in the place where his body is buried, liveth with God in the heavenly places, where after the troubles of this world he rejoiceth with the just in the eternal contemplation of God and in the stead of this earthly and transitory kingdom whereof he patiently bore the loss, he now possesseth one that endureth for ever.

11) *Polydore Vergil*
(*Vergil*, pp. 155–6)

Henry the Sixth, being not long before deprived of his diadem, was put to death in the Tower of London. The continual report is that Richard Duke of Gloucester killed him with a sword, whereby his brother might be delivered from all fear of hostility. . . . Afterwards the corpse of King Henry was, without any honour, brought from the Tower to St Paul's church, where it lay upon the bier all one day, and the day following was carried to an abbey of monks of St Benedict's Order, in a town called Chertsey. Not long after it was transferred to the castle of Windsor and laid in a new tomb in St George's chapel.

12) *Exchequer Records: Henry VI's Funeral, 1471*
(*EHD*, pp. 318–19)

To Hugh Brice, for money paid by him for wax cloth, linen, spices, and other ordinary expenses promised and incurred by him in connexion with the funeral of Henry of Windsor who died in the Tower of London, and for the wages and rewards of various men carrying torches from the Tower to the cathedral church of St Paul's, London, and thence to Chertsey with the body, £15 3*s* 6½*d*.

To Richard Martin, £9 10*s* 11*d*, for money paid by him for 28 yards of linen cloth, and expenses incurred within the Tower at the last departure of Henry, and also at Chertsey on the day of his burial, and for wages given to various soldiers of Calais watching round the body and for the conducting of barges with masters and sailors, rowing along the River Thames to Chertsey; and another time, £8 12*s* 3*d*, for money paid to the four orders of friars in the city of London, and the brothers of the Holy Cross there, and in other works of charity, that is, to the Carmelite friars 20*s*, to the Augustinian friars 20*s*, to the Franciscan friars 20*s*, to the Dominican friars for obsequies and celebrating masses 40*s*, and to the brothers of the Holy Cross 10*s*, and for saying obsequies and masses at Chertsey on the day of Henry's burial 52*s* 3*d*. . . .

Bibliography

'Annales Rerum Anglicarum', in *Letters and Papers Illustrative of the Wars of the English in France*,
Vol. 2, ed. J. Stevenson (Rolls Series, 1864)

Armstrong, C.A.J., 'Politics and the battle of St Albans, 1455', *Bulletin of the Institute of
Historical Research*, Vol. 33 (1960)

Aston, M., 'Richard II and the Wars of the Roses', in *The Reign of Richard II*, ed. C.M. Barron
and F.R.H. Du Boulay (London, 1971)

Bagley, J.J., *Margaret of Anjou Queen of England* (London, 1948)

'Benet's Chronicle for the years 1400–1462', ed. G.L. and M.A. Harriss, in *Camden Miscellany*
(Camden Society, 1972)

Blacman, John, *Henry the Sixth*, transl. M.R. James (Cambridge, 1919)

Boardman, A.W., *The Battle of Towton* (Stroud, 1994)

Britnell, R.H., 'The Economic Context', in *The Wars of the Roses*, ed. A.J. Pollard (London, 1995)

Brut or Chronicles of England, ed. F.W.D. Brie (Early English Text Society, 1908)

Calendar of Patent Rolls, Henry VI, 1446–52, 1452–61, Edward IV, 1461–7, 1467–76 (London,
1897–1901)

Calendar of State Papers and Manuscripts existing in the Archives and Collections of Milan, Vol. 1,
1385–1618, ed. A.B. Hinds (London, 1913)

Capgrave, John, *Liber de Illustribus Henricis*, ed. F.C. Hingeston (Rolls Series, 1858)

Carpenter, Christine, *The Wars of the Roses* (Cambridge, 1997)

Chrimes, S.B., *Lancastrians, Yorkists and Henry VII* (London, 1964)

Christie, Mabel, *Henry VI* (London, 1922)

Chronicle of John Hardyng, ed. H. Ellis (London, 1809)

Chronicles of London, ed. C.L. Kingsford (London, 1905)

Chronicles of the Wars of the Roses, ed. E. Hallam (London, 1988)

Commynes, Philippe de, *Memoirs: The Reign of Louis XI 1461–83*, transl. M. Jones
(Harmondsworth, 1972)

Crawford, Anne, 'The King's Burden?: the Consequences of Royal Marriage in Fifteenth-
Century England', in *Patronage, the Crown and the Provinces in Later Medieval England*, ed.
R.A. Griffiths (Gloucester, 1981)

Crowland Chronicle Continuations 1459–1486, ed. N. Pronay and J. Cox (Gloucester, 1986)

Denton, William, *England in the Fifteenth Century* (London, 1988)

Dockray, Keith, 'The Battle of Wakefield and the Wars of the Roses', in *The Battle of Wakefield*
(Ricardian pamphlet, 1992)

Dockray, Keith, 'The Origins of the Wars of the Roses', in *The Wars of the Roses*, ed. A.J. Pollard
(London, 1995)

Dockray, Keith, 'William Shakespeare, the Wars of the Roses and Richard III', *History Teaching
Review Year Book (Journal of the Scottish Association of Teachers of History)*, Vol. 11 (1997)

Dockray, Keith, *Edward IV: A Source Book* (Stroud, 1999)

Dunn, Diana, 'Margaret of Anjou, Queen Consort of Henry VI: A Reassessment of her Role,
1445–53', in *Crown, Government and People in the Fifteenth Century*, ed. R.E. Archer (Stroud, 1995)

England under the Lancastrians, ed. J.H. Flemming (London, 1921)

England under the Yorkists 1460–1485, ed. I.D. Thornley (London, 1920)

English Chronicle of the Reigns of Richard II, Henry IV, Henry V and Henry VI, ed. J.S. Davies
(Camden Society, 1856)

English Historical Documents, Vol. 4, 1327–1485, ed. A.R. Myers (London, 1969)

Erlanger, Philippe, *Margaret of Anjou Queen of England* (London, 1970)

Fortescue, Sir John, *The Governance of England*, ed. C. Plummer (Oxford, 1885)

Gillingham, John, *The Wars of the Roses* (London, 1981)

Goodman, Anthony, *The Wars of the Roses* (London, 1981)

Gransden, Antonia, *Historical Writing in England 11:* c. *1307 to The Early Sixteenth Century* (New York, 1982)

Great Chronicle of London, ed. A.H. Thomas and I.D. Thornley (London, 1938)

Green, J.R., *A Short History of the English People* (London, 1874)

'Gregory's Chronicle', in *Historical Collections of a Citizen of London*, ed. J. Gairdner (Camden Society, 1876)

Griffiths, Ralph, 'Duke Richard of York's Intentions in 1450 and the Origins of the Wars of the Roses', *Journal of Medieval History*, Vol. 1 (1976)

Griffiths, Ralph, 'The Sense of Dynasty in the Reign of Henry VI', in *Patronage, Pedigree and Power in Later Medieval England*, ed. C. Ross (Gloucester, 1979)

Griffiths, Ralph, *The Reign of Henry VI* (London, 1981, reprinted Stroud, 1998, with a new introduction by the author)

Griffiths, Ralph, *King and Country: England and Wales in the Fifteenth Century* (London, 1991)

Gross, Anthony, 'Lancastrians Abroad, 1461–71', *History Today*, Vol. 42 (August 1992)

Gross, Anthony, *The Dissolution of the Lancastrian Kingship* (Stamford, 1996)

Haigh, Philip, *The Military Campaigns of the Wars of the Roses* (Stroud, 1995)

Haigh, Philip, *The Battle of Wakefield 1460* (Stroud, 1996)

Hammond, P.W., *The Battles of Barnet and Tewkesbury* (Gloucester, 1990)

Harvey, Isobel, *Jack Cade's Rebellion of 1450* (Oxford, 1991)

Haswell, Jock, *The Ardent Queen: Margaret of Anjou and the Lancastrian Heritage* (London, 1976)

Hicks, Michael, *Richard III and his Rivals: Magnates and their Motives in the Wars of the Roses* (London, 1991)

Hicks, Michael, *Who's Who in Late Medieval England* (London, 1991)

Hicks, Michael, 'The Sources', in *The Wars of the Roses*, ed. A.J. Pollard (London, 1995)

Hicks, Michael, *Warwick the Kingmaker* (Oxford, 1998)

Historical Poems of the 14th and 15th Centuries, ed. R.H. Robbins (New York, 1959)

Historie of the Arrivall of Edward IV in England, ed. J. Bruce (Camden Society, 1838)

Horrox, Rosemary, 'Personalities and Politics', in *The Wars of the Roses*, ed. A.J. Pollard (London, 1995)

Incerti Scriptoris Chronicon Angliae de Regnis Henrici IV, Henrici V et Henrici VI, ed. J.A. Giles (London, 1848)

Ingulph's Chronicle of the Abbey of Croyland, ed. H.T. Riley (London, 1854)

Johnson, P.A., *Duke Richard of York 1411–1460* (Oxford, 1988)

Jones, Michael K., 'Somerset, York and the Wars of the Roses', *English Historical Review*, Vol. 14 (1989)

Kingsford, C.L., 'Extracts from the first version of Hardyng's Chronicle', *English Historical Review*, Vol. 27 (1912)

Kingsford, C.L., *English Historical Literature in the Fifteenth Century* (Oxford, 1913)

Kingsford, C.L., *Prejudice and Promise in Fifteenth Century England* (Oxford, 1925)

Lander, J.R., *The Wars of the Roses* (London, 1965)

Lander, J.R., *Conflict and Stability in Fifteenth Century England* (London, 1969)

Lander, J.R., *Crown and Nobility 1450–1509* (London, 1976)

Lander, J.R., *Government and Community: England 1450–1509* (London, 1980)

Lee, Patricia-Ann, 'Reflections of Power: Margaret of Anjou and the Dark Side of Queenship', *Renaissance Quarterly*, Vol. 39 (1986)

Letters of Queen Margaret of Anjou, Bishop Beckington and Others, ed. C. Monro (Camden Society, 1863)

Letters of the Queens of England 1100–1547, ed. A. Crawford (Stroud, 1994)

Lovatt, Roger, 'John Blacman: biographer of Henry VI', in *The Writing of History in the Middle Ages*, ed. R.H.C. Davis and J.M. Wallace-Hadrill (Oxford, 1981)

Lovatt, Roger, 'A Collector of Apocryphal Anecdotes: John Blacman Revisited', in *Property and Politics: Essays in Later Medieval English History*, ed. A.J. Pollard (Gloucester, 1984)

McFarlane, K.B., *The Nobility of Later Medieval England* (Oxford, 1973)

McFarlane, K.B., *England in the Fifteenth Century* (London, 1981)

McKenna, J.W., 'Piety and Propaganda: the Cult of Henry VI', in *Chaucer and Middle English Studies in Honour of R.H. Robbins*, ed. B. Rowland (Kent, Ohio, 1974)

Paston Letters 1422–1509, ed. J. Gairdner, 6 vols (1904, reprinted Gloucester, in one volume, 1983)

Politics of Fifteenth-century England: John Vale's Book, ed. M.L. Kekewich and others (Stroud, 1995)

Pollard, A.J., 'The Last of the Lancastrians', *Parliamentary History*, Vol. 2 (1983)

Pollard, A.J., *The Wars of the Roses* (London, 1988)

Pollard, A.J., *North-Eastern England during the Wars of the Roses* (Oxford, 1990)

Pollard, A.J., 'Percies, Nevilles and the Wars of the Roses', *History Today*, Vol. 43 (September 1993)

Pollard, A.J. (ed.), *The Wars of the Roses* (London, 1995)

Pollard, A.J., 'Fifteenth-century Politics and the Wars of the Roses', *The Historian*, no. 57 (1998)

Rawcliffe, Carole, 'Richard Duke of York, the king's "obeisant liegeman": a New Source for the Protectorates of 1454 and 1455', *Historical Research*, Vol. 60 (1987)

Rawcliffe, Carole, 'The Insanity of Henry VI', *The Historian*, no. 50 (1996)

Registrum Abbatiae Johannis Whethamstede, Vol. 1, ed. H.T. Riley (Rolls Series, 1872)

Richmond, Colin, 'After McFarlane', *History*, Vol. 68 (1983)

Richmond, Colin, 'Propaganda in the Wars of the Roses', *History Today*, Vol. 42 (July 1992)

Ross, Charles, *Edward IV* (London, 1974, reprinted Yale, 1997, with a new introduction by Ralph Griffiths)

Ross, Charles, *The Wars of the Roses* (London, 1976)

Ross, Charles, 'Rumour, Propaganda and Public Opinion during the Wars of the Roses', in *Patronage, the Crown and the Provinces in Later Medieval England*, ed. R.A. Griffiths (Gloucester, 1981)

Rotuli Parliamentorum, ed. J. Strachey and others, 6 vols (1767–77)

Scattergood, V.J., *Politics and Poetry in the Fifteenth Century* (London, 1971)

Six Town Chronicles of England, ed. R. Flenley (Oxford, 1911)

Storey, R.L., *The End of the House of Lancaster* (London, 1966, reprinted Gloucester, 1986, with a new introduction by the author)

Stubbs, William, *Constitutional History of England*, Vol. 3 (Oxford, 1878)

Three Chronicles of the Reign of Edward IV (Gloucester, 1988) for reprints of *Warkworth's Chronicle* and the *Arrival of Edward IV*, with an introduction by Keith Dockray

Three Fifteenth Century Chronicles, ed. J. Gairdner (Camden Society, 1880)

Vergil, Polydore, *Three Books of Polydore Vergil's English History*, ed. H. Ellis (Camden Society, 1844)

Warkworth, John, *A Chronicle of the First Thirteen Years of the Reign of King Edward the Fourth*, ed. J.O. Halliwell (Camden Society, 1839)

Watts, John, 'Ideas, Principles and Politics', in *The Wars of the Roses*, ed. A.J. Pollard (London, 1995)

Watts, John, 'Polemic and Politics in the 1450s', in *Politics of Fifteenth Century England: John Vale's Book*, ed. M.L. Kekewich and others (Stroud, 1995)

Watts, John, *Henry VI and the Politics of Kingship* (Cambridge, 1996)

Waurin, Jean de, *Recueil des Croniques et Anchiennes Istories de la Grant Bretaigne, a present nomme Engleterre*, ed. W. and E. Hardy, Vol. 5, 1447–1471 (Rolls Series, 1891)

Wilkinson, B., *Constitutional History of England in the Fifteenth Century* (London, 1964)

Wolffe, Bertram, 'The Personal Rule of Henry VI', in *Fifteenth-century England 1399–1509*, ed. S.B. Chrimes, C.D. Ross and R.A. Griffiths (Manchester, 1972)

Wolffe, Bertram, *Henry VI* (London, 1981)

Index